Thirty Years of Change for Children

The National Children's Bureau was established as a registered charity in 1963. Our purpose is to identify and promote the interests of all children and young people and to improve their status in a diverse society.

We work closely with professionals and policy makers to improve the lives of all children but especially young children, those affected by family instability, children with special needs or disabilities and those suffering the effects of poverty and deprivation.

We collect and disseminate information about children and promote good practice in children's services through research, policy and practice development, publications, seminars, training and an extensive library and information service.

The Bureau works in partnership with Children in Scotland and Children in Wales.

© National Children's Bureau, 1993

ISBN 1 874579 13 X

Published by the National Children's Bureau, 8 Wakley Street, London EC1V 7QE. Telephone 071 278 9441. Registered Charity No 258825.

Printed by Saxon Graphics Ltd, Derby.

Contents

Notes on contributors

Peg Belson is Vice-Chairman of Action for Sick Children (previously NAWCH). She is closely involved as a researcher and writer with health care issues, particularly as they affect children and young people.

John Coleman is Director of Trust for the Study of Adolescence. Trained as a clinical psychologist, he has been a university lecturer, and the Director of a therapeutic community for disturbed adolescents. He has written several books, including *The Nature of Adolescence,* now in its second edition.

Joan Cooper is an Honorary Visiting Research Fellow, University of Sussex and was formerly Children's Officer, East Sussex County Council; Chief Inspector, Children's Department, Home Office; and then Director of the Social Work Service at the DHSS.

Ron Davie is a consulting psychologist; Visiting professor at Oxford Brookes University; Honorary Research Fellow, University College London. He was formerly Director of the National Children's Bureau; Co-Director, National Child Development Study; and Professor of Educational Psychology, University College, Cardiff.

Michael Freeman is professor of English Law, University College London. He is editor of the new *International Journal of Children's Rights*.

Myer Glickman is a health information specialist, Wolfson Child Health Monitoring Unit, Department of Epidemiology, Institute of Child Health, University of London.

A.H. Halsey is Emeritus Professor of Social and Administrative Studies at the University of Oxford, and Fellow of Nuffield College. He is a life-long sociologist, socialist and student of education and is now working on issues in tertiary education internationally. His most recent book is *Decline of Donnish Dominion* (OUP, 1992).

Sonia Jackson is Professor of Applied Social Studies at University College, Swansea. She moved from a background in child psychology to primary teaching and then social work. Her research and development work with under fives and children in care has been particularly concerned with the education/care divide. She is co-author of *Childminder, Other People's Children*, and *People Under Three*.

Barbara Kahan is Chair of the National Children's Bureau, formerly professional adviser in childcare to the House of Commons Select Committee on Social Services; and consultant in childcare. She is co-author of *The Pindown Experience and the Protection of Children*; and author of a number of books and other publications.

Jane Lane has worked as a geologist and has taught in further education. She currently works in the education section of the Commission for Racial Equality.

Vivienne Little is Director of Studies, Department of Education, University of Warwick and co-editor of *Children & Society*.

Jean Packman is Senior Research Fellow at Dartington Social Research Unit. She has had a lifetime's interest in childcare, through practice, teaching and research. She formerly headed social work courses at the University of Exeter and in now engaged full time on evaluative research on aspects of the Children Act 1989.

Gillian Pugh is Director of the Early Childhood Unit at the National Children's Bureau, and co-editor of *Children & Society*. She has published numerous books and is particularly interested in policy development, coordination of services, early years curriculum, and parent education and support.

John Tomlinson is Director of the Institute of Education and Professor of Education at the University of Warwick. He chairs the Editorial Board of *Children & Society*.

Sheila Wolfendale is professor, Psychology Department, University of East London and is course tutor, MSc Educational Psychology. She has been a teacher and educational psychologist in several LEAs. She has written extensively on special needs, parental involvement, early intervention, and educational psychology.

Caroline Woodroffe is an epidemiologist and health economist, and was until recently at the Wolfson Child Health Monitoring Unit, Department of Epidemiology, Institute of Child Health, University of London.

Foreword

As President of the National Children's Bureau and Chairman of the All Party Parliamentary Group for Children at Westminster, it is my privilege to commend this book to all those concerned with the well being of children, their families and the communities in which they live.

It is fitting that this important book edited by Gillian Pugh should be published in the 30th Anniversary year of the setting up of the National Children's Bureau.

Joan Cooper, whose vision pioneered the setting up of the Bureau in 1953, has outlined in her chapter the history and achievements of the Bureau, notably the research carried out by Dr Kellmer Pringle and her colleagues, as part of the National Child Development Study, started in 1958.

Gillian Pugh is to be congratulated on her choice of contributors, each of whom has shown insight and skill in their analysis of the social trends of today and how they differ from those of 30 years ago. I refer to the rising divorce rate, the number of lone parents, the phenomenon of child sexual abuse and the position of working mothers.

Whilst it would be of value to embark on a second Child Development Study, the contributors to this book have nevertheless signposted the many changes in the education, health and social services in this country, some of which mediate the breakdown in personal relationships. The contributors offer positive ways ahead to deal wisely with these changes.

This book should be heeded by legislators and practitioners alike, committed to the well being of children in this country.

Baroness Faithfull OBE
President, National Children's Bureau
August 1993

1. Thirty years of change for children 1963-1993: an overview

Gillian Pugh
Director, Early Childhood Unit, National Children's Bureau

[It is a] fundamental principle that the lives and normal development of children should have first call upon society's concerns and capacities and that children should be able to depend upon that commitment in good times and bad... (UN Convention on the Rights of the Child, UNICEF, 1991)

How well have children in the United Kingdom fared in thirty years since the National Children's Bureau was established in 1963? Have they had the first call upon society's concerns and capacities? This edited volume celebrates the National Children's Bureau's thirtieth birthday by reviewing some of the main changes that Britain has seen in relation to children and services for children during this period. The chapters were originally commissioned as articles for a double issue of the Bureau's journal *Children & Society*. Contributors were not asked specifically to focus on the Bureau's achievements - although of course reference is made to these where appropriate. Instead, we took the theme of 'thirty years of change for children' and asked fifteen distinguished contributors to reflect on what had changed for children in their field of interest in the last three decades. What legislation had there been, what were the key messages from research, and did developments in practice reflect research findings?

In planning the volume and writing this introductory chapter I have had of necessity to be selective. Some areas receive rather fuller treatment than others, but although the choice is inevitably subjective,

I have been guided by Bureau colleagues and by the editorial board of *Children & Society*, as well as by an awareness of those areas where the Bureau has been particularly active.

Whilst the climate within which the Bureau was established in 1963 may have been different from today, the issues and concerns have a remarkably familiar ring to them. Joan Cooper, a founder member of the Bureau, describes the growing evidence in the 1950s of the link between social deprivation and ill health and disability, and the need for the health, education and childcare systems to work together to meet the needs of all children. She writes of the need to understand and use research, of the importance of preventive work with families rather than being forced to adopt expensive intervention measures; of the plight of children in care and leaving care and of the need for better training for childcare workers; of children with special needs and juvenile delinquents; of early child development; and of families who have nowhere to live. All of these are still on our agenda today.

The original emphasis of the National Bureau for Cooperation in Child Care (NBCCC) - as it was then called - was on:

...the pursuit and spread of knowledge, the desire that good practice should be evaluated and then shared across professional boundaries and that research should permeate all systems concerned with children.

In the early *Annual Reports* of the NBCCC, Mia Kellmer Pringle presented her Director's report each year under five main headings:

- to make information available on children's development, needs and problems;
- to improve communication between professionals and between statutory and voluntary organisations;
- to explore better use of services and encourage the development of new ones;
- to bring about a more preventive outlook in the field of childcare;
- to contribute to new knowledge.

These are still central to the Bureau's purpose, although the emphasis on advocacy and children's rights is now even stronger, and all aspects of the work programme are underpinned by a clear statement of values and principles. The wish of the Bureau's founder members to involve local and health authorities in the Bureau's work, and the multiplicity of voluntary organisations that wished to collaborate, proved so complex that it took a working party three years to resolve. But it was three years well spent, for the over-riding concern of today's Bureau is still to be an advocate for children, to see children's needs as a whole, and to forge links between those who work with children and young people but often in their rather separate compartments.

Since its inception the Bureau has debated whether its concerns should be with all children, or with those who are particularly vulnerable. Its genesis in the work of children's officers and leading voluntary organisations has meant that the main focus was originally - and remains - on the welfare of children, but the five main strands of Bureau work today reflect a balance between the needs of all children - particularly young children - and those whose needs are more acute. Thus the five main areas of Bureau work in 1993 are children's health and development, young children and their families, children living in poverty, children experiencing family breakdown, including those separated from home and those who have been abused, and children with special educational needs and disabilities.

Reference to the summary of highlights in the life of the Bureau, given in the Appendix, shows just how wide a range of issues have been considered by the Bureau's researchers, development workers, policy officers, information staff and conference organisers. From preparation and education for parenthood to solvent abuse; from children in care to children with AIDS/HIV; from equality of opportunity to involving children and young people in decision making; from assessment to children's play; from major contributions to longitudinal research methodology to creating networks and forums, the Bureau has attempted to live up to its early ideals and to become more effective as the 'powerful voice of the child'. But against what kind of national and international backdrop, and what have been the main changes in the lives of children?

Trends in society

As Halsey points out in his chapter and elsewhere (Halsey, 1988) the post war period up until the mid seventies was one of economic growth and prosperity, including full employment and an ambitious building

3

programme for schools and hospitals, against an international background of dwindling imperial power and the relative decline of economic productivity. Average earnings increased, the manual workforce decreased, more women and particularly married women joined the workforce and workers enjoyed longer holidays and shorter working hours. Then after the oil crisis of the mid seventies and the dawn of computer technology, the shift away from nineteenth century urban industrial manufacturing was accelerated, unemployment rose and the population began to move away from the inner cities towards suburbia, and particularly the new towns. But whilst mounting prosperity has led to more holidays abroad and a second home for some, so the economy has weakened, and the 'two nations' first described by Disraeli over one hundred years ago, have become further divided, with a growing gap between the 'haves' and the 'have nots'. The number of children living in poverty continues to rise at an unacceptable rate, with a rise of 50 per cent in the years between 1979 and 1990. I return to this issue below.

The changes have not of course been only economic. In 1969 the UK ratified the European Convention on Human Rights, since when the rulings of the European Court and the principles of the Convention have had a clear impact in the UK, for example in the abolition of corporal punishment in schools, the access of children in care to their parents, court hearings for children being placed in secure accommodation, and children's access to their own files. In 1973 Britain finally signed the Treaty of Rome to join what was then called the European Economic Community. In 1993, as we ratify the Maastricht treaty, commitment to a single Europe takes on broader social and educational dimensions. Our thinking and our practice have begun to be as much influenced by our European neighbours as once it was from across the Atlantic.

Over this thirty year period the government has taken on more of the family's traditional roles and, at least until the mid eighties, the numbers of social workers, doctors, nurses, police officers and teachers continued to rise. At a time of economic uncertainty, the spiralling cost of the welfare state, both in services and benefits, is a problem to which all political parties are currently seeking solutions.

For those who have grown up during the years 1963-1993, this has been a time of increasing opportunity. The proportion of young people leaving school with two A-levels has increased from 6.5 per cent in 1960 to 22 per cent in 1990, and the numbers going on into higher education have grown correspondingly. An elite 7 per cent in 1963 has expanded to 27 per cent today, a fivefold increase in student numbers.

For many children an increase in the numbers of families owning cars and the virtually universal access to television has opened up the world in a way unimagined in the 1960s. But as children have in many ways become more independent, in other respects the environment has become more hostile. Concerns for their safety has made it much more difficult for children to play outside on their own or travel on their own to school or to see their friends. A study of children and the environment published by the Bureau (Rosenbaum, 1993) points out that outdoor play facilities are often in short supply, or very dangerous. They are particularly limited on housing estates where 'planners are principally concerned with protecting children from the environment rather than including them in it'. The *Charter for Children's Play,* published by the National Voluntary Council for Children's Play (1992), calls for adequate play facilities for all children. In 1971 some 86 per cent of primary school children went to school on their own; in 1990 it was only 29 per cent. There have been correspondingly large drops in the number of children allowed to cross roads or ride bikes on their own (Hillman and others, 1990). Rosenbaum (1993) also points to the millions of children suffering from high levels of lead in drinking water, and air pollution from increased exhaust fumes, both issues which new European standards should begin to address.

A growing understanding of physical and sexual abuse of children has been one of the most obvious developments during this period, and a number of highly publicised cases of abuse have led to government action and guidance. Our understanding has been tempered most recently with an awareness of the dangers of system abuse and a welcome shift to a more family and child-centred approach to protection. The need to work together if any progress is to be made in preventing abuse and protecting children remains crucial.

Drugs have become more readily available, and the extent of alcohol and substance abuse continues to alarm. A 1990 Health Education Authority report estimates that 6 per cent of 9 to 15-year-olds had been offered cannabis and that 4 per cent had tried it; and that 6 per cent had been offered glue and that 2 per cent had tried it. The survey also found that 11 per cent of eleven year old boys and 17 per cent of 11-year-old girls had drunk alcohol in the previous week (*Children Now*, 1992).

Family trends

But it is perhaps changes in the institution we call the family (described by one commentator as 'what we find behind the front door') that have had the greatest impact on children, as Halsey reminds us in his chapter. The main features are well known and can be summarised as (OPCS, 1993; Social Trends, 1993):

- a drop in the birthrate to an average of 1.8 children per family, rather less than replacement rate;
- increasing numbers of births outside marriage (three in 10 in 1991). Half of these parents are cohabiting, and three quarters of the births are registered by both parents;
- a considerable increase in the divorce rate (about four in 10 marriages in 1991) and in the rate of remarriage (now a third of all marriages), so that a quarter of children now witness their parents divorce, and some eight per cent of families include a step-child;
- a high proportion of parents bringing up children on their own, some through choice, some through widowhood and some following divorce. The number of lone parents doubled during this period, and now accounts for one in five of all families, caring for 2.2 million dependent children - the highest proportion in Europe apart from Denmark. A decreasing number of single parents are divorced - currently about a half; one third are single, never married;
- changes in the division of labour between men and women, such that some 65 per cent of women with dependent children are now working. For those with children under five the number has risen in the last ten years from 24 per cent to 47 per cent. Some 60 per cent of couples with dependent children both work;
- an increase in the number of men who are economically inactive, with a disproportionate number of fathers with large families out of work.

Halsey's chapter expresses strong concern for the weakening of the norms of traditional family life. He argues that individual freedom, espoused by Margaret Thatcher - who he feels may come to be seen as the major architect of the demolition of the traditional family - works against the collective good of families and society. Marriage becomes a mere contract rather than a life long commitment. Parental responsibility, seen as the most coherent way of ordering relationships to equip children for their own adult responsibilities, is diminishing he argues, with an increasing number of males with no experience of fatherhood. Gains for adults in terms of individual freedom, may perhaps not be in the best interests of children. The role of fathers is clearly back on the agenda.

Research on the impact of marital disruption, separation, divorce and bereavement on children, much of it deriving from the Bureau's National Child Development Study (Ferri, 1976; Kiernan and Chase-Lansdale, 1991), shows that while marital disruption is associated with less good outcomes for children than an intact two parent family, the effect of family disruption due to bereavement is much less marked. Social class and income account for much of the difference in outcomes, and it is now clear that many of these differences are apparent before the marriage actually breaks down. There is little recent research on the outcomes for children born to single, never-married mothers. Of perhaps greater concern is recently published research on children in step-families (Ferri, 1984; Kiernan, 1992). Data suggests that step-children are at greater risk of leaving school and leaving home early, that girls are more likely to become teenage mothers, and boys to cohabit before the age of 21. The more transitions children experience, the more likely they are to report difficulties with school, friendships and family relationships.

In reviewing this research, however, it is important to remember that in 70 per cent of families children are living with both their natural parents; and that most children of divorced parents do not experience particular difficulties. Whether or not children are more at risk from the breakdown in family relationships in the UK than elsewhere it is not possible to say. But it is perhaps worth reflecting on a European survey on attitudes towards family life. Across Europe as a whole the most important role for families was judged to be 'bringing up and educating children'. However only one in four UK respondents thought this was most important, preferring 'to provide love and affection' (Eurobarometer, 1990).

Roles and patterns of family life have clearly changed substantially over this period, and continue to lead to heated debate. Social policy and social security systems, an area of work in which the Bureau has to date been little involved, are devised on the assumption that women give up work on marriage and become financially dependent on their husbands. This is clearly unrealistic today, but the debate continues about the extent to which family policy recognises diverse family patterns. Equality of opportunity for women, with equal access to the labour market and training opportunities, will inevitably impact on the roles of men as fathers, and on the lives of children, but the impact does not have to be negative. We can, as Halsey argues, build closer links with 'third age' citizens - grandparents and other senior citizens over 65, a 'new social and political class free from obligations of paid employment', who now account for almost one fifth of the UK population.

But we must also look to new ways of reconciling work responsibilities and family life, for whilst unemployment limits the quality of life for too many families, the working patterns of some parents severely limit the time they can spend with their children. As a government Minister recently acknowledged, in a speech calling for a more coherent family policy, 'Some of the most deprived children in society have every material convenience available to them, all they lack is their parents' time and affection because it is so committed elsewhere' (Castle, 1993). This family policy will need to increase day care and other family support measures, and ensure that fathers are enabled to play a more central part in family life (see Moss, 1990; Coote, and others, 1990). The punitive approach of the Child Support Agency, launched in April 1993 to pursue fathers who are not paying maintenance, appears to be driven rather more by financial imperatives than by the needs of children.

Children's rights

Perhaps the single most significant step forward for children in this thirty year span has been the United Nations Convention on the Rights of the Child, adopted by the United Nations in 1989 and ratified by the UK in 1991. The three central rights - that all the rights in the Convention apply to all children whatever their racial origin, sex, religion, language, disability, opinion or family background; that all decisions made on behalf of children must be in their best interests; and that children have the right to participate in decisions affecting them - are an historic move forward. Michael Freeman's chapter outlines the historical background to the Convention, and discusses the tensions that can arise between the child's right to self-determination and the need to protect children and support their welfare in order that they can exercise this self-determination. He argues that we are only beginning to recognise the rights of children - but this is surely an important start.

The Children Act embodies many of the principles underpinning the convention, but, in his analysis of the Convention, Peter Newell (1991) argues that in many respects children still lack an effective voice in the political system or in many of the services and institutions designed for them. Two specific examples are discussed in the chapters on adolescence by John Coleman, and on education by Vivienne Little and John Tomlinson.

Adolescence is described as an uncertain stage, searching for a 'theory of normality'. Coleman argues that the view of adolescence as a time of turmoil has been exaggerated, and that one of the main difficulties is that of status ambiguity - are adolescents children or adults, and what is their civil status? He illustrates his point with reference to the Gillick ruling that a girl under sixteen of sufficient understanding and intelligence may have the legal capacity to give valid consent to contraceptive advice and treatment, although as Rachel Hodgkin points out (*Children & Society*, 1993), a subsequent case - the W case where an anorexic 16-year-old had her wish not to be force fed overruled- means that there is now renewed confusion over the rights of adolescents with regard to their own health. Whereas the Children Act does give young people the right to be listened to and to participate in decision-making, the Criminal Justice Act treats young people as the responsibility of their parents, holding them responsible for the offences of their children, and duly punishing them. Society gets the adolescents it deserves, argues Coleman. Young people need respect, status, to be taken seriously, given information and support, and still need protection at times when they may be vulnerable.

The Education legislation, too, takes a different perspective than the Children Act, giving parents but not children the 'charter' and the choice, but denying children any opportunities to be consulted on matters concerning the school, the curriculum or themselves, for example in cases of exclusion. The central message of the Elton report *Discipline in Schools* is that schools are healthier places if they give pupils more respect and responsibility and the whole school community has a clear consensus on behaviour, rules and sanctions (*Children Now*, 1992). The 1993 Education Act includes little that will address the welfare or rights of school children.

And finally, one important development, in which the Bureau has been closely involved, has been the establishment of the Children's Rights Development Unit as a three-year project committed to promoting full implementation of the UK convention. The Unit has embarked on a wide ranging consultation programme and feels that although the Convention has had little impact on many areas of legislation, some progress has been made (Lansdown in *Children Now*, 1992). However, one has only to look at the ambitious multi-million dollar programme of work inspired by the Convention in Canada to realise the potential of putting children's rights at the centre of policy and practice.

Equality of opportunity; or access to life chances

Central to the UK Convention is the concept of the rights of all children, but the work of the Bureau over thirty years has shown clearly that some children finish up with a greater share of 'life chances' than others, and that we still live in a profoundly unequal society in which many children experience poverty, abuse, avoidable ill health and discrimination. The Bureau's National Child Development Study, following the progress of 16,000 born in one week in March 1958 shows perhaps more clearly than any research before or since, the impact of the environment and social circumstances on children's development. Ron Davie's chapter is only able to pick out some of the highlights of this massive study - which continues today, looking at the children of our children (see for example Ferri, 1993) - but he has chosen to focus particularly on the social, health and educational differences that are already so starkly apparent at seven, and are still there at eleven and sixteen. *Born to Fail?* (Wedge and Prosser, 1973), one of the Bureau's best selling books, catalogues the extent and range of disadvantage in health, education, welfare, housing, income and take-up of services amongst Britain's 11- year-olds at the end of the 1960s. Although as subsequent studies showed, some children are able to 'escape from disadvantage' , one can only assume that the link between poverty and disadvantage is stronger today than it was twenty years ago, for Bradshaw's recent study for the Bureau (1990) found that child poverty has more than doubled during the 1980s, with more than one in four children now living below the poverty line. 'Inequalities in children's lives have increased. The lives of children in a two parent, two earner family, living in owner occupied housing, in the south of England, serviced by good public services have improved. In contrast the lives of children in an unemployed or lone parent family, living in rented accommodation, in the inner city with deteriorating health, education and social services have got worse. Black children and families are particularly disadvantaged on many fronts.' (p.52)

A further study of the ten-year period 1979-89 (Kumar, 1993) makes even more chilling reading. Some of the key findings are that:

- the gap between the income of the poor and the rich has widened: the average real income of the bottom 20 per cent of married couples with children declined by seven per cent, while that of the general population increased by 30 per cent, and of the top 20 per cent increased by 40 per cent;
- the relationship between infant mortality and morbidity and social class got stronger, and overall improvements in the health of children were less marked in children in social classes IV and V;
- homelessness increased sharply, especially in inner city areas;
- children in deprived urban areas made less progress than their peers in terms of improved educational standards and entry to higher education, and at the end of primary school the gap between children from different social and ethnic backgrounds has actually widened;
- poverty amongst children from minority ethnic groups was significantly higher, because of the over-representation of their parents among the unemployed and low earners.

Factors related to the increase in poverty include high levels of unemployment, increase in the incidence of low pay and the increase noted above in the number of lone parent families. Changes in the benefit system from universal to selective, means-tested benefits and significant cuts in unemployment benefit, mean that although the value of benefits has doubled in real terms since 1948, in relation to earnings it is lower. Several chapters in this book reinforce this evidence.

Caroline Woodroffe and Myer Glickman in their chapter on children's health point to many impressive technical and scientific advances during this period. Between 1963 and 1991 infant mortality fell by 65 per cent, although is still higher than in France, West Germany or Netherlands. The number of 'cot deaths' has fallen dramatically, largely due to a health campaign to encourage parents to put infants to sleep on their backs. Deaths to 15-19-year-olds have also fallen though only by 18 per cent.. However, reported levels of chronic illness have doubled since 1972, particularly respiratory diseases, partly due to improved survival of children with previously fatal conditions. Despite many improvements, however, the chapter points to increases in homelessness, poverty and unemployment which mean that while some seriously ill children receive transplants, others die in house fires because their parents, unable to afford electricity, use candles. The authors point to the high correlation between poverty and child health and mortality, and to the particular risks facing children of teenage mothers and unsupported mothers. In questioning whether the government's objective should be in increasing healthy life expectancy or in reducing the striking inequalities between children of different social classes, they argue that the greatest health gain would be a commitment to tackle poverty and deprivation.

Many of these issues had been highlighted by the Court Report (Committee on Child Health Services, 1976) on the state of child health and child health services, a major report which made far reaching recommendations and looked to significant change in services for children. Some ten years later, the Bureau's report *Investing in the Future: child health ten years after the Court Report* (Policy and Practice Review Group, 1987) showed how little had changed. It also pointed to a continuing lack of cooperation between professionals working with children:

There has been an unwillingness both by government and by the professions to come to firm decisions about who should have responsibility for different aspects of the preventive services...The inter-professional disagreements that have occurred and the lack of government leadership to deal with them have resulted in uncertainty about using even the limited resources that have been available. There has been no lack of committees, reports and studies on these subjects. We have been impressed by many of them ... We have been most unimpressed by the action that has arisen as a result of these studies and deliberations (p.9-10).

Kumar (1993) pointed to the particular disadvantages faced by many Black families. Jane Lane's chapter takes one aspect of discrimination - racism - and asks what role the law has in getting rid of racism in the lives of children. She argues that whilst the law in unlikely to change attitudes, it can begin to change behaviour, and looks at two major pieces of legislation - the Race Relations Act 1976 and the Children Act 1989 - to make the point that whilst we now have the framework of the legislation, we must use it to ensure that every child is treated equally. The examples of cases that the Commission for Racial Equality has taken to court in its fight against discrimination in school admission policies, exclusions, suspensions, racial harassment, and setting and banding, show how many customs and practices that were not necessarily intended to discriminate against Black children, do in fact do so. The Children Act is the first piece of legislation in which racial equality is a central concern, and Lane points to the importance of training to ensure that it really is implemented. This issue has been of particular concern to the National Children's Bureau, and the training packs and 'good practice' guidelines produced by the Early Childhood Unit have all attempted to provide practitioners and managers with the skills and understanding to combat racism and promote equality.

The level of public funding for services for young children has never been high in the UK. Sonia Jackson, in her chapter on 'thirty years of no progress?' for children under five, argues that young children have been marginalised and that services for them, already amongst the poorest in Europe, are the first target for cuts. The continuing split between 'care' and 'education' have contributed to a failure to develop a coherent policy for pre-school children, and dwindling resources mean that instead of the universal service that is enjoyed by many of our European neighbours, we are increasingly having to prioritise places for 'children in need', with the stigma that goes with this. The lack of a universal service providing adequate childcare also locks single parents into poverty. The Early Childhood Unit at the Bureau has taken up this issue in its report on the costing and funding of day care and nursery education (Holtermann, 1992), which shows that the benefits to the Exchequer of providing day care to enable single parents to work rather than remain dependent on benefits, would be considerable. It is in the early childhood field, as Jackson points out, that much valuable work has taken place in relation to gender roles in the family, and women's opportunities and rights to participate in paid employment. UK membership of the European Childcare Network has done much to broaden the perspectives of early years workers, and there are hopes that the requirements of the European Community Recommendation on Child Care may ultimately make some impact on four areas - childcare services, leave arrangement for employed parents, the environment and organisation of work, and the participation of men in the care and upbringing of children.

Children with disabilities and special educational needs have always been a group for whom the Bureau has been particularly concerned. During this period there have been dramatic changes in the rights of such children, many of whom before 1970 were considered to be 'ineducable' and, if they had complex disabilities, to need very specialist institutional care. The implementation of the Children Act 1989 marked the end of several decades of concern at the lack of protection and childcare principles in many services for children with disabilities. The final closure of children's wards in long-stay hospitals and an emphasis within the Children Act on partnership with parents and community care ensures that children with disabilities are now seen as children first. In achieving integration within their local communities, education has played a key role in increasing opportunities for children with a range of special needs.

In her chapter, Sheila Wolfendale traces the increasing attention and priority given to children with special needs since the first Bureau working party published its report on *Living with Handicap* and the Voluntary Council for Handicapped Children - now the Council for Disabled Children - was established. In the last thirty years, the range and availability of provision for children with special needs has improved, there has been greater cooperation between providers and closer partnership with parents, and the moves towards integration or 'inclusion' have gained considerable ground. In pulling out two themes to illustrate her point - empowering parents, and integration or inclusion of children with special needs into mainstream services - Wolfendale emphasises the rights of all children to be fully valued and included, and points to the work of the network of special needs organisations that have joined forces as the Special Educational Consortium to ensure that the current 1993 Education Act recognises these rights. Much of the debate on this Act in its passage through parliament has been lead by Baroness Warnock, whose 1978 report was a seminal influence on policy in what became the 1981 Education Act. The importance of early intervention, and of identifying and meeting individual needs rather than creating unhelpful labels, are as critical in 1993 as they have ever been.

Children living away from home, particularly those in care, or as it is now known, being 'looked after' by the local authority, are a further group of children for whom the Bureau has had a particular concern since its earliest days, when one of its first projects was the establishment of a working party on the effects of long-term substitute care. Although the percentage of children and young people being looked after is now only about 0.5 per cent (a number that has reduced since the introduction of the Children Act), these children and young people are perhaps the most vulnerable in our society. The Who Cares? project, in which a group of young people living in the care of the local authority were supported in writing a book about their experiences (Page and Clark, 1977) and in setting up a national organisation, was one of the most innovative established under the Bureau's auspices, encouraging greater involvement of young people in care in decisions affecting their own lives.

A growing number of children being looked after - more than half - are now placed in foster care, but the residential care services continue to cause concern. In her chapter, Barbara Kahan points to the irony of a situation in which boarding school education - usually in public schools - is seen as a desired resource for aspirant families, and yet the 13,000 children in residential care with the local authority are consistently dogged by the 'ghosts of long past Poor Law policies and theories'. A long line of reports have consistently shown a failure to support, to understand, to develop and to value residential care, and Barbara Kahan herself, as co-author of the 'Pindown' report (Levy and Kahan, 1991) knows as well as anyone how important it is to focus on the needs of individual children, and not just fit the children into existing provision. A new development at the Bureau - the Residential Childcare Development Unit - will be working in several regions of the UK, helping to identify good practice and promote local initiatives.

Peg Belson's account of care for children in hospital makes encouraging reading in many respects, reflecting on a number of effective campaigns undertaken by the National Association for the Welfare of Children in Hospital (now called Action for Sick Children), just two years older than the Bureau. The number of paediatricians has doubled since the 1960s, and a greater understanding of the needs of young children has led to many changes in practice. Children are now likely to stay in hospital for a much shorter time, are more likely to be cared for in paediatric wards, by staff specially trained to meet their needs, with close and continuing attention from their parents. A far cry from the 1960s when parents were thought to be an upsetting influence on their children in hospital, and when children 'would soon settle down and forget about home'. There are however, still areas of concern, not least the number of children still in adult wards, the amount that it costs parents to visit children in hospital, and the lack of coordination between hospital and community services, an issue which may well get worse before it gets better as the changes in the organisation of the health service continue to unfold.

Changes in legislation: the changing role of the welfare state

As this book goes to press, the Government is reassessing its benefits package, and asking how much of the welfare state it can still afford. In his chapter Halsey describes the consensus that was built up during the war as expressed by Beveridge, Keynes and Butler that 'a prosperous and civilised future required a positive welfare state'. In the 'systematic interference' by government to ensure that resources were appropriately redistributed for, amongst other things, the health, welfare and education of children, Halsey sees the Bureau as a 'public broker' of the clash of ideas concerning upbringing between government and the governed, the churches and the laity, professionals and amateurs, parents and children, the classes, the genders and the ethnic groups. The consensus on the welfare state appears, however, to be broken, as both Halsey and Little and Tomlinson in their chapter on education argue.

The last thirty years have seen dramatic changes in the education system in this country. The first twenty five of these reflected the post-war optimism and expansion following the 1944 Education Act, and a commitment to equality of opportunity for all pupils. The school leaving age was raised to 16 in 1972, the same year as the White Paper *A Framework for Expansion* promised developments in teacher training, higher education opportunities and nursery education. In the years that followed, comprehensive education replaced grammar and secondary moderns in most areas, and a growing understanding of how children learn and how to plan and manage the curriculum led to a new focus on the importance of child centred approaches to teaching. Tomlinson and Little argue that until the 1980s the education system struggled to widen opportunities for all children, with a growing emphasis on the need to direct resources to support children with special educational needs and to help schools cope with the effects of social class and ethnic differences. Standards have risen as the number of children leaving school with two A-levels testifies to, but the view persists that they are falling, and the 'back to basics' brigade has, the authors argue, sustained its life independent of the findings of either research or HMI. Prime Minister James Callaghan in his Ruskin speech in 1976 had begun to question whether school leavers were being given the tools they needed for a working life, but saw reform as needing to be in the hands of the schools and LEAs. 1987 saw a radical break in the consensus and a change of direction and value position which has, in a few years, led to the education system in England and Wales becoming both the most centralised and the most fragmented in Europe. The authors argue that this new approach cannot sustain principles of access, entitlement, social justice or public service.

The implications of the 1988 Education Reform Act, passing budgetary control over to schools, centralising the curriculum and assessment arrangements and requiring the publication of league tables based on these assessments are still providing daily newspaper coverage as teachers struggle to come to terms with the speed of change. The implications of the 1993 Education Act cannot at present be gauged accurately, but its intention is to reduce substantially the role of the local education authority, as schools are offered incentives to opt out of LEA control. The Act was the focus of lengthy debate during its passage through parliament, as the Special Educational Consortium pointed to the possible impact of a system in which schools are encouraged to compete with each other on the more vulnerable children, children who may be expensive or difficult to educate, and who may bring down the school averages when league tables are published. If dwindling resources are to be made available to the children in the greatest need, whether children with special educational needs, or children under five for whom nursery education is still provided only at the discretion of the local authority, then it is difficult to see how this can happen unless the local authority plays a strategic role in planing and reviewing how these resources are used.

The introduction of an approach to service provision which is market driven is perhaps furthest advanced in the health service, where the NHS and Community Care Act of 1990 split the functions of providing and purchasing in the health and community care services and encouraged the establishment of independent self-governing Trusts. In a report commissioned by the Bureau on the publication of the White Paper leading up to this Act, Woodroffe and Kurtz (1989) raise a number of concerns about the impact of these changes on children's services, concerns remarkably similar to those in the education service. For example, will General Practitioners who hold their own budgets want children on their lists with costly long term chronic conditions? How will the need for long term supervision and management from several different services be coordinated? The authors ask whether the percentage of spending on children will change, and whether the balance between expenditure on primary, secondary and tertiary care will change. They ask whether there will be more equitable access to health care by children in different parts of the country, and whether more children will have to travel outside their district to find a hospital bed. They ask whether the differences in access to health services by children in different socio-economic groups will be reduced. They conclude by saying that there is little evidence that child health services will be improved by the new framework. Services for children may become more fragmented, the proportion of expenditure on children may decline, the internal market may lead to an increase in hospital expenditure at the expense of community care, and socio-economic differences in access to health services for children may increase.

Whether or not the reorganisation of the health service will be to children's advantage, the government's health strategy published in 1992 as *Health of the Nation* established five areas for priority attention: coronary heart disease and strokes; cancers, mental illness, HIV/AIDS and sexual health, and accidents. The involvement of children in developing healthy life styles is critical to the long term success of the strategy, and it is to be hoped that success in meeting the targets will improve the health of all children.

Jean Packman's chapter traces developments in the emphasis and direction of child welfare services from 1963, when local authority children's departments were 15 years old, through the establishment of social service departments in 1970 to the Children Act and beyond, a critical thirty year period in which the balance between childcare, child delinquency control and preventive work are seen to have come full circle. The Bureau was founded in the year of the 1963 Children and Young Person's Act, an act which, despite its failure to integrate juvenile delinquents into the childcare system, is seen as having underpinning principles very much in line with those of the Bureau - cooperation with other agencies and, through this, preventive work to diminish the need to bring a child into care. 1963 was also the year in which the first British article on the 'battered baby syndrome' appeared in the medical press, although at this stage preventive work was still dominating the work of children's departments. Packman argues that the decade of prevention gave way in the seventies to the decade of protection or 'benevolent maternalism' and, following the Seebohm report, to the establishment of social services departments. In all of these developments the Bureau's research and information work was to play a crucial role. The Bureau was also to contribute to another feature of the decade - the rise of pressure groups on behalf of children and families involved in the welfare system - through its work with children in care.

In the 1980s the theme was partnership, reaching its culmination in the 1989 Children Act, described by the Lord Chancellor in the

House of Lords as the most important and far-reaching piece of children's legislation in living memory, repealing wholly or in part 55 previous Acts. Reference has already been made to its unifying and underpinning principles in relation to children's rights and the paramountcy of the welfare of the child. The child's welfare is also seen as firmly embedded in its family context, with parents having important and enduring responsibilities (even after divorce), rather than simply enjoying rights.

The concept of partnership brings challenges for professionals and parents alike - but it also raises issues about compatibility with the 'contract culture' embodied in the NHS and Community Care Act 1990. In describing the contract culture as the 'new right ideology', one director of social services writes of the rejection of the political consensus of the post war period, which agreed that, because vulnerable and disadvantaged people could not compete in the market they should therefore receive specific services and protection from the state, and these could not be allocated justly by the market. This new right ideology is also seen as rejecting the key role of professionals (Walby 1993). Although market forces have clearly brought improvements in some areas - Walby cites the reduction in restrictive practices, increase in flow of information to and power of consumers, and inspection of quality services - and clarity of thinking in others (needs assessment, for example), she argues that the contracting role would denude the local authority of all its expertise, and of its ability to plan appropriately and coherently. These arguments are remarkably similar to those above, in relation to health and education legislation.

One final piece of legislation that requires a brief further comment is the 1991 Criminal Justice Act. The Bureau has done very little work on juvenile delinquency since the innovative projects in the late sixties and early seventies on family advice centres and community based intermediate treatment schemes. The 1991 Criminal Justice Act is the last of a series of Acts throughout the eighties which reduced care and custody sentences and increased community-based sentences, leading to a dramatic fall both in the numbers of young people in custody and in the numbers of young people convicted of offenses. The 1991 Act extended the scope of the juvenile courts, renamed youth courts, to include 17-year-olds, abolished custody for 14-year-old boys, and rationalised and tightened criteria for custodial sentences, whilst increasing alternatives to custody. Two issues arise from this Act. One is the view referred to above that parents should be reinforced in their responsibilities for their children who offend. A recent review of crime prevention and the family (Utting and others, 1993) throws some useful light on some of the myths surrounding criminality, showing that it is misleading to concentrate on family structures and to blame rising crime on divorce and lone parenting. Although young offenders are more likely to come from severely disadvantaged homes, and often to have experienced school failure and criminality in the family, the significant factor is family management practices - the parents of young offenders tend to be neglectful or inconsistent in their use of discipline and to show poor parental supervision. Praise and affection are important, but so is knowing how to discipline in a non-violent and consistent and effective way (Patterson, 1982).

The key issue here is another in which the Bureau has had a long term interest - how can parents be helped to be more effective, and when and by whom should preparation, education, and support be offered (see Pugh and De'Ath, 1984, currently being updated).

The research review also confirms that locking young people up creates greater risks in terms of re-offending than not locking them up, and that custody is seldom an adequate deterrent and should only therefore be used as a last resort. It was with some disquiet therefore that the childcare world viewed the proposal by the Home Secretary at the end of 1992 that there would be new custodial sentences for 12 to 15-year-old persistent offenders who would be locked up in centres offering a mixture of punishment, education and training.

Looking to the future

The first thirty years of the Bureau's life has coincided with a period of economic growth and expansion, improvements in service provision, and increasing prosperity for many children and families. The majority of children are healthier and have greater educational opportunities than they did in 1963; and as a society we have a greater understanding of the needs and rights of children - at least at a theoretical level - and of listening to and involving children in decisions that impact on their lives. Much progress has been made, but much remains to be done if children in the UK are to enjoy the level of investment envisaged in the words of the UN Convention quoted at the head of this chapter.

In attempting to identify some of the key issues that affect children, an agenda for the Bureau over the next thirty years has begun to emerge. As we move towards the twenty first century, we find ourselves living in a society in which the number of children living on or below the poverty line continues to increase, in which the gap between those who 'have' and those who 'have not' is growing wider, in which the level of unemployment shows little sign of substantial reduction, and in which considerable numbers of children do not have access to the opportunities that a civilised society would expect to offer all its citizens. As several contributors to this book point out, the consensus on the role of the welfare state in providing for all children and families and in protecting those whose needs are greatest - in which society accepts a collective responsibility for its children as an investment in the future - is being challenged by a concern that we can no longer afford this level of support, and by a competitive approach in which market forces may well further disadvantage the most vulnerable. It is perhaps worth reflecting that the ability of parents to fulfil their responsibilities in bringing up the next generation will depend as much on the 'permitting circumstances' (access to jobs, housing and support services on the one hand and, on the other, time to spend with their children when they are in employment) as it will on their skills, knowledge and understanding as parents.

The challenge for the National Children's Bureau in the years ahead is how to adjust to these changing circumstances, whilst remaining true to the organisation's underpinning values and overall aims. The issues identified throughout this book create a clear agenda at least in the foreseeable future: implementing the UN Convention in the UK, by working towards more child-centred policies across all areas of public life; supporting and empowering parents, and looking for a better balance between work and family responsibilities; ensuring that children's needs are central to the continually changing parameters of service provision in health authorities and local authorities; continuing to work on behalf of those who do not have equal access to resources, and combating discrimination whether in terms of ethnicity, gender, disability or class.

These are not issues that the Bureau can tackle alone, but the original aims and purposes of an organisation committed to multi-disciplinary cooperation on behalf of children are perhaps even more important today than they were 30 years ago. As a membership organisation representing all those who work with and for children, and with new sister organisations in Wales and Scotland, the potential for working collaboratively as 'the powerful voice of the child' is enormous. We must continue to add to our knowledge of children's development and of good practice in meeting children's needs through research and development initiatives, and fully utilise this information as a basis from which policies can be developed, professional practice improved, and parents supported in bringing up the next generation.

References

Bradshaw, J. (1990) *Child Poverty and Deprivation in the UK*. National Children's Bureau

Castle, S. (1993) 'Tory says capitalism wrecks people's lives', *Sunday Independent,* 27 June

The Children's Society and National Children's Bureau (1993) *Children Now 1992*

Committee on Child Health Services (1976) *Fit for the Future*. Court Report. HMSO

Coote, A., Harman, H. and Hewitt, P. (1990) *The Family Way*. IPPR Social Policy Paper 1. Institute for Public Policy Research

Eurobarometer (1990) *The Family and Desire for Children,* European Commission

Ferri, E. (1976) *Growing Up in a One-Parent Family,* National Foundation for Educational Research

Ferri, E. (1984) *Step Children: A National Study*. National Foundation for Educational Research

Ferri, E. (ed.) (1993) *Life at 33: The Fifth Follow Up of the National Child Development Study*. National Children's Bureau

Halsey, A.H. (1988) *British Social Trends Since 1990*. Macmillan

Hillman, M., Adams, J. and Whitelegg, J. (1990) *One False Move: A Study of Children's Independent Mobility*. Policy Studies Institute

Hodgkin, R. (1993) 'Policy review', *Children & Society,* 7(2)

Holtermann, S. (1992) *Investing in Young Children: Costing an Education and Day Care Service*. National Children's Bureau, with AMA and ACC.

Kiernan, K. and Chase Lansdale, P. (1991) 'Children and marital breakdown; short and long-term consequences', *Proceedings of European Demographic Conference. Paris*

Kiernan, K. (1992) 'The impact of family disruption in childhood on transitions made in young adult life', *Population Studies,* 46

Kumar, V. (1993) *Poverty and Inequality in the UK: The Effects on Children.* National Children's Bureau

Levy, A. and Kahan, B. (1991) *The Pindown Experience and the Protection of Children.* Staffordshire County Council

Moss, P. (1990) 'Work, family and the care of children: issues of equality and responsibility', *Children & Society,* 4(2), pp.145-66

National Voluntary Council for Children's Play (1992) *Charter for Children's Play.* National Children's Bureau

Newell, P. (1991) *The UN Convention and Children's Rights in the UK.* National Children's Bureau

OPCS (1993) *General Household Survey 1991.* HMSO

OPCS (1993) *Population Trends.* HMSO

Page, R. and Clark, G.A. (eds.) (1977) *Who Cares? Young People in Care Speak Out.* National Children's Bureau

Patterson, G.R. (1982) *A Social Learning Approach 3: Coercive Family Process.* Castalia Publishing Co

Policy and Practice Review Group (1987) *Investing in the Future: Child Health Ten Years After the Court Report.* National Children's Bureau

Pugh, G. and De'Ath, E. (1984) *The Needs of Parents: Policy and Practice in Parent Education.* Macmillan

Rosenbaum, M. (1993) *Children and the Environment.* National Children's Bureau

Social Trends 23 (1993) Central Statistical Office

UNICEF (1991) *The State of the World's Children.* Oxford University Press

Utting, D., Bright, J. and Henricson, C. (1993) *Crime Prevention and the Family.* Family Policy Studies Centre

Walby, C. (1993) 'The contract culture; mix or muddle?', *Children and Society,* 7(4)

Wedge P and Essen J (1973) *Born to Fail?* National Children's Bureau

Woodroffe C and Kurtz Z (1989) *Working for Children? Children's Services and the NHS Review.* National Children's Bureau

2. The origins of the National Children's Bureau

Joan D Cooper, A Vice President, National Children's Bureau

Formalities

The National Bureau for Cooperation in Child Care was authorised, by unanimous agreement, at a large conference composed of representatives of statutory and voluntary organisations and individuals who had a concern, academic or practical, for children in need. They met at Church House, Westminster on 23 June 1962. The first annual general meeting was held on 18 September 1963, when Sir John Wolfenden presided and Sir George Haynes was elected to the chair. They were then Chairman and Director of the National Council of Social Service (NCSS), now the National Council for Voluntary Organisations (NCVO). The founder members of the Bureau were 111 British local authorities, which then provided child and school health services, all the leading voluntary organisations concerned with children, then largely on a denominational basis, and 47 interested individuals (Haynes, unpublished).

Such unanimity belied the preceding decade of turbulence and frustration. The need for a national institution for childcare arose from the plethora of agencies concerned with children's needs, their rivalries, the ambitions of Government Departments (Parker, 1983, pp.197-202), the lack of a central bank of information, the paucity of research and a vacuum as far as multi-disciplinary communication was concerned.

Concern for children

After World War II, the care of children was a 'women's issue'. A study made in 1946-7 by a sub-committee of the Women's Group on Public Welfare in association with NCSS had published a report on *The Neglected Child and his Family*. This had recommended that local authorities should be made responsible for providing a comprehensive service for the care of all children living in their area but the 1948 Children Act was restrictive and concerned essentially with the care of children deprived of a normal home life. Nevertheless, concern remained about neglected children and part of the problem was the lack of coordination of resources scattered among statutory and voluntary agencies.

The NBCCC was not the first attempt. Early in the 1950s a Children's Foundation had been sponsored by Professor Alan Moncrieff, a leading paediatrician, and by Dame Eileen Younghusband of the London School of Economics. Their public statement pronounced:

There is not even a central source of information about children and their problems so that, among other unhappy results, much research remains buried and many problems are left untouched because unrecognised.

The Foundation did not come to fruition but it was an important opinion forming activity.

There was also a joint consultative committee in childcare which met annually. This largely involved the voluntary sector but had some statutory representatives. This body appointed a sub-committee to examine the idea of a bureau and the members were John Gittins, then Principal of Aycliffe Approved school (now Aycliffe Centre for Children), Ian Brown, Children's Officer for Manchester, Rev. John Waterhouse, Principal of the National Children's Home and myself. There were other groups meeting informally, one in a London public house, and in different parts of the country. Edwin Ainscow, Children's Officer of the London County Council, was an activist in a lead role for London. These groups examined the specific need for a Bureau and the issue of cooperation in childcare with a concern for inter-disciplinary working:

The organisation of the services seemed like a chain store, magnificently departmentalised with the Headquarters of each department separately housed with its own management, but unfortunately neither the Directors nor the Department Heads ever dined at the same club. Professional training for work with children was as varied as in some cases it was expert. The market was being flooded with new knowledge but it percolated slowly and was sometimes misinterpreted on the way (Cooper, 1963, p.142).

The 1948 Children Act was one of the post war reforming measures, along with health, education and social security legislation. What the Children Act did, following the concerns over evacuation, the unfounded fear that a large number of children might be left behind and not returned to their parents, and the need to produce a successor to the old poor law responsibility for children needing substitute homes, was to set up a local authority framework to respond to the needs of children deprived of a normal home life. The legislation enabled certain categories of children under the age of 18 to be received, not taken, into care. These included children who were orphans, abandoned or lost, and those whose parents were prevented from providing proper accommodation, maintenance and upbringing, providing it was in the interest of the child's welfare to be received into care. In addition, there were also those children committed to care by order of a juvenile court.

It quickly became apparent that children received into care were the tip of the iceberg. In 1953, 39,000 children were received and 38,000 returned home. Placement, much over simplified by the Curtis Committee which had preceded the 1948 Children Act, was to be adoption, boarding out or institutional care in that order. By the mid 50s, however, assessment was recognised as the basis of placement and this development owed much to Dr Hilda Lewis and the psychological framework that she outlined (Lewis, 1954).

Evidence was beginning to mount that socially deprived families and children were dogged by ill health and disability and that the health, education and childcare systems must all be involved in meeting their needs.

Early thoughts
The need for a National Bureau was again formally mooted at the 1954 Annual Conference of Children's Officers:

What we need most of all is a sorting house for our ideas and a free market for the exchange of our acquired experience in all forms of family social work;

something like the Child Welfare League of the United States, but I should prefer to see it called the Family Welfare League of the British Isles (Cooper, 1954)

The idea was taken up by Alan Jacka, the Education Secretary of the National Children's Home and Orphanage. He marketed it in *Child Care*, the predecessor of *Social Work Today*, and at various conferences. Barnardo's was also enthusiastic. The leading voluntary organisations hosted meetings to examine the potential for a national organisation. They all wanted to be in on the act and were rather more enthusiastic than the local authorities or professional associations, which each visualised themselves as taking the lead and servicing not only their own members but the rest of the children's field. Most enthusiastic were Baroness Serota and Dame Eileen Younghusband. The Government Departments listened sympathetically but could not be overtly involved until a charitable organisation existed.

Somewhat reluctantly, it was decided that an intermediary negotiator was needed. Hence the decision, taken sadly, as far as the statutory childcare world was concerned, to seek help from NCSS, the leading voluntary organisation experienced in setting up and guiding new ones.

Apart from the financial difficulties, which were beyond the experience of most of the statutory organisations, there was the question of the rivalrous situation between the health, education and childcare professions. Health visitors backed by the maternity and child welfare committees of local health authorities were powerful claimants. These authorities employed home helps and psychiatric social workers. The argument that finally won the day was that a genuinely independent body was needed with membership open to all agencies and individuals concerned with children.

The parameters of a Bureau

Another reason for the slow progress was the long debate on the parameters of a Bureau. Was it to focus on deprived and neglected children or to serve all children? Fortunately the need for an independent Bureau serving all children received powerful support from Lord Cohen, the first Chair and a distinguished professor of medicine from Liverpool. He opened the doors of the British Medical

Association for many early discussions. Sir Alan Moncrieff, another prominent medical leader actively promoted a Bureau with a wide remit. Another powerful influence was Lord Wolfenden, Vice President from 1965, then President until his death in 1983. He disliked narrow boundaries, rather naturally as he had been Vice Chancellor of Reading University and then head of the British Museum.

The original emphasis was undoubtedly on the pursuit and spread of knowledge, the desire that good practice should be evaluated and then shared across professional boundaries and that research should permeate all systems concerned with children. Furthermore, the Bureau was not to serve the professionals exclusively. Both Baroness Serota and Eileen Younghusband pressed for a model which would have a social and cultural function and be open to anyone with an interest in children and their development. Given the statutory divisions between health and welfare in the local authorities and the multiplicity of voluntary bodies, issues of boundaries and membership were not easily resolved. In fact they had proved so defeating that Lord Wolfenden had chaired a three-year working party to study feasibility nationally and to explore funding and he also chaired the actual organising committee appointed in May 1961. By June 1962 the NBCCC was formally established with a legal constitution and registration as a charitable body. It was supported, thanks to the efforts of NCSS, by the Leverhulme Trust, the Carnegie UK Trust, the Buttle Trust, the London County Council, and 12 leading voluntary organisations.

The scene in 1954

The proceedings of the 1954 annual conference of children's officers give a picture of current concerns. These included adoption and in particular the need for cooperation with adoption societies, then the placing agencies; the recruitment and training of childcare officers; the gnawing fear that there were too many children in care for the wrong reasons which included homelessness, illegitimacy, the incapacity of a parent on account of social or health problems; and the growing determination that fostering and residential care should be seen as incidental to the care of children in their own homes. More precise concerns were that children in boarding schools and in private children's homes were left relatively unprotected and there was recognition that young people's needs should be considered at the time of leaving care on attaining independence (ACO conference, 1954).

Not only was there growing pressure for research into family patterns and into the special needs of identifiable groups of children and families but there was also the continuing problem over disseminating research findings and creating multi-disciplinary dialogues about research based practice. Very influential was Spence's Newcastle study of 1,000 families which argued that the decline in disease and death in infancy during the last 40 years was due less to improvements in medical or hospital practice than to the increasing spread of knowledge about the proper care and feeding of infants, a decrease in poverty and better housing. Spence made a rough division of 'problem families' into the 'friendly type' usually poor, feckless and of low intelligence, the sullen type usually defensive and suspicious and the vicious type when the mother and her partner could be cunning and sometimes cruel (Spence, 1954, p.146). So called problem families were of great concern in the early 1950s. An admonition to children's officers at their 1954 conference indicates the need for research and development:

Prevention so far has been envisaged by you as immediate prevention - prevention at the point of imminent deprivation. I would advise you to join with your colleagues in probation, education, health and planning to put all your weight and experience behind prevention at the source - namely the fostering of those conditions of informal community relationships which give the family the same natural sustenance and moral guidance as the parents in their turn provide for their children (Mack, 1954).

New housing was being built to a better standard, but Kenneth Brill, then Children's Officer for Devon, made a spirited plea to press for housing the homeless as a priority. Professor Craig, Professor of Paediatrics and Child Health at the University of Leeds, argued that solving the housing problem would reduce demands on other services, and dramatically reduce the need for hospital beds. Incidentally, he warned that there could be a danger of a child, especially in adoption placement, 'becoming the victim of too zealous and too numerous specialist interests'.

Residential care was also a conference theme. The small family group home, usually for fewer than 12 children and often situated on a council housing estate, was queried as a concept. So also were hostels for older boys and girls since they were not regarded as a better alternative to homely lodgings.

Another concern was low educational performance and the learning difficulties of deprived children. Mia Kellmer Pringle, then Deputy Head of the Centre for Child Study at the University of Birmingham had been researching this issue. It was a time when, as in the current scene, educational standards were under scrutiny. She argued that the factors causing educational difficulties in general were intellectual, physical, emotional and environmental, and tended to be associated with poverty which afflicted many children received into care. She suggested that children excluded from school might have home tuition as an alternative.

Dr William Moodie, Consultant Physician at University College Hospital, complained that enthusiasts for psychological theory often possessed only scant knowledge of what the theory really meant when attempting to translate it into practice; a comment not unheard of today. For development of sound mental health, children needed affection, security, occupation and freedom within limits, and parents must always be involved with the treatment of the child, he argued. It will be noted that there was little attention paid, except for educational difficulties, to physical handicap or ill health probably because these conditions were perceived as the responsibility of the NHS and the local health authority together with the considerable support of some of the long established voluntary agencies widely scattered throughout Britain.

Childcare training

Childcare had become accepted coinage after the Curtis Committee produced its first report 'Interim Report of the Care of Children Committee' recommending distinctive childcare training under a central council in collaboration with a number of universities. Unlike medical or psychiatric social work, the term 'child care social work' was not used. What happened was that psychiatric social work teaching came to dominate the early childcare courses, notably at the London School of Economics and at the University of Birmingham.

Case work was predominant. Childcare training meant the education and training of childcare visitors or field workers thus reflecting emphasis on adoption and fostering rather than institutional care. Newcastle and Bristol Universities became honourable exceptions and broke the deadlock by initiating courses for the training of residential staff at an advanced level. The advanced courses were first based within the university education departments. The influence of the approved schools and their need for qualified staff was marked. This offers a commentary on the educational role of the approved schools and a degree of professional competition between education and social work in the childcare field. Apart from these two advanced courses, training for residential work lay largely in colleges of further education. The knowledge base for childcare training was at this time derived largely from psychiatry and both Bowlby and Winnicott were influential.

The Bowlby influence

Dr John Bowlby's research and publications were seized on by the childcare world almost as basic dogma. His 1951 report *Maternal Care and Mental Health*, prepared for the World Health Organisation under the United Nations programme for the welfare of homeless children emphasised the importance of mother love in the development of a child's character and personality and assessed the effects of maternal deprivation (Bowlby, 1951, p.32). Homeless children were categorised as 'children who are orphaned or separated from their families for other reasons and need care in foster homes, institutions or other types of group care'. His scholarly report was quickly translated into popular reading in paperback (Fry, 1953). Bowlby's research had covered France, the Netherlands, the United States and the United Kingdom and he found considerable consensus on the damaging effects of maternal deprivation. Once again adoption and substitute families were seized upon as preventative measures. The impact of Bowlby's work on mental health, child guidance and health visiting was considerable but on childcare it was dramatic. Here was a workable theory which could be translated into practice, and childcare quickly claimed ownership. It was a theory that justified the resources needed to invest in children deprived of a normal home life and in preventive work with families. The impact of Bowlby served to highlight the communication problem among the various professions. Modified practice in the hospitalisation of children was needed, for example, as well as in institutional care for deprived children. Rutter (1972) later modified the theory by distinguishing between failure to make bonds of affection and deprivation after such bonds have been made, but the National Children's Bureau was well established by then and continuing debate, discussion and cross boundary examination of research had become more feasible and frequent.

Interestingly, it was the Children's Centre in Paris which had first reported on the issue in England and France, but this only served to highlight the need for a similar centre in Britain. Furthermore the National Foundation for Educational Research (NFER) had been set up following the 1944 Education Act to promote a working partnership with all concerned with public education, and research was seen as a unifying factor. In Scotland there was the Scottish Council for Research in Education. The point was not lost. If new education legislation was followed by national research foundations, then they were obviously needed for childcare following its own legislation. Nevertheless, the Bureau was not established as a research organisation as such but a body to promote and organise research, disseminate the results and provide the means for cooperative working among the various agencies and disciplines. Yet it was the Bureau's early distinguished research that gave it national and international recognition.

The Winnicott ascendancy

Another major contribution to childcare knowledge and practice in the 50s was that of Dr Donald Winnicott, paediatrician and psychoanalyst who wrote prolifically for professionals of all backgrounds, and frequently broadcast on the developmental needs of young children. He published his articles in nursery and in educational journals to reach teachers and in *Case Conference* to reach social workers. Much of his early work centred round mother and child relationships and led again to a concentration of concern on motherhood in relation to the health, growth and development of children (Winnicott, 1959). Winnicott's collected papers and subsequent flow of books were grist to the mill of childcare courses and their place was further assured when Clare Winnicott, his wife, became Director of the Central Council for Training in Child Care in the 60s.

The scene that developed between the proposal for a children's Bureau and its launch in 1963 reflected growing social concern over neglected children and their treatment, an increasing demand for emphasis on preventive work, on the education and training of childcare staff and anxiety over adoption and fostering since it was clear that breakdowns were further damaging already damaged children. There was also concern over child health, mass education and its effect on children with special needs, the prominence of psychoanalytic theory in child development and yet its uneven spread. The need for professional education in its broadest sense as a continuing requirement was also prominent.

The sixties

First steps

Carrying a heritage from the 50s, NBCCC came into being in October 1963 and so was a child of the opportunist 60s, largely attributable to the research reputation and the prodigious work output of its first Director. Dr Mia Kellmer Pringle was invited to leave her academic and research post at Birmingham and to accept the challenge of what had to be a risky enterprise. What especially appealed to her was the Bureau's multi-disciplinary task, the emphasis on the pursuit of knowledge, the information task including the all important library and the prospect of increasing the chances of all children whatever their talents or difficulties. Before the thirteen years spent at Birmingham, she had been a practising educational psychologist in Hertfordshire, but it was at Birmingham that she acquired her distinguished research record.

The NBCCC had a modest start with three staff in four small rooms first in Fitzroy Street, London, near the Post Office tower. A move to Adam House in Fitzroy Square was an improvement, and the move to Wakley Street more so, and manifestly improved when the Barnardo Hall was opened in 1974.

Early accommodation restrictions were, however, counterbalanced by a highly significant research fillip from Dr Neville Butler and the National Birthday Trust Fund. Mia and NBCCC were entrusted with the intellectual and research management of the National Child Development Study (1958 Cohort) about which Dr Ronald Davie, who also played a distinguished role in this and subsequent research programmes, writes in this issue.

The fashionable words in the early sixties were disadvantage, disability and deprivation: all candidates for preventive rather than remedial work, and finally reflected in legislation. On 1 October 1963, almost co-incidental with the founding of NBCCC, Section 1 of the Children and Young Persons Act became operative. It was made an express duty of local authorities to develop preventive work designed to reduce the need to receive children into care or bring them before a court. Many local authorities had developed such strategies but their legal position had been doubtful and needed clarification. Statutory recognition was now given to the principle that the best place for a child is with his family. It had taken more than 10 years to enshrine preventive work as a duty under children's legislation. This legislation also authorised the Home Office, the government department then responsible for child care, to conduct or support research. The Home Office had had its own research department but this was restricted to juvenile delinquency and adult crime because this was legally authorised and the Treasury could allow the expenditure. Once it got the new research powers under children's legislation the Home Office wasted no time. It immediately asked the NBCCC to produce a review of research into adoption. This resulted in *Adoption - Facts and Fallacies - A Review of Research 1948-65,* making use of Mia Kellmer Pringle's (1967) research expertise. Adoption continued to be a matter of concern. The statutory provisions for adoption date only from 1926 in England and Wales and 1930 in Scotland and came only after the deliberations of several committees and at least six unsuccessful Private Member's bills. Local authorities, as distinct from voluntary agencies, were not empowered to act as adoption placing agencies until 1968. Such was the fear of social engineering.

The research element

NBCCC quickly attracted wide ranging research commitments embracing child development, handicapped children and those receiving substitute care. The major research remained, however, the

National Child Development Study of the 1958 cohort of children born in early March in that year. This heralded broad cooperation as it involved four charitable bodies concerned with health, education and social development of children and was financed by several government departments. It resulted in the publication of *11,000 Seven Year Olds* (Pringle and others, 1967). This and the research into adoption quickly gave the Bureau a name for research and the flow of Bureau publications has continued to reflect this early and continuing trend towards inter-disciplinary research into child health, child development, education and childcare. From the start, the Bureau established a reputation for relevant academic research intended to have policy and practice implications. The dissemination of results was widespread through publications, articles in journals and conferences. Not least important was the growing recognition of the library and information centre, always central to the purpose of the Bureau, but now to have available a specialist service on child development in its widest sense which was of considerable benefit to multidisciplinary concern with research and practice. The Bureau's reputation for issuing statements based on knowledge and research was thus established from the outset.

Covering the various disciplines and organisations, the library gained recognition as a specialist one and publications such as *Highlights* added to the dissemination of research findings all over Britain and abroad too. By now the Bureau was set fair to build up its basic aims of making available existing knowledge of children, their development and their needs, facilitating communication among health, education and childcare agencies, between statutory and voluntary organisations, and making research available as a basis for the development and evaluation of practice (Pringle, 1980, pp.16-18).

Interest continued to grow in the care of young children as evidenced by the work of the Newsons (Newson, 1963). This presented a sociological perspective and work in the education field was also continuing to contribute to child and teenage development (Jackson and Marsden, 1962). Childcare was broadening out well beyond the psychoanalytic interpretation to include not only health and education development but the social, economic and cultural development of children with special needs.

The resolution founding NBCCC stated that the aim was to benefit children or young persons in need of special care. It was not to seek to co-ordinate the policy of its corporate members, but would aim to promote and organise cooperation, to initiate research and increase knowledge and understanding in the care of children.

The flavour of the times when the Bureau was founded can be caught from the reports of the Home Office and the Ministry of Health. In his personal foreword to the Home Office Report 1964, Henry Brooke, the Home Secretary, concentrated largely on the rising numbers of juvenile delinquents. In 1938 only 11 boys per thousand in the 14-16 age group were found guilty of indictable offences. By 1962, the figure was 26 per thousand and rising yearly, particularly among girls. 'There is also a general shortage of people willing to undertake residential work with boys and girls' he commented (Brooke, 1964). A cause for celebration was the Children and Young Persons Act 1963 which required local authorities:

...to make available such advice, guidance and assistance as may promote the welfare of children by diminishing the need to receive children into or keep them in care ...or to bring children before a Juvenile court.

This legalised preventive work with families and all relevant local authority departments were to be involved as were voluntary agencies.

The Children Act 1948 had made it a duty to board out with foster parents children in public care except when it was not practical or desirable for the time being. The percentage boarded out had risen from 35 per cent to 52 per cent between 1949 and 1963 and children with disabilities were being included. The voluntary organisations concentrated on residential care and placed only 20 per cent of children in foster homes. This disparity in aim between public and voluntary care for deprived children increased the need for cooperation based upon research and evaluated practice. Childcare still retained its own identity as a collection of papers *Child Care and Social Work* (Winnicott, 1964) demonstrated, concentrating as these papers did on casework in residential as well as individual placements and a psychiatric view of casework.

There had been a significant expansion of statutory residential provision. In 1963, there were 1,145 local authority children's homes in England and Wales and of these 809 were small family group homes despite the querying of their concept in 1954. In 1948 only about 400 residential establishments had been in use but some were very large institutions.

Medical encouragement and support for the Bureau continued to be marked. The Advisory Council in Child Care and the Central Training Council, reconstructed in 1962, were chaired by Professor Alan Moncrieff who had chaired the former since 1948 and the latter since 1953. NBCCC owed much to the contribution of distinguished medical figures who understood research based practice and the need to evaluate it as a basis for development and training.

Training, however, was still very limited. In 1964, students qualifying as childcare officers numbered 190 and there were five residential training courses for the whole country. 'The proportion of trained staff in residential childcare is still very low' was a comment made in the Home Office Report but the numbers qualifying, including those on senior courses, reached 320 in 1964.

Adoption continued to be a matter of concern. Legal adoptions, as distinct from informal arrangements, had increased from 14,109 in 1959 to 16,894 in 1962 and were heavily weighted in favour of children under five years. The 1963 Children and Young Persons Act conferred powers on the Secretary of State and the local authorities to conduct or assist others in conducting research into any matter connected with the adoption of children and thus dealt a blow in favour of the acquisition of knowledge as distinct from the over zealous preservation of confidentiality.

As part of its general survey of childcare, the Home Office commented in its 1964 report (p.7) that NBCCC was a national centre to 'improve communication between the various services concerned with children, to develop understanding among workers and to improve the quality of their services'. Its object was to promote the benefit of children or young persons who are in need of special care in any manner which now is or hereafter may be deemed by law to be charitable and adding that the Bureau was concerned with a wide range of needs beyond those covered by children's legislation.

By the mid sixties, academic research into child development and childcare practice had established itself. Research into fostering practice (Trasler, 1960; Parker, 1966) and into family life and educational development (Douglas, 1964) offers examples.

The health perspective

The Report of the Ministry of Health for 1963 (Cmnd. 2389) disclosed that the total number of day nurseries maintained by local authorities and voluntary organisations was continuing a downward trend from 472 in 1961 to 459 in 1963. Day nurseries had been a war time measure to enable women to work outside home and had been reduced during the 50s. The figures demonstrate that this switch was not in tune with the times or women's changing needs. By contrast registration under the Nurseries and Child-Minders Regulation Act 1948 rose from 17,618 to 31,045 during the same period. The Home Help Service also expanded from 21,893 to 24,620 during this period. Local health authorities could justifiably continue to stake a claim for preventive work with families and young children when in difficulty.

It will be noted that children with disabilities did not loom large but a breakthrough was coming. The British Council for the Rehabilitation of the Disabled published a Report on the Handicapped School Leaver in 1963. NBCCC established a working party to examine the special needs of handicapped children with Dame Eileen Younghusband in the chair resulting in 1970 in the publication *Living with Handicap*. The Voluntary Council for Handicapped Children was established independently, but in association with the Bureau, in 1975. It is now titled the Council for Disabled Children.

Small beginnings

The Bureau had to struggle from its beginnings to create bridges across the various professions and disciplines concerned with children in need. Yet from the start, almost briskly, it demonstrated at its conferences and lectures that policy and practice, to be informed, have to cross knowledge boundaries. Local groups were not part of its original strategy but they, nevertheless, developed and are now being resuscitated and supported. Given the current difficult economic and social climate, it is hard to believe that there is not as much need for the National Children's Bureau, and possibly more, than there was when it was founded. In any case, it will be apparent that over 30 years many of the concerns identified in the early 50s and 60s remain. They include early child development, and in this area the Bureau has an international reputation, but there remains concern over opportunities for pre-school learning, coupled with childcare facilities for working mothers. There remains concern over rising rates of juvenile delinquency and over children living in single parent families.

Thirty years on

From these vignettes of the early 50s and 60s, it becomes apparent that the Bureau was a child of the sixties. The social sciences had by then become recognised as a discipline, and research the tool for evaluation. Health and education were well advanced in research whereas childcare was a laggard. The Bureau made the breakthrough and ensured from the start that results were disseminated across the disciplines. This is an enduring and outstanding Bureau characteristic and is as vital now as 30 years ago. Newly recognised social problems such as child abuse and AIDS illustrate the continuing multi-disciplinary approach. Historically identified issues still persist such as the long standing concern about adoption, residential services, funding and evaluating preventive work to help families survive. There remains concern over children's health and development and regional variations, and soon there will be the European variations and the contribution of the European Children's Centre. Thirty years on, the opportunities are exciting and challenging and the staff of the Bureau are still prodigious workers who translate ideas into action.

References

Association of Children's Officers (1954) *Proceedings of Fifth Annual Conference*. BASW, 16 Kent Street, Birmingham B5 6RD

Brill, K. (1954) *Back Home*. Association of Children's Officers, Proceedings of Fifth Annual Conference, pp.12-25

British Council for Rehabilitation of the Disabled (1964) *The Handicapped School Leaver*. Report of a Working Party. London: Tavistock

Brooke, H. (1964) *Against the Evil of Delinquency*. Foreword to the Report on the Work of the Children's Department of the Home Office, pp.iii-xii. London: HMSO

Children Act 1948. London: HMSO

Children and Young Persons Act 1963. London: HMSO

Cooper, J. (1954) in Association of Children's Officers *Proceedings of Fifth Annual Conference*, p.4

Cooper, J. (1963) 'The founding of the National Bureau for Co-operation in Child Care', *Social Services Quarterly*, 38(4), pp.141-145

Craig, W.S. (1954)'The needs of the under fives', *Proceedings of Fifth Annual Conference*, pp.28-35. Association of Children's Officers

Curtis Report (1946) *Report of the Care of Children Committee*. Cmd 6922. London: HMSO

Curtis Report (1946) *Interim Report of the Care of Children Committee*. Cmd 6760. London: HMSO

Douglas, J.W.B. and Blomfield, J.M. (1958) *Children Under Five*. The results of a national survey made by a Joint Committee of the Institute of Child Health (University of London), the Society of Medical Officers of Health and the Population Investigation Committee. London: Allen & Unwin

Fry, M. (1953) *Child Care and the Growth of Love*. London: Pelican

Haynes, G. *How It Came About*. Unpublished paper

Home Office (1964) *Report on the Work of the Children's Department*. London: HMSO

Jackson, B. and Marsden, D. (1962) *Education and the Working Class*. London: Routledge & Kegan Paul

Leissner, A. (1967) *Family Advice Services: An Exploratory Study of a Sample of Such Services Organised by Children's Departments in England*. London: Longmans for National Children's Bureau

Lewis, H. (1954) *Deprived Children: The Mersham Experiment - A Social and Clinical Study*. London: Oxford University Press

Mack, J.A. (1954) 'The family in a changing society', *Proceedings of Fifth Annual Conference,* p.8. Association of Children's Officers

Moodie, W. (1954) 'The Mental Health of the Growing Child', *Proceedings of Fifth Annual Conference*, pp.59-67. Association of Children's Officers

Newson, J. and Newson, E. (1963) *Infant Care in an Urban Community*. London: Allen & Unwin

Parker, A.R. (1966) *Decision in Child Care*. London: Allen & Unwin

Parker, R. (1983) 'The gestation of reform: The Children Act 1948' in Bean, P. and MacPherson, S. (eds.) *Approaches to Welfare*. London: Routledge & Kegan Paul, pp.197-202

Pringle, M. Kellmer (1954) 'Educational difficulties of the deprived child',

Proceedings of Fifth Annual Conference, pp.51-56. Association of Children's Officers

Pringle, M. Kellmer (1967) *Adoption - Facts and Fallacies.* London: Longmans

Pringle, M. Kellmer, Butler, N. and Davie, R. (1967) *11,000 Seven-Year-Olds.* London: Longmans

Pringle, M. Kellmer (1980) 'Opening the doors to child care', *Social Work Today,* 11(43), pp.16-18

Rutter, M. (1972) *Maternal Deprivation Reassessed.* Harmondsworth: Penguin

Spence, J. (1954) *A Thousand Families in Newcastle-Upon-Tyne: An Approach to the Study of Health and Illness in Children.* London: Oxford University Press

Trasler, G. (1960) *In Place of Parents: A Study of Foster Care.* London: Routledge

Winnicott, D.W. (1958) *Collected Papers: Through Paediatrics to Psycho-Analysis.* London: Tavistock

Winnicott, C. (1964) *Child Care and Social Work.* Hitchin: Codicote Press

Women's Group on Public Welfare (1948) *The Neglected Child and His Family. A Study Made in 1946-7 of the Problem of the Child Neglected in His Own Home.* Cumberlege, London: Oxford University Press

3. The impact of the National Child Development Study

Ron Davie, Consulting Psychologist
formerly Director of the National Children's Bureau and Co-Director
of the National Child Development Study

Introduction

The National Child Development Study (1958 Cohort) - usually shortened to NCDS - is by any standards a major research study. It has an international reputation. The study is following the lives of a complete week's births in Britain (technically, a birth 'cohort') from 1958 through to the present day. Its story is a fascinating one.

The fascination derives from a number of aspects, many of which will be beyond the scope of the present article. For example, two of the members of this very large cohort became internationally famous 'pop stars' and several were exceptionally gifted in sport, the arts and academically. For the most part, of course, since the group is a complete cross-section of the British population, the cohort members as children were ordinary boys and girls, growing up nevertheless in their different ways. They are now in their mid-thirties and have more than 20,000 children of their own.

A particular point of interest derives from the seemingly universal fascination - exploited in several small-scale studies by television - of seeing how children or young people turn out in later life. This 'longitudinal' aspect has a more serious value from a research perspective in that it is the only way in which certain scientific and practical questions can validly be addressed. For example, separate studies of, say, seven-year-olds and of 11-year-olds can tell us a great deal about the characteristics of those age groups. However, they cannot tell us whether those children who are doing well - or badly - in school at seven years of age are for the most part the same ones who prove to be doing well, or badly, four years later. This latter kind of information would open up important further questions about the characteristics and life situations of those children whose educational performance improves or deteriorates over the junior school years.

In this chapter, I - the almost inevitable personal perspective seems to demand the first person singular - shall often be examining this kind of 'longitudinal' issue. However, the impact of the study has also taken other forms, which have sometimes included relatively simple, straightforwardly descriptive findings. In these instances the findings have carried great weight because of the size and nationally representative nature of the sample. This left no room for doubting the validity of the results.

Both the size of this article and the brief of the editor preclude any attempt to produce an overall summary of even the major scientific or policy implications of the many NCDS findings in the past 30 years. To give some indication of the potential size of such a task, a recent review of the child health findings alone (Power, 1992) produced 338 references, almost all of which were publications of the study. Therefore, as the title indicates, I shall confine myself (largely) to findings which covered the cohort's school years and which have had a clear 'impact' on the world of policy or practice in education, health or social services. Even within that brief, a very rigorous selection has been made, so that as I look back on a familiar terrain, I pick out some of the peaks which stand out - for me and, I know, for a number of that small group of researchers who have spent a significant part of their life's work on this study. Nevertheless, the responsibility for the selection must remain mine and, of course, any implicit or explicit weight which is attached to the implications.

The birth and growth of the study

The study of this 1958 birth cohort was not the first of its kind in Britain. A similar, though less extensive, study was started in 1946 b;

J.W.B. Douglas. This earlier study was initially an investigation of ante-natal and maternity services in Britain. It gathered data on all the births in the country during the week 3 to 9 March 1946. The project was subsequently transformed into a longitudinal study, investigating education and other factors as well as health. This project is still continuing (for example Wadsworth, 1991).

The 1958 study followed a similar pattern. It, too, started life as a health project, its focus being reflected in its original name: the 1958 Perinatal Mortality Survey. The 1958 cohort was drawn from the same birth week - twelve years later - in order to facilitate any subsequent comparisons between the two. The 1958 week's births numbered some 17,000 in all.

After the obstetric data had been subjected to a first analysis (Butler and Bonham, 1963), Butler turned his attention to the possiblity of a follow-up study of the children. At around this time the 'National Bureau for Co-operation in Child Care' (now the National Children's Bureau) was established. Neville Butler was introduced to the Bureau's first Director, Mia Kellmer Pringle, and together they began to seek research funds for what they saw as a major project which would cover the whole of the children's childhood and beyond - possibly, even extending 'from the cradle to the grave'. The present name of the study, NCDS, was created at around this period.

Butler's and Kellmer Pringle's conception differed from that which had been adopted by Douglas for the 1946 study in a number of important respects. First, NCDS was to be avowedly interdisciplinary, whereas the earlier one had been largely steered by one person. Second, the whole of the birth week was to be followed up, whereas Douglas had used a stratified sample from his original cohort of births. Third, for NCDS the large-scale studies ('sweeps') of all the cohort at intervals were to be supplemented by much smaller-scale studies of particular groups of special interest. This has remained a feature of the work: for example, Hitchfield's interviewing and assessment of the 'gifted' children in the cohort (1974) and Ferri's study of the stepchildren (1984).

Butler and Kellmer Pringle obtained their initial funding from a government committee (the Plowden Committee) which was looking at primary education in England. The children were of infant school age by this time and therefore of special interest to this committee.

RON DAVIE

The first NCDS research team was established in 1964 to undertake the work of tracing all of the children, designing this sweep, gathering and analysing the data and providing a report for the Plowden Committee within 18 months. I was appointed to lead the team, as Senior Research Officer (and subsequently became a co-director). The deadline for reporting to the Plowden Committee was achieved (Plowden, 1966; Pringle and others, 1966). These first follow-up data were later much more intensively and extensively analysed (Davie and others, 1972).

The pattern of data gathering established for this first 'sweep' was to become the established pattern for subsequent 'sweeps' of the cohort at 11 and 16 years. Educational data were obtained from the children's schools, including special tests and (at the later ages) written work and opinions from the children themselves. A full medical and physical examination was carried out by a medical officer of the child's local authority; and a health visitor, usually, interviewed the parent(s) and completed a social questionnaire.

The funding source for the major sweeps changed from the original Plowden Committee to the Social Science Research Council and then to a consortium of government departments, including the sweep at 23 years. The latest sweep at age 33 yeas had its major funding from the Economic and Social Research Council but this was supplemented by central government department money and from American sources. However, it has to be said that funding for the study has always been most precarious and its continuation has often hung by a thread. Its survival, whilst Mia Pringle was at the Bureau, often depended more upon her persistence and persuasiveness than upon any appreciation of the value of the study by government officials or research councils.

In any event, what had originally started out in 1964 as a modest budget of £60K or so, over three years, can now be counted in £millions and encompasses not only the cohort members themselves but their spouses/partners, their children and their parents (most of whom are now reaching retirement age).

Thus, although information about the parents of the cohort children has always been gathered, it has until now been collected and used largely as background material for use in analysing the data on the cohort children. Now, data on the parents are being analysed in their own right. The sweep at age 23 also collected basic information about the cohort member's own children. Now, for the first time, these children are being studied in some detail. Thus, what was already a rich longitudinal data source has been transformed into a multi-level, multi-age project in which each level is both of interest in itself and can also feed into the other levels to illuminate inter-generational trends and relationships. Nevertheless, the main focus continues to be on the cohort members themselves.

To complete briefly the historical framework of NCDS, the earlier mention of the 1946 cohort should be complemented by mention of a subsequent cohort study, cast in a very similar mould in that it was also based upon one week's births in Britain, which were subsequently followed up longitudinally. This project was launched in 1970 and the prime mover was again Neville Butler (for example Butler and Golding, 1986).

Effects of social circumstances on children's development

Few can doubt that the environment, especially the social environment, in which children grow up affects their developing abilities and other personal characteristics. Indeed, the environment is also likely as a consequence to affect their life chances, although there are many children who subsequently defy these kinds of predictions (as we shall see later).

NCDS was therefore following a long line of researchers, not to mention social commentators and philosophers, in examining the effects of environmental factors. J.W.B. Douglas was perhaps the most notable immediate predecessor to tread this research path with his book *The Home and the School* (1964), which became a favourite text for countless student teachers and other in the late 1960s.

Nevertheless, it is often the case that each new generation has to rediscover certain basic truths. Furthermore, NCDS had the potential for more impact on this issue than probably any other research project before it. The size of the sample, its national character, the range and depth of the health, educational and social data, the sophistication of the statistical analyses which had become more readily possible on such a group with the rapid advance in computing technology - all of these features together gave the NCDS research findings potential importance. When this amalgam was combined with a topic which itself carried human or political interest or controversy the 'echo chamber' was in place for considerable impact.

The early findings from the study exemplified this. As mentioned above, the first report from NCDS was produced for the Plowden Committee and appeared as Appendix 10 of the Committee's Report (1966). These first findings were also published separately (Pringle and others, 1966) but because they had been geared to an English committee, the analyses were confined to the children who were living in England. Whether for this reason, or because the results were 'buried' with many others in the Plowden Report, or because the political climate was not right, the impact was not notable, although *Eleven Thousand Seven-year-olds* began to appear on book lists for student reading.

However, some six years later, *From Birth to Seven* (Davie and others, 1972) based upon the same data, albeit now covering all of the children and with analyses in much more detail, evoked a response with a much greater resonance, notably from the Press. For example, the findings were covered in what was planned as an 'exclusive' feature article in a Sunday *Colour Supplement* (*Sunday Times*, 4 June 72). Most of the daily papers - incensed, apparently, that a mere colour supplement should have exclusive rights to such important and newsworthy results - decided to break the embargo on the Press Release and to cover the 'story' on the previous day. The findings were presented in considerable detail and in some cases the newspapers commented in their leader columns, too. *The Times*, for example, carried separate features by their education correspondent and by their health and welfare correspondent opposite the leader page.

The message which had attracted their attention was the extent of the social, health and educational differences which were already so starkly apparent in the nation's children at such an early age. The message is well exemplified in the title of the *Sunday Times* 'exclusive' article, 'The unequal start'. Brief extracts from the opening paragraph give the flavour of the theme:

The chances of an unskilled manual's worker's child (Social Class V) being a poor reader at seven years old are six times greater than a professional worker's child (Social Class 1). The chances of a Social Class V child being a non-reader are 15 times greater... Although children are getting taller each decade, the gap between the classes is not narrowing .... Families liable to need the medical and welfare services most were least likely to use them.

The following week, the industrial correspondent of the *Daily Mirror*, under the headline 'The Haves and the Have Nots', wondered if this kind of unequal start and its later consequences were one of the causes of industrial unrest in Britain's workplaces, creating an atmosphere of 'them' and 'us' between management and workforce.

Effects on educational policy

The most obvious effect upon educational policy of these early findings was to prompt politicians of both major parties to look at the possibilities of offering nursery education on demand, or at least to embark on a rapid expansion of this service. The justification was that such universal, or near universal, provision would create a more equal start for the nation's children.

Of course, the NCDS findings alone did not bring about this change and there are interesting comparisons between this move in British policy and the situation in the United States where President Johnson had in 1967 initiated the 'Head Start' programme for disadvantaged pre-school children (see Rutter and Madge, 1976, p.131). Furthermore, in both countries there had been a growing interest in 'compensatory education' (Rutter and Madge, 1976, p.130).

Therefore, the time was right for the NCDS findings (and others) to strike home. For example, Edward Short, the then Labour Party Shadow Education Secretary, said at an Annual Conference of the National Children's Bureau that the findings had prompted the Labour Party to review its education policy document in order to give greater priority to nursery school provision.

Margaret Thatcher, Secretary of State for Education and Science at that time, produced a White Paper entitled *A Framework for Expansion* (DES, 1972), which was centrally concerned with building up nursery schooling in the years ahead. The National Children's Bureau was told informally by DES officials that the NCDS findings had influenced Ministerial thinking in this area.

Cycles of disadvantage

Across Whitehall at the Department of Health and Social Security, another Secretary of State, Sir Keith Joseph, was taking a particular interest in the issue of disadvantage from a social policy perspective. In his 1972 speech to the Annual Conference of the Pre-school Playgroups Association, he spoke with some force about 'cycles of disadvantage', which trapped children and families from one generation to another in social deprivation. The opening lines of his speech made reference to the NCDS findings.

The speech led on to a joint DHSS/SSRC working party on Transmitted Deprivation, which then commissioned a review of the literature (Rutter and Madge, 1976) and established a seven-year programme of research. The link with the American scene was clear here, too, for Sir Keith in partnership with an American Foundation initiated in 1972 a trip to the States by a small British group of policymakers and academics (of which I was a member) to visit Head Start programmes in the States. An American group later paid a reciprocal visit to Britain.

Poverty and disadvantage

I certainly cannot leave the issue of social disadvantage without picking out the NCDS publication which sold in far greater numbers, and almost certainly had more impact with practitioners, than any other publication from the study. Although the title *Born to Fail ?* (Wedge and Prosser, 1973) might suggest - notwithstanding the question mark - a sombre note, this is not the description which comes most readily to mind. 'Concerned', 'urgent', 'challenging' characterise the book's message better.

It was a modest publication in size, some 60 pages and originally priced at 30 pence. It was written in an easily readable style and had an easily accessible format with good graphics and photographs. The results portrayed emerged from a special study of social disadvantage amongst the cohort children, when they were 11-years-old.

Despite the book's brevity, its message was skilfully punched home. It catalogued the extent and range of disadvantage in health, education, welfare, housing, income and take-up of services amongst Britain's 11-year-olds at the end of the 1960s. The final few sentences convey very well the flavour of the book's theme:

If children are indeed the nation's future, then everyone has a stake in their welfare.....Do we mind if children grow up in bad housing when we could do something about it ? Do we mind the stress caused by low incomes when we could afford to change it? As a society do we really care sufficiently about our children to reduce drastically the hardships of their families? Do we care that so many are born to fail ?

Mention was made above of the book's major impact on practitioners. However, this is not to imply that it did not also affect policy. Following so closely after *From Birth to Seven*, the policy message of which was very similar, the impact on central government and on the media of *Born to Fail?* was more one of reinforcing a largely accepted view than of breaking new ground. Nevertheless, policy does not necessarily begin or end in Whitehall, and at local authority level in particular the 'punch' which *Born to Fail?*'s style and format gave to the message was often influential. Perhaps the most dramatic example was that of Strathclyde Regional Council (covering approximately half of Scotland's population) which considered the Report's implications in detail and built them into its policy and services. *Born to Fail?* was still being cited in Strathclyde policy documents some ten years later.

A subsequent sub-study (Wedge and Essen, 1982) examined the extent and nature of disadvantage in the cohort at age 11 and 16 years. This work, without having the same resounding impact as the earlier one, nevertheless both reinforced the messages of *Born to Fail?* and carried them forward into new dimensions.

Escape from disadvantage

One aspect of the study's longitudinal perspective is of particular interest. It is therefore surprising that the one NCDS sub-study which has been able to address it directly and in depth has seemingly had little impact (Pilling, 1990), at least thus far.

Earlier reference was made to the fact that television companies have exploited the universal appeal of the question 'How do they turn out?' by mounting small-scale longitudinal studies of their own, starting with a group of young children.

Perhaps the most fascinating question of all is to ask: how do some children manage to succeed in later life despite the most socially disadvantaging conditions in their childhood? Essen and Wedge (1982) had carried out an analysis using already available data from the 16-year-old sweep but inevitably many of the most interesting questions had had to remain effectively unasked as well as unanswered. However, Pilling's study was mounted on the basis that she would go out and interview a group of adults from the study who could be defined as 'successful' (at age 23) and for comparison a reference group with similar earlier disadvantages but who had not been successful by the same criteria. Since her criteria of 'success' were based upon educational and vocational qualifications, she also selected a small group of 'alternative achievers' who had achieved a measure of success in some other way, including material possessions (for example, income, housing).

No magic elixir emerged, but the results were very interesting indeed. For example, it seems that boys are more likely to suffer long-term effects from social disadvantage experienced in early childhood, whilst for girls adolescence is a more critical period. Most intriguingly, since the findings appear to conflict with at least some of the implications of the NCDS Study on one-parent families, almost all of the 'achievers' had been living with both their natural parents at the age of 16, whilst only a half of the comparison group had been in this family situation. The issue was not as simple as this might seem, of course, as Pilling points out. Another important result from this study is its confirmation of the value of family involvement. For example, there was strong evidence of the importance of the father's interaction and involvement with his child. Also, more generally, the importance emerged of some kind of participation and of some shared value system within the family for the child's later 'success', notwithstanding an apparently disadvantaging environment.

Smoking in pregnancy

Thus far, I have considered findings which, though important and influential, were not on the whole longitudinal in nature. In considering the study's contribution on the effects of smoking in pregnancy, we move to this latter category.

At the time of the original perinatal survey of the cohort babies and their parents, some research had been reported showing an association between smoking during pregnancy and obstetric factors. However, the establishment of a statistical association is only the first step along what may be a complex research path. The contribution of NCDS has been to tread that path to considerable effect with its rich data source and its longitudinal framework.

The problem facing most researchers, particularly those who are not carrying out experimental work, is that causal factors are notoriously difficult to pin down. A correlation between A and B may simply mean, for example, that both factors are themselves correlated with another factor C, and there may be little true relationship and no causal link between the initial pairing at all. NCDS' first strength therefore was the number of potentially spurious social and health factors that it was able to control for - to eliminate from the search, as it were (see Butler and Alberman, 1969). Major findings to emerge from the study included (Power, 1992), 'that the effect of smoking 10 cigarettes a day or more in the second half of pregnancy increased the perinatal mortality rate by 28 per cent and decreased birthweight by an average 170g compared with non-smokers'.

The second strength of the study has been its ability to continue tracking these correlations in the years which followed the original perinatal survey. These follow-up data have confirmed the longer term adverse effects of smoking in pregnancy upon children's later development in characteristics as diverse as height and reading attainment (for example, Butler and Goldstein, 1973; Fogelman, 1980). Work on NCDS data has thus - in an international as well as a national context - played a very important role in helping to establish the adverse effects of smoking in pregnancy and also in highlighting some of the mechanisms through which these effects are mediated, such as in lowering birthweight.

Selective and non-selective education

This topic was tackled by NCDS using data gathered largely when the cohort members were 11 and 16-years-old. They entered secondary education in 1969 at a time when many local authorities were beginning to change to comprehensive schooling. Some had already done so.

In some ways, the cohort was an ideal vehicle for a research enquiry in this area. Here was a representative group of children passing through the three principal existing types of secondary school: secondary modern, grammar and comprehensive. Furthermore, the type of schooling which each individual child would receive was less a matter of their parents' choice, more a matter of the policy adopted in the area in which they lived. Therefore, in a sense, an educational 'experiment' was taking place in which the cohort members were for the most part necessarily involved, and the study was ideally placed to assess the outcome.

There was one important shortcoming from an 'experimental' point of view, namely, that the comprehensive schools would be a relatively new phenomenon in most areas. Therefore, as everyone connected with education during that period will recall, the early years were often unsettled because many teachers had to adjust to teaching a wider range of ability than they were accustomed to. In that sense, then, the 'experiment' was less than balanced in that some of the children in comprehensive schools were likely to be somewhat disadvantaged. The extent of this was unknown. Nevertheless, set against this shortcoming was a very significant research advantage, namely, that a great deal of relevant and comparable educational and social information about the cohort children was available for the analysis.

In the current educational debate about the publication of examination or test results for individual schools, the crux of the argument between the government and its critics on this issue is whether the results are best published as they stand, or whether some kind of 'value added' weighting should be built in. Proponents of a 'value added' analysis point out that the intake to different schools can be vastly different, and that simply measuring the eventual outcome may merely reflect initial differences and not the quality of education received. Therefore, they argue, some way is needed of weighting the examination or test results, so that they will more nearly reflect the contribution of schools.

It was this 'value added' model of analysis which NCDS used in the late 1970s in order to carry out valid comparisons between the educational progress made by cohort children in the three different kinds of secondary school. A special sub-study was set up, funded by the Department of Education and Science (DES), which also appointed a steering committee to oversee the work.

It is rare that a complex issue yields a simple result, and this piece of research was no exception. One of the necessary complexities of the research was to analyse whether children of different levels of ability fared equally well in the three types of school. Perhaps the most 'politically' sensitive question to address was whether children at the top levels of ability - previously in grammar schools - suffered academically by going to comprehensive schools. The outcome measures used in the initial study to facilitate comparability were a reading and a mathematics test (Steedman, 1980). A second study looked at public examination results (Steedman, 1983).

On the question of how well the most able children fared, the study's analysis proved clear and reassuring:

...amongst those whose test scores at 11 put them in the top 20 per cent, the ones who went to comprehensives did much 'better' than those who went to secondary moderns. Compared to grammar school pupils from this top fifth of 11 year-olds, the comprehensive pupils did about as well in mathematics and in reading comprehension by the age of 16. There is, by these lights, no great cause for concern over the progress in comprehensives of bright children who might have gone to grammar schools (Steedman, 1980, p.218).

The overall results of the sub-study were not seen by the researcher as 'favouring' comprehensives as against grammar schools, or vice versa. However, those who supported the non-selective ideology, conscious that those early years were a time of teething troubles, drew comfort from the fact that the comprehensives' results had held up so well.

On the other hand, some who were committed to grammar schooling appeared to find difficulty in accepting the findings. For the first and only time in the history of the study it found itself plunged into political controversy. The implication of political bias was levelled by some against the sub-study, notwithstanding the existence of a steering committee appointed by the DES. However, more balanced commentators prevailed, and the government funded a second study (using public examination results) with the same researcher and committee. The publication of the results of this second study was met with no outbursts at all.

It is difficult to gauge the impact of these two pieces of work. However, it may be that it gave pause for thought to at least some of those who regard the selective/non-selective debate as essentially a political issue with a simple outcome, rather than an educational one with a complex outcome and with no clear 'winners'. Furthermore, as we have seen, the findings did indicate that the switch to comprehensive schooling was not adversely affecting the most able of the nation's children - at least, not in ways that one could readily measure. In trying to assess the impact of NCDS in such a central area of British life, one only has to consider what might have been the consequences of this government-funded study finding that these most able children *were* being significantly disadvantaged by attending comprehensive schools.

Family situations

We now move to NCDS findings which have on the whole had a less public exposure and impact. A group of these findings, some of which date back to the earliest days of the study in the late 1960s focus upon what researchers at that time often referred to as 'anomalous family situations'. This generic term encompassed all those families which did not have two (married) parents bringing up their own (biological) child(ren). The term has tended to drop out of use as such family situations have become less and less anomalous, and as such terms in any event have been felt to imply a value judgement.

One of the first NCDS sub-studies in this area helped to establish the pattern which I referred to earlier as being favoured by Butler and Pringle for NCDS. These projects, separately financed and staffed from the main sweeps, were usually small in scale, typically involving interviewing the parents of a particular sub-group of children - or the children themselves. Alternatively, the sub-studies have meant gathering additional (or confirmatory) information, such as from hospital records, on a sub-group of particular interest. A third model has been to instigate further work on most if not all of the cohort in order to research in more depth a topic of special relevance to policy or practice (that is, the research on social disadvantage which produced *Born to Fail?* and the research on selective schooling).

In fact, the first sub-study published in book form was cast in this third mould. It looked at the issue of illegitimacy (Crellin and others, 1971). The health, education, development and social circumstances of those cohort children who had been *Born Illegitimate* were analysed in detail. The findings confirmed the major problems on virtually all fronts encountered by the children and their families. The analyses were also subsequently used by Seglow and her colleagues (Seglow and others, 1972) as a point of reference or comparison in looking at some aspects of the progress of the adopted children in the cohort, many of whom had, of course, been born illegitimate.

The sub-study on adoption - like another very early one on gifted children, already mentioned - involved the principal researcher in interviewing the adoptive parents of cohort children all over the country. As in so many of the studies being reviewed here, it is difficult in a few short paragraphs to do justice to the findings or their impact. Nevertheless, this study of adoption was especially important in its time and in its field in helping to 'normalise' people's perception of adoption. Most studies done hitherto had almost inevitably had to take samples of 'clinic' referrals or other special groups. There are well known and formidable difficulties of extrapolating to the population at large from samples which are not only small but unrepresentative - and worse, where typically the bias in the sample is difficult to assess both as regards its extent and its nature. NCDS sub-studies have a tremendous strength and an enhanced impact in their fields in being free from such difficulties. We shall return later to this point.

The adoption study was rare therefore in being able to assert that its description and analysis of adoption amongst young families was representative, and it was also able to dispel many myths and concerns. The families had problems, of course, and a few of these could be traced to the attitudinal and other stresses of the adoptive situation itself but by and large these children were growing up normally. In terms of comparisons with the children's socio-economic group of birth, the adopted children were doing very well.

Sub-studies of single-parent and step-children within NCDS have not involved further interviews but have analysed existing information in more depth. The findings and impact of the work on NCDS children in single-parent families (for example Ferri, 1976, 1979; Lambert, 1978) have been influential in helping to correct the view, often implicit rather than explicit, that somehow single parenthood per se necessarily has adverse consequences. The attitudes which underlie this view may sometimes have a moral dimension.

It is important to clarify the point at issue here. There can be no doubt that single parenthood often creates financial and sometimes other material difficulties. Furthermore, since it tends more often to occur in lower socio-economic groups, the characteristics of those groups in terms of take-up of services and other social disadvantages discussed earlier will also tend to affect children of single parents. Therefore, the question which the NCDS sub-study was able to address was whether, when due allowance was made for all of these other correlated factors, the fact of being brought up by a single parent was disadvantageous.

The findings on this latter point could not be conclusive. Indeed, it would perhaps have been surprising to find that bringing up a child single-handedly was not at times accompanied by problems of a kind not so often experienced by two-parent families. On the other hand the reverse may well also be the case. What the sub-study was able to show very clearly was the extent and the nature of the major problems which beset such families. In comparison with these problems, any other factors which might be specific to the one-parent situation itself were both less easy to identify and much smaller in their actual effects.

The sub-study on step-children came later (Ferri, 1984). Again, this is an area well-endowed with myths and where good, representative data are difficult to find. Ferri, using existing data which had been gathered on the whole cohort at age 16, looked in detail at those children (some five per cent) who at any time had been living with one natural parent and one step-parent. She compared them on a considerable number of dimensions with the large group of children who had always lived with both natural parents and with two other smaller groups. She found amongst other things that the step-families were economically and socially deprived compared with unbroken families but this only applied amongst manual workers' homes. The step-children also tended to be more 'deprived' in more personal ways. For example, their relationship with their step-father, or step-mother, was relatively poor, as was the parental interest and aspiration shown in their schooling and in future employment or education plans. Predictably, perhaps, step-parents were more worried about their children's behaviour. However, interestingly, at school their children's behaviour was not a significant source of concern to teachers. Also, their educational attainments showed no differences with comparable groups.

The impact of methodology

There is one category of finding from the study which, almost by its very nature has been unsung. In the context of research results, it is more concerned with means than with ends, namely, the statistical and other methodologies used to produce the findings.

The statistician principally concerned with all of the statistics of the study for the first ten years or so of its life states modestly in a recent personal communication (Goldstein, 1992), that 'most of the analyses were simply a question of applying standard techniques to the data with understanding'. As someone who has worked now in many different research contexts and supervised much post-graduate research work, I can assert that what is simple to a statistician of outstanding ability is not necessarily so to ordinary mortals. Furthermore, the phrase 'with understanding' is the understated key to Goldstein's contribution. A good example of the latter is his contribution on the 'statistical controversy' surrounding the effects of smoking in pregnancy (1977).

In addition, there are specific ways in which the methodologies used made an impact. For example, Goldstein's work with Healy on the construction of scales for attitudes and behaviour broke new ground (Healy and Goldstein, 1976). Of obvious policy and immediate practical relevance was the NCDS work carried out on screening for disease or disability, an issue which in the late 1960s and into the 1970s was very topical, even at times contentious. Although the work on this was substantive and not simply methodological, I include it in this section because the statistical models used were at the heart of much of the thinking (for example Alberman and Goldstein, 1970; Goldstein, 1975). The impact of this research was to move forward people's thinking about the screening process for disability or illness and its implications for the differential allocation of resources to 'high risk' and 'low risk' groups.

The other aspect of the methodology of the study which is worthy of special note is the one referred to earlier in different contexts of having the main sweeps complemented by more sharply focused sub-studies. In addition to the points made above, I should mention that in the research world there is sometimes a schism between those who undertake large-scale work, which is necessarily a 'broad brush' approach, and those who carry out small studies where interviews and observations are possible and where the reliabilities of the measures used are more often within one's control. The schism is pointless, of course, because both methodologies have their merits and their disadvantages.

The great strength of the NCDS framework, envisaged initially by Butler and Pringle, and exploited by Pringle to great effect right through to her retirement as Bureau Director in 1981, was that NCDS was able to build on the strengths of both approaches and to minimise their shortcomings. Perhaps I may best characterise this as follows: to publish a study of a few hundred children in particular circumstances may be interesting; when the findings on those children accurately reflect the national picture, they become news. Moreover, the strength of the NCDS sub-studies of this kind has not just derived from the fact that the samples were nationally representative. It was also always possible to supplement the more detailed data gathered for the small groups with other data gathered both on them and on the 14,000 or more other children in the national cohort.

A myriad of findings

The results presented in this article are more than simply the tip of an iceberg in terms of the study's impact on policy and practice. Many are major by most standards, certainly of socially oriented research. Nevertheless, numerically they represent only a small fraction of the whole. Furthermore, most of the ones not mentioned are extremely important in their own fields and in their own right. There are studies of hearing impairment and of handedness, of unemployment and unforthcomingness, of convulsions and creativity, of wheezy bronchitis and working mothers. Certainly, the weight of influence of this myriad of lower profile NCDS studies may well over the course of time be shown to have carried more impact than the better known ones. For example, since its initial report to the Plowden Committee, the study has contributed significant evidence - often specially commissioned - to every major enquiry on child health, education or welfare in Britain. As Wedge (1992) in a recent personal communication says, 'Mostly we operate on the gentle drip principle by which research crucially influences policies, practices and perceived ideas'.

All of the major summaries and reports of NCDS sweeps are

included in the bibliography below and an up-to-date list of publications is available from the current study team at City University. In addition, the NCDS data themselves - virtually ready for further analysis, of which much is possible - are available to bona fide researchers from the ESRC Data Archive. NCDS has now become a national resource. It will grow in value and in stature as it is used nationally.

A collaborative enterprise

NCDS is now sited at the same place (City University, London) as the 1970 cohort study and there are strong links with the ongoing 1946 study. Active cooperation between these three studies has as yet hardly been exploited at all. But for the first time conditions are favourable for such exploitation. Or rather they would be, if it were not for one inescapable feature of such studies, namely, that the cohort members grow older. The necessity to gather fresh information at key points in the cohort members' lives is a continuing task of preparation (including, notably, seeking funding), detailed planning, data gathering and processing, and finally analysis and publication. This leaves the core teams little if any time for cooperative research, much as they may wish it. However, the pattern of this current sweep of NCDS, when the cohort were aged 33, is importantly different in that the design of the data which were gathered was the result of a consortium of research institutions combining their expertise. As the data become ready for analysis, these same institutions are instantly able to commence work on those aspects of the study for which their particular expertise fits them. This pattern, essentially a collaborative model, will be immensely valuable and productive in its own right for NCDS. However, it should also make joint research activities more readily possible between the three national cohort studies. This would undoubtedly further enhance the value of three projects which already, individually (arguably), and collectively (unquestionably) are unrivalled in any other country in the world.

Note

Further information may be obtained from the Social Statistics Research Unit, City University, Northampton Square, London EC1V OHB. The next stage of the study is due to be published in October 1993 by the National

Children's Bureau, Social Statistics Research Unit and the Economic & Social Research Council entitled *Britain's 33-Year-Olds: The Fifth Follow-Up of the National Child Development Study*

References

Alberman, E. and Goldstein, H. (1970) 'The 'at risk' register: a statistical evaluation', *British Journal of Preventive and Social Medicine*, 24. pp.129-135

Butler, N.R. and Alberman, E. (1969) *Perinatal Problems*. Edinburgh: Churchill Livingstone

Butler, N.R. and Bonham, D.G. (1963) *Perinatal Mortality*. Edinburgh: Churchill Livingstone

Butler, N.R. and Golding, J. (eds.) (1986) *From Birth to Five*. Oxford: Pergamon Press

Butler, N. and Goldstein, H. (1973) 'Smoking in pregnancy and subsequent child development', *British Medical Journal*, 4, pp.573-575

Crellin, E., Pringle, M. and West, P. (1971) *Born Illegitimate*. Windsor: NFER

Davie, R., Butler, N.R. and Goldstein, H. (1972) *From Birth to Seven*. London: Longman

Department of Education and Science (1972) *A Framework for Expansion*. (White Paper). London: DES

Douglas, J.W.B. (1964) *The Home and the School*. London: MacGibbon & Kee

Ferri, E. (1976) *Growing Up in a One-parent Family*. Windsor: NFER

Ferri, E. (1979) 'Children in one-parent families', *Ginger*, Feb, pp.4-6

Ferri, E. (1984) *Stepchildren: A National Study*. Windsor: NFER/Nelson

Fogelman, K. (ed.) (1976) *Britain's Sixteen Year Olds*. London: National Children's Bureau

Fogelman, K. (1980) 'Smoking in pregnancy and subsequent development of the child', *Child Care, Health and Development*, 6, pp.233-251

Fogelman, K. (ed.) (1983) *Growing Up in Great Britain*. London: Macmillan

Goldstein, H. (1975) 'A mathematical model for population disease screening', *Bulletin of Institute of Mathematics and Its Applications*, 11, pp.64-66

Goldstein, H. (1977) 'Smoking in pregnancy: the statistical controversy', *British Journal of Preventive and Social Medicine*, 31, pp.13-17

Goldstein, H. (1992) Personal Communication

Healy, M. and Goldstein, H. (1976) 'An approach to the scaling of categorical attributes', *Biometrika*, 63, pp.201-211

Hitchfield, E. (1974) *In Search of Promise*. London: Longman

Lambert, L. (1978) 'Living in one-parent families: school leavers and their futures', *Concern*, 29, pp.26-30

National Children's Bureau (1972) *Report to the Social Science Research Council on the 2nd Follow-Up of the National Child Development Study*. London: National Children's Bureau

Pilling, D. (1990) *Escape from Disadvantage*. London: Falmer Press

Plowden, B, (Chmn.) (1966) *Children and their Primary Schools*. 2 Vols. London: HMSO

Power, C. (1992) 'A review of child health in the birth cohort: National Child Development Study', *Paediatric & Perinatal Epidemiology*, 6, pp.81-110

Pringle, M., Butler, N. and Davie, R. (1966) *11,000 Seven Year Olds*. London: Longman

Rutter, M. and Madge, N. (1976) *Cycles of Disadvantage*. London: Heinemann

Seglow, J., Pringle, M. and Wedge, P. (1972) *Growing Up Adopted*. Windsor: NFER

Steedman, J. (1980) *Progress in Secondary Schools*. London: National Children's Bureau

Steedman, J. (1983) *Examination Results in Selective and Non-Selective Schools*. London: National Children's Bureau

Sunday Times (1972) 'The unequal start', Colour Supplement, 4 June, pp.25-31

Wadsworth, M. (1991) *The Imprint of Time*. Oxford: Clarendon Press

Wedge, P. and Prosser, H. (1973) *Born to Fail?* London: Arrow Books

Wedge, P. and Essen, J. (1982) *Children in Adversity*. London: Pan Books

Wedge, P. (1992) Personal Communication

4. Changes in the family

A.H. Halsey, University of Oxford

We live now in a new demographic age, centred on Western Europe and those parts of the world which were once British colonial possessions. This new reproductive order has momentous potential implications for the twenty-first century world as a whole. There are revolutionary comings in and goings out concerning ideas of birth, marriage, divorce, child-rearing, age, gender and death which constitute the foundations of a new demographic era.

In essence the new regime is a balance of low fertility and low mortality. In other words it is an historically unprecedented combination of fluctuating and small reproduction with steadily advancing longevity. An ageing population, along with proportionate reduction in the place of children, is a necessary demographic consequence. But economic affluence and increased geographical mobility add hitherto largely unrecognised implications and possibilities. The further social contingency of the decline of the traditional family as a reproductive unit (which some contend is cause rather than consequence) must also be included as a defining characteristic of the new regime. Finally the new order is one of incipient population decline if the now well-established trends of natural reproduction are not counteracted by reversal of traditional patterns of international mobility. There are, of course, already signs of such a reversal in the absorption of growing minority ethnic groups in the metropolitan economies of Western Europe. Meanwhile low fertility, population ageing, and family frailty together bequeath a changing structure of production, reproduction, and distribution between age groups, ethnic groups, and the genders.

What then is new about the new order? It can be dismissed as a dramatised version of the industrial population cycle as described by sociologists since Malthus. Agrarian societies had sparse populations balanced by high fertility and high mortality yielding relatively young populations in which upbringing took place in strong families, small communities, and with well defined skills combined with relatively restricted information and social connections. Britain and early European industrialism led the way out of agrarianism. Reduced mortality and population explosion, with its menace to the rest of the world, followed in the late nineteenth and early twentieth centuries by accelerated reduction in fertility, led after the Second World War to the new low birth-death balance. None of that is particularly novel but the associated features of unprecedented economic prosperity and the renegotiation of the division of labour between men and women portended a new society, smaller in numbers, older in years and offering new egalitarian freedoms to women as well as a new political class of the 'Third Age'.

The fate of the family as the social unit of childrearing is thus brought into question. A first conventional indicator is marital breakdown. Divorce has risen rapidly over the past thirty years. When calculations are made of the future proportions of marriages that will end in divorce, it turns out that four out of ten will collapse, even though one in every two couples will celebrate their silver and one in seven their golden wedding; the future of grandparenthood is buoyant.

A second indicator is that of births outside marriage. By 1990 the percentage had risen to 28. In Sweden the figure is 50 per cent compared with 10 in Italy. Births outside marriage in Britain have trebled in a decade while births within marriage have actually fallen. Three-quarters of births to teenage mothers are outside marriage, which is roughly double the proportion of a decade ago. On the other hand, no single statistic can be taken as a sure index of the stability of child rearing circumstances. Thus for example the 'illegitimate' birth rate (now 'outside marriage') of earlier years took no account of the stability of the relationship between the parents. The recent records of birth registration suggest that at least half of the children born outside marriage have parents living together in a stable relationship.

A third indicator of family stability is the record of one-parent families. The number of such families has grown from around 600,000 to over a million since the early 1970s and the children number over one and a half million, that is about one in eight children now living in such families and such reproductive circumstances are typically (though not exclusively) concentrated in the lower echelons of class and income with higher rates of unemployment and poorer housing conditions. All in all the evidence is of mounting multiple instability of marriage and increasingly tenuous support for mothers and children outside wedlock. To be sure it is a situation of great complexity and heated dispute. There are pessimistic traditionalists who believe that the family is collapsing with consequent chaos, crime and crisis of civilisation. There are also optimistic modernists who see a new dawn for opportunity and equality for women, the end of the stigma of illegitimate birth, and the demise of male tyranny.

Could it be that the gains for adults are at the expense of the interests of children? It could end in disaster. Modern society has strange superstitions. Perhaps the central one is the belief that if ego maximises his or her choices we are all better off (Dennis and Erdos, 1992). Put more portentously it is the fallacy that individual freedom is collective good. The family is the age-old disproof of this contemporary nonsense. The traditional family is the tested arrangement for safeguarding the welfare of children. Only a post-Christian country could believe otherwise. The individualist doctrine is an hallucination with two main sources. First is the spectacular advance of human power over nature, which has relieved so many of us so much from the life of toil that our grandparents had to take for granted. They invented the workplace, the career, the substitutes for human muscle and sweat and we, with our micro-chips and washing machines, have both inherited and refined these escapes from the 'curse of Adam'. We call it the economy or the productive system and we employ economic statisticians and Treasury politicians to celebrate its continual growth. We use a language of productivity, employment, capital and education which encourages us to imagine that the family has nothing to do with national prosperity.

Then second there is the developing assumption, so rampant in the 1980s, that the adult ego is self-sufficient. Children thereby become commodities - quality objects to be sure - but nonetheless things just like cars or videos or holidays which adults can choose to have in preference to other consumables. And if they do, that is their choice and their responsibility. Contraceptive control of our bodies enhances the illusion. So who needs a family or a community or, for that matter, a government other than to prevent ruin of the market for these good things by thieves and frauds? Surely technology has conquered nature and we can safely allow individuals to choose a consuming style, limited only by their willingness to work for money. Everybody is then free to buy the good life of their own definition. Marriage becomes a mere contract. The quality of life is measurable by calculation through methodological individualism rather than contained in organic conceptions of man and nature.

Our ancestors were poorer but wiser. They understood the notion of political economy. They knew what the modern fantasy forgets, that we are all dependent on one another. Atomised individuals calculate only for themselves and only for their own lives. Yet their very existence depends on calculation across generations. Few women and fewer men would rationally choose to have children in a world of exclusively short-term egotistical calculation. The costs and foregone satisfactions are too high. Hence rich countries which carry the modern ethos have declining or incipiently declining populations (for a stable population there must be a total period fertility rate of 2.1 children per woman; Britain has 1.8, West Germany 1.6, Italy and Spain 1.4 or even 1.2). The individualised as distinct from socialised country eventually and literally destroys itself.

Nor is this the whole of the modern mirage. In reality the family is part of, not separate from, the economy. Parents are the main producers of tomorrow's wealth and we all consume what they produce. That is why we need a just political economy to ensure that the beneficiaries pay their dues. Behind the fiscal and monetary facade, old age pensions are dependent on the future work of today's children. Yet paradoxically our political economy, far from paying parents, actually punishes them for their folly in producing the producers of the future. Such people as Frank Field on the left, Sir Brandan Rhys Williams on the right and Professor Richard Whitfield in the academic non-political centre have shown that our system of taxation and social security is systematically biased against the family in favour of the childless adult, and increasingly so since the 1960s.

How can all this be turned round? The first step is to get the facts right. I appreciate that 'facts' always appear in the context of assumptions about what is good or bad for human beings. We deal today with heated value discord in these matters. I share with my colleague Norman Dennis the value position of the ethnical socialist as set out in our *English Ethical Socialism* (Dennis and Halsey, 1988). Central to that position is the doctrine of personal responsibility under virtually all social circumstances. People act under favourable and unfavourable conditions but remain responsible moral agents. History heavily conditions them, their own actions eventually become history and therefore determine the future balance of favour and disfavour in the ceaseless effort to become good people in a good society. The whole question of the quality of life remains for ever open. There are no ineluctable laws of history, only a continual reloading of the dice by millions of individual decisions. It follows that reproductive decisions are crucial to human destiny. Whatever the character of society or state, polity or economy, religion or culture, parents cannot escape responsibility for the quality of their children as citizens.

In the light of this political morality I see incontrovertible evidence of a weakening of the norms of the traditional family since the 1960s. It is not that I see a golden age of traditionalism. Material deprivation, and inequality between the classes and the sexes were integral to British society in the first half of the century. There was no utopia. There was cruelty, a double standard of sexual morality, incest and child abuse, savage treatment of unmarried mothers, desertions and separations. Nevertheless the traditional family system was a coherent strategy for the ordering of relations in such a way as to equip children for their own eventual adult responsibilities.

The much needed reform of the system required comprehensive strengthening of supporting health, education and security services if quality children were to be produced, women were to have freedom to combine motherhood with career, and men were to be encouraged to take fuller part in the domestic rearing of their offspring. Instead the evidence of more recent change is that the supporting services have deteriorated, the increment of economic growth has been transferred disproportionately to the individual pocket horizontally and to the rich vertically through the running down of family allowances, the raising of regressive national insurance contributions, the abandoning of joint taxation for spouses, the failure to fund adequate community care and so on. In the 1980s the economic individual was exalted and the social community desecrated. Mrs Thatcher may well be seen by dispassionate future historians as a major architect of the demolition of the traditional family.

She was, to be sure, vigorously aided by other social and personal forces. No one can deny that divorce, separation, birth outside marriage and one-parent families as well as cohabitation and extra-marital sexual intercourse have increased rapidly. Many applaud these freedoms. But what should be universally acknowledged is that the children of parents who do not follow the traditional norm (that is, taking on personal, active and long-term responsibility for the social upbringing of the children they generate) are thereby disadvantaged in many major aspects of their chances of living a successful life. On the evidence available such children tend to die earlier, to have more illness, to do less well at school, to exist at a lower level of nutrition, comfort and conviviality, to suffer more unemployment, be more prone to deviance and crime, and finally to repeat the cycle of unstable parenting from which they themselves have suffered (Elliot and Richards, 1991; Bradshaw and Millar, 1991; Kiernan, 1992).

The evidence is formidable as well as tallying with commonsense (Burghes, 1993). But we must be clear what the thesis does not say. The comparison is of averages. It is not maintained that traditionally reared children will all be healthy, intelligent and good; nor that children from parentally deprived homes will all turn out to be sickly, stupid and criminal. Like all social science the relevant studies deal with multiple causes of multiple effects and give us estimates of statistical association for particular groups at particular moments in history. Nevertheless it must be insisted that no contrary evidence is available to contradict the average differences postulated by the stated thesis. Accordingly the conclusion must be drawn that committed and stable parenting must be a priority of social policy. If that view is accepted, it is no comfort either to the right or the left. Committed parenting cannot be the outcome of the market policies of economic liberals nor of what Norman Dennis has dubbed the 'egotistic socialism' of irresponsible fathers. The challenge to social policy is to avoid both of these evils.

The National Children's Bureau thinks of itself as 'the powerful voice of the child'; it has been a characteristic institutional response to 'the century of the child'. It has also been a witness to the decline of the traditional family. A look back over these twin features of recent demography and sociology with a view to explaining an apparent paradox is the purpose of this essay.

Thirty years is a misleadingly short period for our purpose - scarcely more than a single generation. But as a social force, childhood is subjectively stretched in that it is carried as an evolving and more or less shared notion in the minds of children, parents and grandparents (Wadsworth, 1991). Thus there were even a few people in Britain in 1960 who had had experience of the 1860s. They had been alive at a time before the State made its first serious incursion into the education of children, when married women were still legally the chattels of their husbands, when puberty was for the vast majority the end of formal schooling and the beginning of laborious life, when men worked and women waited, when a child's corpse was a domestic commonplace, Freud was unknown, health visitors and the germ theory unrecognised, and when fertility was both high and inversely correlated with family income.

Thus corresponding and conflicting definitions of childhood coexist and contend in a period of rapid change: and the National Children's Bureau can be aptly described as a public broker of the clash of ideas concerning upbringing between government and the governed, the churches and the laity, professionals and amateurs, parents and children, the classes, the genders, and most recently the ethnic groups. A conception of the changing scene in these terms must accordingly be one of great complexity. All I can offer here is a selective simplification.

In a summary of social trends (Halsey, 1988) I described Britain as having emerged from the Second World War as a classical industrial economy, a centralised democratic polity and a familistic social structure. The long historical roots of the country had been in a social order with minimal government and with wealth and welfare principally determined by the relation between the family and the market for labour. In prototypic industrialism as in the preceding agrarianism the institutional division of labour consisted essentially of a triangle joining the family, the workplace and the state. Families raised children; men worked in separate workplaces; women ran households. The economy produced; the family reproduced; and the state protected.

The National Children's Bureau was an agent of transformation. A consensus was built during the war, expressed by Beveridge, Keynes and Butler, that a prosperous and civilised future required a positive welfare state. It meant systematic 'interference' by government and its agents in the traditional exchanges between the family and the economy. That was the context defining the role of the Bureau as the voice of the child. The rise of the welfare state entailed an elaboration of tax collection to be used as redistributive resources for the education and health of children, the relief of men temporarily out of work, the maintenance of mothers without men to connect them to the economy, the sustenance of the old, and the protection of the health and safety of the population as a whole.

In the following generation legislation and social practice ushered in a more elaborate division of labour between the members of the institutional triangle of traditional life. The family, it was recognised, produces as well as consumes. People live as well as work in factories and work as well as live in houses. The family has fewer children, and it reforms on separation and divorce as well as on death and departure. Women no longer merely wait but have entered the formal economy while men have been drawn into domesticity. Adults as well as children learn. The state provides parent substitutes as teachers, nurses, housing officers and so on, in an unprecedented expansion of social services supporting and even replacing the family. Altogether in the past thirty years there has been a renegotiation of the division of labour which has transformed the meaning and nature of childhood.

By no means all these changes were the expected outcome of deliberate political planning. In one sense the Bureau emerged to take on the role of a monitoring agency for the unanticipated consequences of deliberate legal and administrative innovation. At all events the social statistics (meaning, historically, facts about the state) began to show intended trends such as the increase of women, especially married women, in employment and declining birthrates; but also the unintended increase in illegitimate births (now recorded as lone-parent births), divorces, remarriage and single-person households. Between the end of the war and 1990 the proportion of economically-active women rose from just over a third to 52.8 per cent: and the proportion of economically inactive married women, which was 51 per cent in 1971, decreased sharply to 29 per cent in 1990 when the total female work force was 12 million. Meanwhile between 1961 and 1989 the incidence of divorce rose from 2.1 to 12.7 per thousand married people. In 1972, 16 per cent of women who were married had previously cohabited with their future husband and this proportion climbed steeply to reach roughly a half by 1987. Most women now have children, though families continue to get smaller. Rather less than a fifth of women born at the end of the 1950s are expected to remain childless. And, most significant, the percentage of births outside marriage which was 4 or 5 per cent for the first half of the century has risen from 5 per cent in 1960 to 11 per cent in 1979 and to 28 per cent in 1990.

The record also shows more men and women in adult education as well as more children in extended schooling and a rising level of qualification in the population at large. By 1990, 72 per cent of men and 65 per cent of women of working age held a qualification. Just as there had been a traditional inverse relation between family size and prosperity so now there was an inverse correlation of educational qualification and age.

Meanwhile, and unplanned, there emerged a socially depressed tail (a so-called underclass) of children in poverty and with poorer educational and life chances as the benefits of traditional two-parent families were withdrawn and inadequately substituted by public services even in a burgeoning welfare state.

There was a lively discussion at the annual meeting of RELATE in 1992 (13 October 92) where I put part of the responsibility for the decline of the traditional family (that is the family with two committed parents) on the Baroness Thatcher and the cult of Individualism. One-parent families make up a fifth of all families, over a quarter of births now take place outside marriage and every year 150,00 children under 16 are added to the number who experience, above their heads, the divorce of their parents. Of course not everyone wants to change this world but nearly everyone would like to be able to explain it.

One clue, which many fewer notice, is that there is a vast global correlate to this national trend. While the human species as a whole continues on its accelerating path towards astronomical numbers, the trends in the richer (that is industrial) countries are in the opposite direction. Countries like Britain, America and Japan are in the early stages of population decline (which means also an ageing of their people). There are two million less West Germans than there were 20 years ago. In southern Catholic Europe birth rates have plummeted. Even in Ireland, the classic case of the Malthusian law that reproduction expands to the limits of the food supply, births have now fallen below the threshold of 2.1 per woman which would ensure a stable population size. The British figure, as we have noted, is 1.8. So there is a pattern of hugely different contributions to the human population of the 21st century such that the industrialised West, including Japan and Taiwan, begin to subtract from future numbers while the developing (that is poor) countries of Asia, Africa, and Latin America, add to them.

What then is the explanation? Conventional wisdom offers two theories. One is economic - low fertility arises from economic growth. Rich countries can afford greater freedoms including the freedom of sexual equality which permits women not to have children and to enter increasingly into the non-domestic world of men. The other theory is cultural (and indeed racist). Western cultures are nicer to women because they are more individualistic. They favour romantic love and women's careers, not arranged marriages, suttee, proscription of birth control and so on.

Either way the consequence is that in the past the poor have reproduced themselves more than the rich, and that modernisation liberates women to become more like men. Neither theory works completely. Obviously Japan and Taiwan are oriental, not Western, and there are some poor countries, in the Indian sub-continent and in sub-Saharan Africa, where women are relatively more equal with men.

The 'cultural' theory is the weaker of the two. It is appreciation of the role of individualism that can rescue it and combine the two theories into more powerful explanation. Individualism is an ethic at the heart of human development. Individuals invent, produce, and choose. Individualism explains our leap forward in production, in control over nature and finally our entry into the modern demographic regime of low fertility. Ever since the renaissance and the reformation of the 16th century it has become increasingly clear that Christianity is the premier carrier of individualism, the cradle of freedom, the bearer of representative democracy, the potential agent of escape from feudal and kinship tyranny in traditional peasant society. Western Christendom, from Galileo, fostered aggressive measurement, deserted fatalism, broke the bonds of superstition and helplessness, invented the steam engine, the telescope and double-entry book keeping. In short, Individualism promised to bring heaven to earth.

So what is wrong with all that? The answer is, first, that free egotistical calculation apparently ensures the eventual disappearance of the species, for rational adults avoid parenthood. The answer, second, is that individualistic policy, despite its many benefits to industry and commerce, also spreads by its own logic into the family. Marriage becomes not a sacred long-run compact but merely a contract, to be broken at the will of either party; and children become consumables. If people choose to 'buy' them that is their right and their responsibility. Caveat Emptor. If only one parent is left (usually the mother) it is largely up to her to look after the interest of the child. Some libertarians deem this a reasonable price for freedom. Many turn their faces away from the evidence that *on average* the children of broken or one-parent families have impoverished life chances - literally chances of survival, of health, of educational attainment, of conviviality, of jobs, of avoidance of marital breakdown in their own lives, and so on.

The point about Mrs Thatcher in this context, as my colleague Norman Dennis insists, is that she tacitly assumed that the individualistic ethic untrammelled could not enter the family; but in fact it did, and was vigorously encouraged by 'egotistic socialists' as well as libertarian individualists. Meanwhile, and pre-dating Thatcher, the state moved systematically to undermine support for the traditional family by the shifts in financial, fiscal and social services policies to which we have alluded. So increasingly we see a closer association of parenting with poverty and, most ominously, a new generation of males with little experience of or interest in responsible fatherhood. The organic solidarity between generations has been largely broken by reforms inspired by economic liberalism.

It could be all turned round by determined action. But not mindless reaction. The old respectable working-class family system worked, but at high cost (the double standard of morality, the harsh treatment of 'fallen women' and 'bastards', the kitchen containment of mothers, the taboo on male participation in 'women's work'). Clearly those traditional conflicts and confinements are neither desirable nor any longer possible. Nevertheless there are positive policy possibilities open to a richer country through serious reform of the schools, of working arrangements (Hewitt, 1993), through 'third-age' grandparents, properly provided 'family-friendly' social services - a whole new programme of reform which dethrones the market mania of present government and turns instead to a wiser civilisation.

Childhood is at a crucial moment in the history of post-industrial society. In Britain and all across Western Europe there are two dramatic demographic developments, threatening both quantity and quality in the rising generation. While much of the rest of the world remains Malthusian, that is with rising populations based on high fertility and death delaying technology. But Britain belongs to the sixteen or seventeen countries (including Western Europe, the 'Anglo Saxon Empire' and Japan) which are properly called Third Age Societies (Laslett, 1989). Their foremost characteristic is the rise of a new social and political class of people who are free from the obligations of paid employment and are possessed of sufficient health and wealth to dominate social policy, at least in political democracies. A democratised leisure class is historically unprecedented. The retired British constitute a fifth of the whole. A primary schoolchild can normally expect to join the third age, to live longer as a grandparent than as a parent or a child.

At the same time the other great demographic characteristic of these countries is that they have actual or impending population decline. For a qualitatively stable population the average number of children per women (the total period fertility rate) has to be 2.1. We have noted the irony that it is as low as 1.4 in traditionally Catholic southern Europe. And decline is also *qualitative* because the traditional family system is in rapid process of erosion. The British statistics illustrates a sombre story. In 1990 the birth rate per 1,000 population was 13.6, but births outside marriage were 27.4 per cent of the whole. The divorce rate per 1,000 married population was over 12, the proportion of all families with dependent children and a single parent was over 14 per cent.

The primary school has to be seen against the background of these two demographic developments. The quality of childhood in the family is highly varied because, although the 20th century is the single 'century of the child', it is still more the century of the individual, which also means a flight from parenthood. There is little prospect of reversing the natural and indeed the laudable aspiration of modern women to find ways of combining maternal domesticity with an independent career outside the home. In a serious sense that is what the primary school was invented to provide. But all the research points to a melancholy outcome. The average two-parent child does better in health, personality, and educational attainment than the one-parent child.

The question therefore arises as to whether the Third Age can be brought in to help the First Age or primary school child. I believe it can. The old concept of the primary school was of a simple partnership between teacher and parent, with the teacher as the bridge to a wider world beyond the family. The new concept must go much further. It must continue the old idea and add to it the notion that, for an increasing minority, the teacher has to take on a much more direct parenting role (Young, 1990). Of course, the immediate and justified response of many teachers is that they are already doing what the new world demands or that the demand is impossible because incompatible with limited professional time and responsibility. It is against the whole temper of modern individualistic times: it means extended hours of opening, operating in holidays as well as conventional school days, 'interfering' with family relations and so on.

That is all true. But if the challenge of deterioration in the quality of childhood is to be realistically met, then the new concept must be nationally applied and one vital contribution to the solution can surely be sought from the new class of Third Age people - the grandparents.

Third age people are, to be sure, often busy, if only with looking after their Fourth Age elders. Yet they are a vast reservoir of potential social service some of which can and must be recruited for the primary life as an auxiliary labour force for after-school supervision, clubs and activities. Many schools have pioneered the necessary extended partnership. But these experiments must now become an integral part of the new system. It means a new professional leadership role for the primary teacher, new training arrangements for them and their Third Age assistants, new attitudes to the whole life experience of children, the end of the scandal of the 'latch key' child. And, if it works, the status of the teacher will be enhanced, the stress on families, especially employed mothers, and most especially single mothers, will be reduced: and the quality of childhood will be restored to the high priority it requires if future civilisation is to be safe-guarded.

References

Bradshaw, J. and Miller, J. (1991) *Lone Parent Families in the UK.* Report 6. Department of Social Security Research: HMSO

Brown, J. (1989) *Why Don't they go to Work: Mothers on Benefit.* Social Security Advisory Committee

Burghes, L. (1993) *One Parent Families: Policy Options for the 1990s.* Joseph Rowntree Foundation

Crellin, E., Kellmer Pringle, M.L. and West, P. (1971) *Born Illegitimate.* A Report by the National Children's Bureau, National Foundation for Educational Research in England and Wales

Dennis, N. and Erdos, G. (1992) *Families without Fatherhood.* Choice in Welfare No12, IEA Health and Welfare Unit

Dennis, N. and Halsey, A.H. (1988) *English Ethical Socialism.* Oxford

Elliot, J. and Richards, M. (1991) 'Children and divorce: educational performance and behaviour before and after parental separation', *International Journal of Law and the Family*, pp.258-276

Furstenberg, F.F. and Cherlin, A.J. (1991) *Divided Families. What Happens to Children When Parents Part.* Harvard University Press

Halsey, A.H. (ed.) (1988) *British Social Trends Since 1900.* Macmillan

Hewitt, P. (1993) *About Time: The Revolution in Work and Family Life.* IPPR/Rivers

Kiernan, K.E. (1992) 'The impact of family disruption in childhood on transitions made in young adult life', *Population Studies*, 46

Kolvin, I. and others (1990) *Continuities of Deprivation? The Newcastle 1000 Study.* ESRC/DHSS Studies in Deprivation and Disadvantages, Avebury

Laslett, P. (1989) *A Fresh Map of Life.* Macmillan

Wadsworth, M.E.J. (1991) *The Imprint of Time: Childhood, History and Adult Life.* Oxford

Young, M. (1990) *The Future of the Family.* Economic and Social Research Council

5. Laws, conventions and rights

Michael Freeman, University College London

Introduction

Thinking about children's rights has come a long way in the past quarter of a century. Hillary Rodham's famous aphorism that children's rights were 'a slogan in search of a definition' (Rodham, 1973) now seems a dated remark as the concept has been debated, analysed and fought over in academic literature and political discussion. Children's rights may not have become the 'primary social value' informing social policy and social planning that Wilkerson looked to twenty years ago (Wilkerson, 1973, p.305) but the concept is better understood and more widely accepted than was the case when Rodham and Wilkerson were writing. The United Nations Convention in 1989 is likely to be the fulcrum upon which debate about children's rights in the foreseeable future will rest, but it is only a beginning, not even the end of the beginning, and, in truth, as Hawes has remarked, there is no 'obvious end in sight'. (Hawes, 1991, p.123).

A pre-history

But we have come a long way both in our recognition of children's rights and our understanding of childhood. Early legal statements are conspicuously silent on children's rights: the Ten Commandments, arguably the most influential of all legal codes, contains a clear normative pronouncement on parent-child relations but it is in terms of respect for parents and is silent on the obligations of parents to love and nurture children (Silverman, 1978). Is it then surprising that well in to early modern times children were being prosecuted in England before the ecclesiastical courts for abusing parents, but that prosecutions of parents for beating children appear not to have taken place? (Helmholz, 1993).

One of the earliest recognitions of children's rights is found in the Massachusetts *Body of Liberties* of 1641. Parents are told not to choose their children's mates and not to use unnatural severity against their children (Pleck, 1987). Children, furthermore, are given 'free liberty to complain to the Authorities for redress'. But this is also the law that prescribes the death penalty for children over 16 who disobey parents. There is no evidence that children did successfully litigate against their parents but nor is there any that disobedient children were executed (Hawes, 1991). The document, nevertheless, remains interesting in showing, as it does, that even 350 years ago protection of children went hand in hand with adding the power of the state to parental authority.

The next two centuries can hardly be said to be identified with children's rights. There are concerns to protect children, though these are often clumsy or inchoate. It is pertinent to remark that the documents emanating from the great libertarian revolutions, the American and the French, have nothing specifically to say about children.

The nineteenth century saw the birth of the child-saving movement, the growth of the orphanage, the development of schooling and the construction of separate institutions, including the juvenile court, for delinquent children (Platt, 1969). Child protection legislation also comes about. Yet cruelty remains a social construct and founders of societies to protect children from abuse still vigorously defend corporal chastisement. Thus, one of the founders of the New York SPCC, Henry Bergh, can uphold 'a good wholesome flogging' as appropriate for 'disobedient children'. Children's rights begin to be advocated: Jean Vallès in France, in the aftermath of the Paris Commune (Vallès, 1878) and Kate Douglas Wiggin in the United States are two of the more eloquent expositors of the ideal (Wiggin, 1892). Wiggin's view of childhood, a century ago, is refreshingly modern. Its flavour is well-captured by this:

As to keeping children too clean for any normal use, I suppose nothing is more disastrous. The divine right to be gloriously dirty a large portion of the time, when dirt is a necessary consequence of direct, useful, friendly contact with all sorts of interesting, helpful things, is too clear to be denied (Wiggin, 1892, p.11).

She also urged a gentler approach to discipline: 'it seems likely', she wrote, 'that the rod of reason will have to replace the rod of birch' (Wiggin, 1892, p.19). Janusz Korczak in Poland was expressing similar sentiments (Lifton, 1988). But it was not the voices of Wiggin or Korczak which prevailed.

Some early history

Korczak himself formulated his ideas during the first world war. *How To Love A Child* (Korczak, 1919) took as one of its main theses the idea that you cannot possibly love a child - your own or another's - until you see him as a separate being with the inalienable right to grow into the person he was meant to be (Veerman, 1992 pp.93-111). It was more than half a century before others, Farson (1978) and Holt (1975) for example, were to recognise the importance of a child's autonomy.

The first international declaration, the Declaration of Geneva of 1924, was more limited in its aspirations. In its preamble it states that 'mankind owes to the Child the best it has to give'. Its five terse principles emphasise welfare: the requisite means for normal development, food and medicine, relief in times of distress, protection against exploitation and socialisation to serve others. The principles, the fifth above all, reflected the aftermath of an imperialist war. One contemporary commentator (Fuller, 1925) compared it with the tendency in Britain to emphasise nationalist and imperialist ideals in education to the detriment of its ideal of world service. According to him, it was from 'the point of view of the world future no less than of the individual the most important and far-reaching of all Principles of the Declaration of Geneva' (Fuller, 1925, p.116).

It was another 35 years before children's rights received international recognition again. We get considerable insight into attitudes towards children's rights in the late 1950s (before civil rights issues became rampant) from the discussions which took place at this time. Thus, for example, the French delegate to the Commission on Human Rights in 1959 believed that:

...the child was not in a position to exercise his own rights. Adults exercised them for the child .... A child had special legal status resulting from his inability to exercise his rights.

Iraq argued that children's rights posed particular problems for Third World countries which did not have the means, for example, to implement compulsory education. The ideological differences between capitalism and communism were also striking: the communist world saw the primary responsibility for the child as lying with the state; for western delegations this responsibility rested with parents. There were also differences about the treatment of illegitimate children, Israel and Poland wishing to protect them against discrimination, and Italy arguing that it was equally necessary to protect the legitimate family which, the Italian delegate said, constituted 'the foundation of an organised society'. It was Italy also which pressed, ultimately successfully, for the recognition of rights from the time of conception.

What emerged on 20 November 1959 was the United Nations Declaration of the Rights of The Child. In the end only two countries abstained (Cambodia and South Africa). The ten principles adopted were:

1. Non-discrimination.
2. Special protection and opportunities to develop physically and mentally, morally, spiritually and socially in a healthy and normal manner and in conditions of freedom and dignity. (The principle adds 'In the enactment of laws for this purpose the best interests of the child shall be the paramount consideration'. This is in contrast to the Convention of 1989 where 'a primary consideration' is substituted for 'the paramount consideration').
3. A right to a name and nationality.
4. The right to the benefits of social security; adequate nutrition, housing, recreation and medical services.
5. The right of a special needs child to the treatment, education and care required by his or her particular condition.
6. The need for love and understanding so that the child, wherever possible, is to grow in the care and under the responsibility of his parents and in an atmosphere of affection and of moral and material security. (The principle stresses that payment of state and other assistance toward the maintenance of children of large families is desirable).

7. Entitlement to education, free and compulsory, at least in the elementary stages.
8. To be among the first to receive protection and relief.
9. Protection against all forms of neglect, cruelty and exploitation (including that associated with employment).
10. Protection from practices which may foster racial, religious and any other form of discrimination.

The coverage is broader, though there is distinct overlap with the Geneva Declaration. The emphasis is still firmly on protection and welfare and, what has been called, the 'investment motive' (Meyer, 1973) remains apparent. There is no recognition of a child's autonomy, of the importance of a child's views, nor any appreciation of the concept of empowerment.

The children's liberation movement

1959 is barely a generation ago but, in the period immediately following it, there was a growth in consciousness of the evils of discrimination, first against Black people and other minority ethnic groups and then against women and other disadvantaged groups. The 1970s saw the growth of the child's liberation movement, spearheaded by John Holt (1975) and Richard Farson (1978). The term 'Toward the Liberation of the Child' appeared for the first time as a sub-title of the book *Children's Rights*, published in 1971 (Adams and others, 1971). In this collection Robert Ollendorff argues (and he was probably the first to do so) for the adolescent's right to self-determination (p.120).

It was self-determination that Farson saw as at the root of all other rights that children were entitled to claim. Responding to the anticipated criticism that such rights might not be 'good' for children, for children's rights hitherto had been geared to furthering 'the good' for children, Farson argued:

...asking what is good for children is beside the point. We will grant children rights for the same reason we grant rights to adults, not because we are sure that children will then become better people, but more for ideological reasons, because we believe that expanding freedom as a way of life is worthwhile in itself. And freedom, we have found, is a difficult burden for adults as well as for children (1978, p.31.).

Farson went on to enumerate nine rights, all derived from the right to self-determination:

1. The right to alternative home environments allowing the child to 'exercise choice in his own living arrangements' (1978, p.62) (of particular interest now that children 'divorcing' parents has hit the headlines).
2. The right to information that is accessible to adults (for example, children should be allowed to inspect records kept about them).
3. The right to educate oneself (he favoured the abolition of compulsory education). Part of this right is freedom from indoctrination with children choosing their 'belief systems' (1978, p.110).
4. The right to sexual freedom: pornography would be made available to children as it is to adults and children would be allowed to experiment with their sexuality without fearing punishment.
5. The right to economic power including the right to work, to develop a credit record and to achieve financial independence (1978 p.154).
6. The right to political power including the right to vote (see also Franklin, 1986; 1992). Nothing, he suggests, indicates that children will 'vote less responsibly than adults' (1978, p.182).
7. The right to responsive design (see also Ward, 1978).
8. The right to freedom from physical punishment (see also Newell, 1989).
9. The right to justice (see also Freeman, 1981).

Holt's catalogue is not dissimilar but it includes the right to travel, to drive, to use drugs as well as the rights which Farson enumerates.

It is easy to ridicule Farson, Holt and the liberation school of the 1970s and, indeed, it has been criticised (Hafen, 1976; Freeman, 1983; Purdy, 1992). But it must be remembered that they wrote when child sexual abuse had yet to be discovered and when drugs were less of a social problem than they are today (and see Zamora Chavarria, 1992). We would want to protect children from sex and drugs and, indeed, from work and possibly other rights which they would confer on children, but protection was not in their vocabulary. Thus, Holt, writing of drugs, says:

On the whole I believe that people ought to be able to use the drugs they want. I don't think we should 'protect' children against whatever drugs their elders use, and in a society in which most of their elders do use drugs and many use them excessively and unwisely, I don't see how we can (1975, pp.194 & 201).

The Farson-Holt thesis has its limitations and more recent advocacy of children's rights acknowledges the need to protect children (Freeman, 1983; 1992a; Houlgate, 1980; Eekelaar, 1986; 1992). To some, indeed, it is the duties of parents and others towards children that must be emphasised, rather than children's rights as such (O'Neill, 1988), but this too may be criticised (Campbell, 1992; Freeman, 1992a). The importance of the liberation school was in making us address discrimination and recognise the importance of autonomy. To believe in autonomy is to believe that anyone's autonomy is as morally significant as anyone else's.

It is significant that philosophical and legal thought on the requirements to exercise autonomy should have converged. Thus, Haworth (1986) writes of the need for 'critical competence' and Lindley (1986) of capacity for reasoning almost at the same time as Lord Scarman in the *Gillick* decision (1986) is formulating, what has come to be called, 'Gillick-competence'. There has been a judicial backlash against this since (*Re R*, 1991; *Re W*, 1992; and see Bainham, 1992; Murphy, 1992). The Children Act 1989 nevertheless continues to recognise the right of a child 'of sufficient understanding to make an informed decision' to refuse to submit to a medical or psychiatric examination or other assessment (Freeman, 1992b). It has come to be realised that the dichotomy between protecting children and protecting their rights to autonomy is false. Children who are not protected, whose welfare is not advanced, will not be able to exercise self-determination: on the other hand, a failure to recognise the personality of children is likely to result in an undermining of their protection with children reduced to objects of intervention. This is to some extent recognised by the United Nations Convention on the Rights of the Child of 1989.

The UN Convention on the Rights of the Child

Thirty years separates the UN Declaration and the UN Convention. The thinking of the period in between is reflected in the differences. It was Poland which, in 1978, proposed that there ought to be a

Convention - to mark, it said, the International Year of the Child a year later. But Poland would have been satisfied with the Declaration turned into a Convention with the addition of an implementation mechanism (Cohen, 1990; see also Cohen and Naimark, 1991). Early on concern was expressed that the passing of a Convention would undermine the 'moral impact' of the Declaration (Singer, 1986; Weisberg, 1978). These reservations were soon overcome but drafting the Convention proved to be difficult.

The world's first international legal instrument on children's rights was the product of ten years of negotiation among government delegations (though only a small number actively participated), inter-governmental organisations and non-governmental organisations. There were five issue areas where consensus was difficult to achieve (Johnson, 1992): freedom of thought, conscience and religion (where there were Islamic concerns); inter-country adoption (with Latin American countries expressing reservations); the rights of the unborn child (where there were splits on both lines of religion and between more developed and developing countries with policies for curbing over-population); traditional practices (with some African concern on female circumcision); and on the duties of children (favoured by Senegal, and found in the Charter on the Rights and Welfare of the African Child Article 31).

Each of these five areas provided a test case for resolving conflicting cultural and religious perspectives, and in each case a compromise was found. In one case (freedom of religion) the compromise was effected by the adoption of a minimal text, but in the others a minority perspective was incorporated in some way into the final text.

Whether these accommodations are necessarily good for children is contested. To take an example: the Preamble to the Convention states that 'due account' is to be taken of 'the importance of the traditions and cultural values of each people for the protection and harmonious development of the child'. But these 'traditions and cultural values' are not problematised. Take female genital mutilation (circumcision is a euphemism) for example (Dorkenoo and Elworthy, 1992). Medically unnecessary and extremely painful operations are routinely carried out on babies and young girls; in their most severe forms they involve the partial to complete removal of the external female genitalia. The practice impacts on over 80 million women and girls in over 20 countries in Africa and has spread to other countries including the United Kingdom (graphically documented in a BBC 2 Forty Minutes programme 'A Cruel Ritual' broadcast on 21 February 1991). Do these 'traditional values' not undermine the child and, if so, are we to be tolerant of them?

There is thus in the Convention a clear recognition that the child's welfare may well be 'trumped' in certain situations by 'cultural values and traditions'. States are, however, by Article 24(2) to 'take effective and appropriate measures with a view to abolishing traditional practices prejudicial to the health of children', but this is itself qualified by Article 24(4), which provides that states undertake to promote and encourage international cooperation with a view to achieving progressively the full realisation of the rights in Article 24. The elimination of harmful traditional practices is seen, then, as the recognition of social or cultural rights, and therefore falls within the realm of progressive obligation (McGoldrick, 1991). Is this acceptable? Surely, practices which are prejudicial to the health of girls and which limit their life choices thereafter should be seen as infringements of a civil right, and therefore be accorded priority.

The Convention is nevertheless important. It is described by Veerman as 'an important and easily understood advocacy tool - one that promotes children's welfare as an issue of justice rather than one of charity' (Veerman, 1992, p.184). The rights in the Convention may be categorised as:

1. General rights (the right to life, prohibition against torture, freedom of expression, thought and religion, the right to information and to privacy).
2. Rights requiring protective measures (including measures to protect children from economic and sexual exploitation, to prevent drug abuse and other forms of abuse and neglect).
3. Rights concerning the civil status of children (including the right to acquire nationality, the right to preserve one's identity, the right to remain with parents, unless the best interests of the child dictate otherwise, and the right to be reunited with the family).
4. Rights concerning development and welfare, including the child's right to a reasonable standard of living, the right to health and basic services, the right to social security, the right to education and the right to leisure.

5. Rights concerning children in special circumstances or 'in especially difficult circumstances'. These extend to such children as handicapped children, refugee children and orphaned children. Included are special regulations on adoption, the cultural concerns of minority and indigenous children, and rehabilitative care for children suffering from deprivation, as well as a prohibition on the recruitment of soldiers under 15 years of age.

6. Procedural considerations, particularly the establishment of an International Committee of ten experts to monitor implementation of the Convention (Muntarbhorn, 1992).

The innovative nature of the Convention is brought out well by Philip Veerman (1992, pp.184-5). He pinpoints first that it says that state agencies will be responsible for the physical, psychological and social reintegration of a child where rights are violated; second that it goes beyond earlier formulations which emphasised the duties of adults and the state to emphasise child participation in decision-making. The Convention is, as he notes, the first explicitly to state that children have a right to 'have a say' in processes affecting their lives. In this way the child is regarded as the 'principal' in the Convention (Pais, 1992). Thirdly, placements in residential care and foster care will now be subject to constant review - a principle very much in line with the new English Children Act (Freeman, 1992b). Fourth the right to identity has never before been formulated in an International Convention (and see Cerda, 1990).

Of these innovations Article 12, providing for a child's participation in decisions affecting him or her, is, I believe, the most significant. It is a development from the child liberation philosophy formulated in the 1970s and is in line with the *Gillick* decision and a strand, but only a strand, in the Children Act 1989 (Fox Harding, 1991; Freeman, 1992c). The Article states:

1. States Parties shall assure to the child who is capable of forming his or her own views the right to express those views freely in all matters affecting the child, the views of the child being given due weight in accordance with the age and maturity of the child.

2. For this purpose, the child shall in particular be provided the opportunity to be heard in any judicial and administrative proceedings affecting the child, either directly, or through a representative or an appropriate body, in a manner consistent with the procedural rules of national law.

The right enunciated here is significant not only for what it says, but because it recognises the child as a full human being, with integrity and personality, and with the ability to participate fully in society. The constituting features of 'freedom of expression', as defined in Article 13 to include 'the right to seek, receive and impart information and ideas of all kinds', and the right in Article 14 to 'freedom of thought, conscience and religion' also look upon children as persons in their own right.

Attention has been focused also on Article 3 which states:

1. In all actions concerning children, whether undertaken by public or private social welfare institutions, courts of law, administrative authorities or legislative bodies, the best interests of the child shall be a primary consideration.
2. States parties undertake to ensure the child such protection and care as is necessary for his or her well-being, taking into account the rights and duties of his or her parents, legal guardians, or other individuals legally responsible for him or her, and, to this end, shall take all appropriate legislative and administrative measures.

In England in matters of 'upbringing' before the courts the child's welfare is the 'paramount' consideration (it 'determines the course to be followed' (*J v C*, 1970)). Although the Convention makes the child's best interests only *a* (not *the*) primary consideration, the scope of this direction is considerably wider. The child's best interests are not even a primary consideration in decisions made by this country's education, housing or immigration authorities, an omission perhaps most remarkable in the field of education where a plethora of Acts since 1980 have purported to extend parents' rights in matters relating to schooling whilst ignoring the rights of its primary consumers.

Articles 12 and 3 encapsulate a tension in the whole debate which has been examined here. Article 12 emphasises the centrality of a child's views. Article 3 points to the priority to be given to concerns of welfare. The first principle is not overriding (a Polish attempt to make welfare paramount failed), but its imperative and the philosophy of Article 12 can conflict. How, then, will conflicts be resolved? It is a real concern. Those who constructed the Convention themselves paid scant regard to children's views: do we not know that the rights enumerated in the Convention are those that children themselves would have constructed? But Article 12 cannot be underestimated.

Children who are capable of forming views must be 'assured' the right to express them on 'all matters affecting' them, and these views must be given 'due weight'. Again this goes beyond the new English Children Act where a child's views and the representation of them is largely confined to the public law arena. A child has a greater 'say' in care than in school or for that matter at home (the Finnish law of 1983 makes a striking contrast - Savolainen, 1986).

The child's best interests test is well-known. There have been many attempts to 'pour content' into it (Goldstein and others, 1980). It has been criticised for its indeterminacy and for being inevitably value-laden (Mnookin, 1985). But 'the Convention does not seek to provide any definite statement of how a child's interests would be best served in a given situation' (Alston, 1992, p.8) This is an acknowledgement that the precise implications of the principle will vary over time and from country to country. However, the Committee on the Rights of the Child, established under the Convention, can be expected over time to identify more precise guidelines to give direction to the principle in specific contexts.

Conclusion.

The Convention is an achievement. But it is a beginning, no more. We must get 'beyond conventions, towards empowerment' (Freeman, 1992d). We must re-examine structures, institutions and practices to make children's rights more meaningful. We have ratified the Convention; we have passed a Children Act. But children are still passed around 'like packages or pieces of property' (Lord Justice Butler-Sloss in *Re W*, 1992b), sexually abused by those 'caring' for them, whisked from their home in 'dawn raids' and held incommunicado. More live in poverty, more are homeless and fewer are entitled to social security than was the case even a decade ago. The Children Act recognises both sides of the children's rights equation: welfare and self-determination. But is there a serious commitment to either? We have as far to go in the next quarter of a century as we have come in the last if we are truly to take children's rights seriously.

References
Adams, P. (1971) *Children's Rights: Toward the Liberation of The Child.* New York: Praeger

Alston, P. (1992) 'The legal framework of the Convention on the Rights of the Child', *Bulletin of Human Rights*, 91(2), pp.1-15

Bainham, A. (1992) 'The judge and the incompetent minor', *Law Quarterly Review*, 108, pp.194-200

Campbell, T. (1992) 'The rights of the minor: as person, as child, as juvenile, as future adult' in Alston, P. et al., (eds.) *Children, Rights and the Law*. Oxford: Clarendon Press

Cerda, J.S. (1990) 'The draft Convention on The Rights of the Child: new rights', *Human Rights Quarterly,* 12, pp.115-119

Cohen, C. (1990) 'Relationships between the child, the family and the state: the UN Convention on the Rights of the Child' in Bayles, M. and Moffatt, R. *Perspectives on the Family*. Lewiston, NY: Edwin Meller Press

Cohen, C. and Naimark, H. (1991) 'The United Nations Convention on The Rights of the Child: individual rights concepts and their significance for social scientists', *American Psychologist*, 46(2)

Dorkenoo, E. and Elsworthy, S. (1992) *Female Genital Mutilation: Proposals for Change*. London,: Minority Rights Group

Eekelaar, J. (1986) 'The emergence of children's rights', *Oxford Journal of Legal Studies*, 6, pp.161-182

Eekelaar, J. (1992) 'The importance of thinking that children have rights' in Alston, P. et al. (eds.) *Children, Rights and the Law*. Oxford: Clarendon Press, pp.221-235

Farson, R. (1978) *Birthrights*. Harmondsworth: Penguin

Fox Harding, L. (1991) 'The Children Act 1989 in context; four perspectives in child care law and policy', *Journal of Social Welfare and Family Law*, pp 179-94, 285-302

Franklin, B. (1986) *The Rights of Children*. Oxford: Basil Blackwell

Freeman, M. (1983) *The Rights and Wrongs of Children*. London: Frances Pinter

Freeman, M. (1992a) 'Taking children's rights more seriously', *International Journal of Law and the Family,* 6, pp.52-71

Freeman, M. (1992b) *Children, Their Families and the Law - Working With The Children Act*. Basingstoke: Macmillan

Freeman, M. (1992c) 'In the child's best interests? Reading the Children Act critically', *Current Legal Problems*, 45, pp.173-212

Freeman, M. (1992d) 'Beyond conventions - towards empowerment' in Fortuyn, M.D. and de Langen, M. (eds.) *Towards the Realization of Human Rights of Children*. Amsterdam, DCI - Netherlands, pp.19-39

Fuller, E. (1925) 'Great Britain and the Declaration of Geneva V', *The World's Children*. VI (7), p.116

Goldstein, J., Freud, A. and Solnit, A. (1980) *Before The Best Interests of Child*. New York: Free Pres

Hafen, B.C. (1976) 'Children's liberation and the new egalitarianism: some reservations about abondoning youth to their rights', *Brigham Young University Law Review*, pp.605-58

Hawes, J. (1991) *The Children's Rights Movement*. Boston: Twayne

Haworth, L. (1986) *Autonomy*. New Haven: Yale University Press

Helmholz, R. (1993) 'And were there children's rights in early modern England?', *International Journal of Children's Rights*, 1, (forthcoming)

Holt, J. (1975) *Escape From Childhood*. Harmondsworth: Penguin

Houlgate, L. (1980) *The Child and The State*. Baltimore: Johns Hopkins University Press

Johnson, D. (1992) 'Cultural and regional pluralism in the drafting of the UN Convention on the rights of the child' in Freeman, M. and Veerman, P. *The Ideologies of Children's Rights*. Dordrecht: Martinus Nijhoff, pp.95-114

Korczak, J. (1920) 'How to love a child' in *Selected Works of Janusz Korczak*, Wolins, M. (ed.). Warsaw

Lifton, B.J. (1988) *The King of Children*. London: Chatto and Windus

Lindley, R. (1986) *Autonomy*. Basingstoke: Macmillan

McGoldrick, D. (1991) 'The United Nations Convention on the Rights of the Child', *International Journal of Law and the Family*, 5, pp.132-169

Meyer, P.B. (1973) The exploitation of the American growing class' in Gottieb, D. (ed.) *Children's Liberation*. Englewood Cliffs, NJ: Prentice Hall

Mnookin, R. (1985) *In The Interest of Children*. New York: W.H.Freeman

Muntarbhorn, V. (1992) 'The Convention on the Rights of the Child: reaching the unreached?, *Bulletin of Human Rights*, 91(2), pp.66-74

Murphy, J. (1992) 'W(h)ither adolescent autonomy?', *Journal of Social Welfare and Family Law*, pp.529-544

Newell, P. (1989) *Children Are People Too*. London: Bedford Square Press

O'Neill, O. (1988) 'Children's rights and children's lives', *Ethics*, 98, pp.445-463

Pais, M.S. (1992) 'The United Nations, Convention on The Rights of The Child', *Bulletin of Human Rights*, 91(2), pp.75-82

Platt, A. (1969) *The Child Savers*. Chicago: University of Chicago Press

Pleck, E. (1987) *Domestic Tyranny*. New York: Oxford University Press

Purdy, L.M. (1992) *In Their Best Interest? - The Case Against Equal Rights for Children*. Ithaca, New York: Cornell University Press

Rodham, H. (1973) 'Children under the law', *Harvard Educational Review*, 43, pp.487-514

Savolainen, M. (1986) 'Finland: more rights for children', *Journal of Family Law*, 25(1), pp.113-126

Silverman, P. (1978) *Who Speaks for the Child?* Don Mills, Ontario: Musson.

Singer, S. (1986) 'The protection of children during armed conflict situations', *International Review of the Red Cross*, May-June

Vallès, J. (1878) *L'Enfant*. Paris

Veerman, P. (1992) *The Rights of the Child and the Changing Image of Childhood*. Dordrecht: Martinus Nijhoff

Ward, C. (1978) *The Child in the City*. New York: Partheon

Weisberg, D.K. (1978) 'Evolution of the rights of the child in the western world', *Review of the International Commission of Jurists,* December, pp.43-51

Wiggin, K.D. (1892) *Children's Rights*. Boston: Houghton Mifflin

Wilkerson, A. (1973) *The Rights of Children*. Philadelphia: Templar University Press

Zamora Chavarria E.M. (1992) 'The rights of the child in democratic societies' in Fortuyn, M.D. and de Langen, M. (eds.) *Towards The Realization of Human Rights of Children*. Amsterdam: DC I-Netherlands, pp.65-75

Cases

Gillick v West Norfolk and Wisbech AHA(1986) AC 112

J v C (1970) AC 668

Re R (1991) 4 All ER 177

Re W (a) (1992) 4 All ER 627

Re W (b) (1992) 2 FLR 461

6. Under fives:
thirty years of no progress?

Sonia Jackson, University College, Swansea

We normally think of ageism as a form of discrimination practised against people in their 70s and 80s, but nowhere is it more clearly demonstrated than in attitudes to people under five. The majority of children in this country receive no direct form of public service, other than health care, until they begin school. At both national and local levels, any provision made for them is considered marginal, and the first target for cuts when money is short. In a world where almost everything is changing, the unwillingness of British governments to formulate a coherent policy for early childhood is a constant factor.

Over the past 30 years there have been many false dawns, each to be followed by disappointment. The recommendations of a long series of research studies and reports of advisory bodies have been resolutely ignored, and as a recent *Times Educational Supplement* editorial commented despondently: 'With public spending ever more squeezed, local authorities in turmoil and government ministers apparently unembarrassable, the chances of improvement look pretty unlikely' (TES, 1992).

Contact with colleagues in other countries through the European Community provides a standard of comparison which vividly highlights the weaknesses of our own system. France and Belgium for example have publicly funded provision for 95 per cent of three and four-year-olds and 20 per cent of under threes (Moss, 1992). Only 25 per cent of three and four-year-olds in this country have access to nursery education, most of them part-time. Another 20 per cent are in reception classes of infant schools, where government pressure to reintroduce formal subject-based teaching methods is making the regime and curriculum increasingly inappropriate for such young children (David, 1990).

More fundamentally, a cross-national perspective enables us to see that neglect of our under fives is only a special case of an essential difference in philosophies of childhood. Historically British family policy has been shaped by the fear of over-population, especially of the underclass irresponsibly reproducing itself, while other European countries have pursued actively pro-natalist policies (Jackson, 1992). In this country official pronouncements on pre-school issues still reflect the attitude that having children is an act of private self-indulgence, like keeping a dog. Most other European countries, by contrast, look on children as a precious national asset, the responsibility not simply of their mothers and fathers but of society as a whole, and are prepared to invest in them at a level which would be politically unthinkable in this country. Here, interests, energies and resources are focused on the voting, economically active adult. The more distant people are from that status, the less they count when financial decisions are made. The failure to secure, or often even to seek, an adequate share of national resources for young children, can only be understood in this political context.

Care and education

However there are other factors in the British situation which contributed to our failure to develop a comprehensive system of care and education before school, unlike other countries who started from much the same point. One was the influence of attachment theory, derived originally from the work of Bowlby (1951), generalised to quite different circumstances and elevated into a dogma by a series of official pronouncements. Once their labour was no longer needed for the war effort, mothers were made to feel guilty about leaving young children for any reason, even for short periods, but especially in order to earn money. Studies of working mothers (McCrae, 1986; Brannen and Moss, 1991) have shown how that view continues to some extent today, and has been internalised even by women holding jobs carrying the same level of pay and responsibility as those of their husbands.

The effect throughout the '60s and '70s was to diffuse demand for services between two groups with very different perceptions of their needs and interests. For women who wanted to work full-time, nursery education on the traditional pattern with short hours and long school holidays was of limited relevance, whereas the great majority who were not contemplating out-of-home work until their children started school, were prepared to settle for whatever relief they could get from the constant demands of childcare. Moreover they were inclined to be critical of those who rejected the dominant ideology for supposedly putting their own interests before those of their children. The result was that discussion of day care and of nursery education went on along separate tracks, and for a time even polarised, with campaigners for day care accused of ignoring the well-being of children (Leach, 1979) while some writers on nursery education seemed unaware that women had any existence outside their role as mothers.

Looking back 30 years, however, we become aware of the shift which has taken place in attitudes and assumptions. In 1963 when Sir Edward Boyle, the Conservative Minister of Education, set up his enquiry into primary schooling, the split between care and education was unquestioned, as was the duty of women with young children to stay at home to look after them. After much debate dominated by the perceived need to keep costs to a minimum, the Plowden Report, *Children and their Primary Schools* (Central Advisory Council for Education, 1967) eventually recommended a substantial expansion of nursery education. The problem of resources was dealt with by proposing a shift system, most children attending either mornings or afternoons. The hostility to working mothers which permeates this section of the Report is quite striking:

Some mothers who are not obliged to work may work full-time, regardless of their children's welfare. It is no business of the educational service to encourage these mothers to do so (p.127).

It is not simply a question of work; the assumption is that women's time and energies should be totally devoted to their young children. For example, the discussion of full-time versus part-time provision completely ignores the difference in usable time for mothers between a full day including a meal and a session so short that it might, if the family lived at any distance, leave barely an hour between returning home from taking the child and setting out again to collect her.

The Plowden Report is informed by a generous, child-centred spirit, in contrast to the tone of much present-day educational debate. However in retrospect its influence on the future shape of pre-school provision, which can still be clearly seen today, was not helpful. Its recommendations reinforced the division between day care for under threes, concerned primarily with physical health, and nursery education for three and four-year-olds. The experience of 'foreign countries', where full-time nursery schooling was already widely available, was considered irrelevant to British conditions, and this dismissive attitude to cross-national experience continues to pervade official statements.

The Plowden recommendations did result in the provision of some new nursery schools and classes, almost entirely in areas of social deprivation, and in the availability of many more *places* because the proposed shift to half-day sessions was generally accepted. For a very brief period, following the 1972 White Paper, *Nursery Education: A Framework for Expansion,* the Plowden targets were adopted as official government policy, but one of Margaret Thatcher's first acts as Prime Minister was to relieve local authorities of their responsibility to provide nursery education (Penn and Riley, 1992). This stop-go pattern has continued right up to the present, with the House of Commons Select Committee (1989) recommending yet again that nursery education should be made available to all three and four-year-olds whose parents want it (identical with Plowden), while the Education Bill currently before Parliament makes virtually no reference to nursery education, and the combined effect of the Education Reform Act 1988 and the latest round of budget cuts will act strongly to discourage local authorities from providing it (Tytler, 1993).

Playgroups and nursery education

The result has been that playgroups, originally intended as a temporary stopgap, have become the main form of provision for children not in school, currently attended by about 60 per cent of the age group, usually for two or three sessions a week.

The playgroup movement has many strengths. It was undoubtedly a lifeline to millions of isolated mothers who would otherwise have been left to cope entirely alone. In its early years it provided an alternative model to the professional-dominated, parent-excluding stance of many nursery schools. Because parent rotas were often the only way of running groups on a shoestring, mothers had to be included. Even if they were confined to subsidiary tasks like washing paintpots and distributing juice, as they sometimes were (Smith, 1980), they could not help observing what was going on and gaining some insight into the process of learning through play which paradoxically, they might not have done in a professionally staffed nursery school at that time.

During the 1970s a considerable amount of research on early childhood was commissioned by the Department of Education and Science and the Social Science Research Council in anticipation of the expected expansion of nursery education. One of the studies which formed part of the Oxford Pre-school Research Project, directed by the eminent American educational theorist, Jerome Bruner, compared nurseries and playgroups. It concluded that the professional training of nursery school teachers and the generally superior facilities and equipment of nursery schools and classes, did not necessarily lead to a better learning experience for the children (Bruner, 1980). Many playgroups attained high standards and also had the advantage of a better ratio of adults to children, providing more opportunities for adult-child conversations and adult involvement in small group activities. However, because most playgroups were in middle class areas and most nursery schools in working-class ones, it could be argued that the comparison was not a fair one. More recently it has been pointed out that the quality of provision in playgroups has always been extremely variable. Many struggle to operate in freezing church halls, where every item of play equipment has to be laboriously excavated from under the stage for each session and stowed away again while the children wait to be collected. Staffing depends on availability of women prepared to work for token pay or none. Such people were never easy to find in less affluent areas and are becoming increasingly hard to recruit as the number of women in the workforce continues to rise (Statham, 1990).

There is a serious question whether the strength of the Pre-school Playgroups Association has been an obstacle to the development of nursery education in this country. Playgroups have always been popular with the government. Sir Keith Joseph used the PPA 1972 annual meeting as the platform for his famous speech on the Cycle of Deprivation, taking the occasion to announce a 'modest' grant to the Association. From a Treasury point of view, playgroups are exceptionally cost-effective. They are a flexible form of provision, more easily able than nursery schools or classes to expand or contract in response to population shifts, making use of marginal accommodation and cheap or volunteer labour. Official spokespeople have been able to make spurious claims that they offer choice, variety and opportunities for parent (mother) participation which compare favourably with provision in other countries. The reality is of course different, with very few families having any effective choice, especially in rural areas (Fanshawe, 1993). Low cost, as Holtermann (1992) has shown, is also largely illusory, since a well-resourced playgroup costs much the same as a nursery class. However, as the difference in price is paid by children and women, it need not be counted.

It is impossible to say if nursery education in Britain would have fared better if the playgroup movement had not become so entrenched and strongly organised. However the failure to develop a stable, widely available system of pre-schooling, can be seen to have had an impact on the nursery teaching profession, the full implications of which are now becoming apparent. Because employment opportunities for nursery teachers have fluctuated in unpredictable ways over the years, specialist training for teaching very young children has ceased to be a viable option. Courses for the three to five age range had already disappeared by the mid-60s and teacher-trainers with early years expertise often went with them, so that the relatively small number of nursery-infant courses, covering the years from three to eight, which survived were already tending to concentrate on the upper age range. More recently this trend has been exacerbated by the introduction of the National Curriculum and the insistence by the Council for the Accreditation of Teacher Education (CATE) that all teachers following a BEd course must have a National Curriculum subject specialism which accounts for 50 per cent of their study time. Although a higher level of education for early years teachers could be seen as an advance, these regulations leave little space for a range of subjects and skills (such as developmental psychology, sociology, music, art or communicating with parents) which might be considered more relevant to work with very young children than French or history. The rigidity of the CATE rules creates severe difficulties for developing appropriate training for work in pre-school and day care settings.

Day care and childminding

As long as the vast majority of mothers with young children were prepared to stay at home, day care was not a topic which attracted much attention. However some women were not in a position to give up paid work on having a baby, and this was particularly true of Afro-Caribbean mothers; in 1970, 80 per cent of those with children under five worked full-time (Hood and others, 1970). Brian Jackson (1973) first drew attention to the fact that most of their children were left for long hours with childminders. Small-scale studies revealed some horrifying situations - rows of carry-cots in the garage, toddlers without toys confined to a white sheet in the hall or spending their days strapped in pushchairs. These extreme cases, widely reported in the media, aroused an interest which gave impetus to more systematic enquiries.

Previously, childminders had been an invisible element in the pre-school world, only achieving momentary attention as a result of dramatic and tragic incidents, such as when minded children died in fires. Under the Nurseries and Child-minders Regulation Act 1948, amended in 1968, there was a requirement for registration and provision for minimal inspection by local authorities, mainly concerned with the premises rather than the person providing the care. The revelation was to discover that childminding was the major form of care for pre-school children outside the family, and for babies, the only one that existed (Jackson and Jackson, 1979).

The starting point of the first study, carried out in two northern cities, with unregistered as well as official minders, was that childminding was an evil to be rooted out. In time the researchers came round to the view that, on the contrary, it was a valuable service, developed by working class communities to meet their own needs, and had important strengths which could be built on. The research revealed a very mixed picture, some childminders providing excellent care and crucial support to families in difficulties, others overburdened, ignorant of children's needs, neglectful and occasionally abusive. The quality of care did not necessarily coincide with the legal status of the minder.

This was action research, exploring ways of helping childminders to provide better care for the children they were already looking after in large numbers. It aimed to attach positive benefits to registration by setting up drop-in centres, training courses, toy libraries, bulk-buying schemes, social and recreational facilities and opportunities for discussion and mutual support. A television series for childminders, *Other People's Children*, presented by well-known personalities, and accompanied by a handbook issued free through social services departments (Jackson and Allen, 1976) raised the status of childminding in the eyes of the general public, and resulted in a marked improvement in the minders' own self-image. The National Childminding Association, launched in the last programme of the television series, can now count almost half of all registered childminders among its members (Ferri, 1992).

Like most of the expedients evolved to make the best of a bad situation, the growth of childminding as a respected occupation could be seen positively or negatively. The development of childminding closely parallels the story of the playgroup movement, and arouses similar controversy. One view is that the promotion of home-based day care as an alternative to centre-based provision, enabled the government to support childminding as a low-cost, low-quality service and to ignore demands for a significant increase in day care at the cost of a small annual grant to NCMA. Just as playgroups were seen as a poor substitute for nursery schools, childminding appeared to many to be a form of day care inferior to day nurseries with their hygienic premises and trained staff. A much-quoted survey (Bone, 1977) showed that, given the choice, the majority of mothers would opt for nurseries in preference to childminders. An ideological confrontation developed in which any proposals for supporting childminders were seen as undermining the case for group day care (Penn and Riley, 1992).

This line of thinking perhaps accounts for the hostile tone of much of the research on childminding in the 1970s. Mayall and Petrie (1977), for example, stressed what they saw as the distant relationship between the child and minder, as compared with that between the child and mother. Bryant, Harris and Newton (1980) also described many minded children as 'passive and detached'. However they also found many instances where parent and minder had become friends and the child's care was shared between loving adults to the benefit of all.

Much of this discussion now seems rather beside the point. There is no necessary connection between the *form* of provision and its quality, as Melhuish (1991) has shown. Concern about standards in childminding carried an implicit assumption about the superiority of day nurseries which remained largely unchallenged. However a number of studies published in the early 1980s raised anxieties about the quality of care and education offered in local authority nurseries. Bain and Barnett (1980) and Marshall (1982) found very young children treated impersonally and handled by many different people. There was little conversation between children and adults and a restricted range of toys and activities. The same criticisms were made by Elsa Ferri (1981) in her study of combined nursery centres. And as she pointed out, the very children who were in day nurseries because they came from families with severe problems and were most in need of high quality, educational care, were least likely to get it.

By 1980 most day nursery places were reserved for children in 'priority' categories, many of them with single mothers more likely to be living on welfare benefits than working. Yet the majority of nurseries continued to operate on traditional lines, providing day care geared to an industrial working day and having only superficial contact with parents. That this obviously dysfunctional situation persisted for so long reflected the low status of nursery workers and their lack of access to policy-making levels in local authorities.

The community nursery movement which flourished briefly in the early 1980s in London and some other big cities might have provided a better model, but in the absence of secure funding it never really got off the ground. The Department of Health Under Fives Initiative ran into the same problem: what was needed was not start-up money for new projects but an ongoing, stable service (Edwards, 1993).

Family centres

The new form of provision to emerge in the 1980s was the family centre, although a few had been set up earlier by the children's voluntary organisations. Centres tended to fall into three different groups: those aiming to serve a neighbourhood, usually with a high incidence of social and environmental problems (Holman, 1988); centres offering a range of facilities and services to families referred by social workers or health visitors; and therapeutic centres working intensively with a small number of parents and children in the hope of averting family breakdown or child abuse. The rapid increase in the number of family centres, to nearly 500 by the end of the decade (Warren, 1989), was partly accounted for by redesignation or renaming of day nurseries and could be merely cosmetic, but more usually it did represent a genuine change in function and orientation.

Like other non-traditional forms of early years provision, the family centre concept has come under sharp attack from social policy theorists (New and David, 1985; Cannan, 1992) as yet another device to lock women, especially single mothers, into their disadvantaged role. It is argued that instead of providing them with a possible route to economic independence through day care, family centres emphasise the parental function at the expense of personal identity, and often urge people to adopt a style of parenting which may be culturally alien to them.

Taking a more pragmatic view, the family centre can be seen as a versatile model which has the potential to be more responsive to the needs of parents and children than either nursery schools or day nurseries. There is no reason why they should not provide day care and education, and some do, but they can also offer support, counselling, health advice and a range of social, recreational, and educational facilities which may be more useful than day care when there are no jobs to be had (Whalley, 1992). Because there is no standard model, family centres are less bound by accepted practices and norms. They are more likely to think creatively about user involvement and participation, even if not many achieve the ideal of 'partnership' (Goldschmied and Jackson, 1993). Evaluations of family centres have usually found that they are viewed very positively by those who use them (Walker, 1991). Mothers typically describe them as a 'lifeline', particularly valuing the social contact and the opportunity to discuss childrearing problems with others in the same situation. However, the quality of the educational experience they provide for the children is variable, and, especially in centres run by social workers, one sometimes has the impression that very little thought has been given to it at all.

Family centres are recognised by the Children Act, 1989, as an important form of preventive service for children in need. In more favourable times this might be welcomed, but with the current pressure on social services budgets there are already signs that the Act will have the undesirable effect of accelerating the trend towards treatment-oriented centres targeted on families perceived to be failing instead of providing a non-stigmatising service to a whole community (Parton and Parton, 1988-89).

Equal opportunities and gender roles in the family

The debate that in the long run is likely to have most impact on decision-makers is not about under fives at all, but concerns women's rights to equality in the workplace and the division of family responsibilities between men and women. It is clear that a renegotiation of gender roles is taking place and that this is a worldwide phenomenon (Lamb, 1986). Although it is far from complete, and numerous writers have shown that women with male partners still take much more than a half share of responsibility for home and children (Hochschild, 1990, Brannen and Moss, 1988), the effects can be seen in steadily rising numbers of mothers with young children working outside the home and increased involvement of men in domestic and childcare tasks. Even in Britain, where the absence of day care has slowed down the process, 12 per cent of mothers with children under five work full time, 29 per cent part-time, and for those with older children the figures rise to 31 per cent full time and 43 per cent part time (Department of Health, 1991).

The ideological component of this shift has been evident in the pre-school literature for many years, running somewhat in advance of reality. For example the term 'mother' is rarely used, even though everybody knows that is what is normally meant by 'parent'. But genuine efforts are being made to develop non-sexist practice in nursery schools, playgroups and day nurseries (Aspinwall, 1984), to involve fathers as well as mothers, and to recruit men to work in pre-school settings. Training and curriculum materials subscribe to the principle of gender equality and urge positive action against sex-stereotyping. Changing attitudes is a very slow process, but overcoming the perception of child care and early education as women's business is an essential step towards moving it up the agenda.

Gender roles in the family are intricately bound up with women's opportunities and rights to participate in paid employment. This is widely recognised in other countries, although so far Sweden is the only one to have an explicit policy to encourage the role of fathers. Nine European countries now have statutory parental leave following maternity leave, and the right to time off to care for sick children. The proposed Directive which would have made this legally binding throughout the EC was vetoed by Britain in the Council of Ministers. The European Childcare Network, which is coordinated by Peter Moss, has done much to broaden the perspectives of early years workers and to demonstrate that the inadequacy of provision is not primarily a matter of resources, as it is so often presented, but of family and employment policy (European Commission 1988, 1990). The current Council Recommendation on Child Care urges member states to take initiatives in four areas: childcare services, leave arrangements for employed parents, environment, structure and organisation of work, and promotion of increased participation of men in the care and upbringing of children. Changes in all these areas would have a very important impact on the experience of under fives in Britain, yet the debate on the Maastricht Treaty has been overwhelmingly concentrated on economic and constitutional issues, with almost no discussion of its effects on children and families.

Cross-national perspectives on childcare and education

International comparisons have been increasingly important in demonstrating the shortcomings of British services for under fives. The statistics speak for themselves:

In 1990 public expenditure on services for children under five was six times higher in Denmark than in Britain, yet as recently as 1979 early childhood services in Britain and Denmark were at much the same level and similarly fragmented. The difference is that Denmark took a political decision to create a high quality, generally available service.

Cross-national research has demonstrated the positive value of pre-school education for all children and thrown light on some long-running debates (Sylva and Moss, 1992). Does day care have adverse effects on children's development, for example? Research in Sweden and the United States indicates that it depends on the balance between the quality of care offered in the home and out-of-home setting (Moss and Melhuish, 1991). Where both home care and centre care are good, as for most Swedish children, the effect is neutral.

Considering the alternative models of pre-school care and education offered in the USA and, say, France, there is no doubt which provides a better experience for more children. Reliance on an ill-coordinated patchwork of private and voluntary provision, as is the policy of the present government, means poor care and education, or none, for most young children, and locks poor parents, especially single mothers, into poverty (Jackson, 1992). Significantly, the Clinton administration is planning a massive expansion of Head Start, one Federal programme that has most clearly proved its worth. But perhaps the most important effect of declining insularity has been to redefine pre-school education and care as *normal* not as it is always categorised in this country, as a marginal service for disadvantaged or failing families.

The Children Act and under fives

The integrative perspective which has been such an important feature of the work of the European Childcare Network is conspicuously absent from the Children Act, 1989, despite its self-description, 'a new framework for the care and upbringing of children'. The failure of the Act to define its key concept of 'children in need' is of course no accident, because the 'need' has to a large extent been created by government policies on income support, housing and employment formulated with no concern for their impact on children. The emphasis on family support is still directed at families at risk of failing, with no recognition of the responsibility of the state to provide social and economic conditions which facilitate the task of childrearing rather than making it more difficult. Parton (1991) comments on how the cross-party consensus which enabled the smooth passage of the Bill through Parliament was threatened as soon as such issues were raised. Even when the argument for broad-based local authority day-care provision was argued on child protection grounds it was adamantly resisted by the Government.

Nevertheless, within its limitations the Act has to be seen as an important advance. For the first time the many different forms of facility existing to serve young children (0 - 8) and their families are brought within the scope of one piece of legislation. By their inclusion in the Act, services for pre-school children are recognised as an integral part of the overall system of child welfare and education.

Volume 2 of the Guidance and Regulations (DH, 1991), is an enlightened document which, if fully implemented, would bring about major improvements. The need for day care is accepted as given without the disapproving tone of earlier pronouncements. Care and education are clearly recognised as interrelated: children in day care settings, as recommended by the Rumbold Report (DES, 1990), should be offered experiences 'comparable in quality with those offered to children attending school'. Quality of care is defined in some detail, with reference to research evidence on the experiences which facilitate children's development and enhance their well-being. There is emphasis on coordination between education and social services departments and practical suggestions on how to achieve it.

The Children Act stimulated a great deal of thinking, planning and training, some of it interdisciplinary, and the requirement for social services and education departments to review jointly services for children under eight prompted some moves towards integration. However, as with so many promising developments over the last 30 years, plans conceived in a spirit of optimism have begun to crumble in the face of economic recession. Severe restrictions on expenditure are already forcing many local authorities to confine themselves to fulfilling their *duties* under the Act rather than using their *powers* to improve quantity and quality of services. Moreover other government legislation appears to conflict directly with the intentions of the Act. For example the implementation of the Education Reform Act, 1988, is reducing the role and size of local education authorities to a point where they are unlikely to be able to provide the support and advice envisaged in the Guidance. The Education Bill at present before Parliament appears to put even the existing level of nursery education at risk. It certainly undermines the strategic planning role of the local authority.

This would appear to be directly contrary to the intentions of the Children Act. However one of the Act's more disappointing aspects is that although local authorities may provide services for children not defined as being 'in need' (the Guidance acknowledges the arguments for preserving a mixed population) they have no duty to do so. The Government has made clear its view that any expansion should be in the private sector, and governed by market forces. What is already obvious (and predictable) is that care and education of the quality envisaged by the Children Act Guidance cannot be provided at a price which will give a reasonable return to the care provider and be affordable by parents on average wages. The Government has, also predictably, refused to recognize the contradictions inherent in its own policy and instead has responded to complaints from the private sector by instructing local authorities to lower their standards. The result will inevitably be that the children who have most to gain from good quality care will be least likely to get it.

If the Children Act is falling short of expectations, at least as far as under fives are concerned, we can still hope that the framework will be left intact and available for use in more propitious times. The Department of Health officials who drafted Book 2 of the Guidance and Regulations had clearly been listening to people in the forefront of thinking about early years provision, however much they were constrained by their political masters. There is some comfort in the reflection that civil servants tend to last longer than politicians.

The contribution of the National Children's Bureau and the Early Childhood Unit

What part has the National Children's Bureau played in this chequered history? Rather surprisingly, in its first few years young children did not assume a very high profile in the Bureau's work. It tended to respond to developments in the field rather than initiating them. For example, the first follow-up report of the National Child Development Study (NCDS, 1966) made no use of information about pre-school experience, although mothers were questioned about it. However, there was some evidence that children who started school earlier were doing better at seven, and the discussion of findings asked 'If "equal educational opportunity" is to become a reality, ought not pre-school education specially geared to the needs of culturally deprived children to be given higher priority?'

The second NCDS report (Davie and others, 1972), reporting on further analysis of the same data, again made only passing reference to the need for more pre-school provision, to be concentrated on those in greatest need. The idea that nursery education might be of value to all children does not seem to have been entertained.

Interestingly, this report challenged the prevailing orthodoxy on working mothers, pointing out that their children showed no sign of poor adjustment and scored rather higher on tests of attainment than those whose mothers stayed at home. This important finding was not emphasised, perhaps because it did not coincide with the views of Mia Kellmer Pringle, the Bureau's founder and first Director. She was keenly interested in early childhood development, but saw the way forward mainly in terms of supporting mothers (and fathers) in their parental role, educating them to do it better, and providing financial inducements to mothers to stay at home rather than go out to work. As late as 1979 she attacked the campaign for improved day care facilities on the grounds that it devalued mothering and parenthood. She wrote in the Bureau's journal, *Concern*:

Most mothers find it rewarding to have the time to enjoy and to be closely involved in their child's rapid growth, which takes place during these vital years (Pringle, 1979).

By this time she was already fighting a losing battle since the proportion of women in paid work was rising steadily, and evidence was mounting that most women found it more rewarding to combine caring for their children with at least part-time participation in the workforce.

However her conviction of the importance of parenthood and the need for better preparation and support for the parental role gave a strong impetus to a continuing strand of the Bureau's early years work - the emphasis on listening to and involving parents in services for young children.

The Bureau's parenting project resulted in a useful and influential book, *The Needs of Parents* (Pugh and De'Ath, 1984). More importantly the model of continuous interplay between consultation, research and dissemination which characterised the project was effectively taken by Gillian Pugh into her work in the Under Fives Unit. It was at this point that the Bureau finally began to take a leading role in the early childhood field.

The Unit was launched in May 1986 with the modest aim of providing information and advice on developments in services for children under five, but with a challenging statement of principles which has given it a strong sense of direction. A number of consistent themes can be seen to run through its work: anti-racism and anti-sexism, partnership with parents, integrating children with special needs, co-ordinating services, a concern for raising the quality of provision, but by enhancing understanding, not by prescription.

Under Gillian Pugh's leadership the Unit has played an increasingly important role in bringing together the numerous organisations involved in early years work to speak with something approaching a common voice. It has achieved the difficult feat not only of providing a direct service, but operating simultaneously at the levels of policy and practice. In its short life the Unit has established itself as a major resource and meeting point for early years specialists in Britain and overseas. In 1990-91, for example, the year before its name was changed to the Early Childhood Unit, visitors came from fifteen different countries and over 1000 enquiries were answered (National Children's Bureau, 1990). The Unit has operated at every level, from briefing government ministers to running study days for nursery nurses and childminders. It has produced a stream of publications targeted at different readerships and pioneered a collaborative, interactive model of research and training.

These activities have done much to support and encourage people working in the pre-school field, and the widespread use of curriculum and training materials produced by the Unit has had a significant impact on the quality of early years provision, especially for under threes. Indeed the very idea of a curriculum for under threes is an important innovation (Rouse and Griffin, 1992).

The Unit has coordinated a range of initiatives, among them the Early Years Training Group, which brought together people from very different backgrounds to look at what kind of education and training would be appropriate for workers in new forms of provision crossing the care\education divide. With nursery\infant teacher training in what looks like terminal decline (Curtis and Hevey, 1992) and the National Vocational Qualifications (NVQ) structure incomplete, the question becomes an increasingly urgent one. The Group meetings revealed the complexity of the issues involved and the formidable difficulties presented by existing institutional divisions. Nevertheless, the support offered by the Group and the Early Childhood Unit was a significant factor in the development of the first UK undergraduate degree course in Early Childhood Studies at Bristol University, soon to be followed by Manchester. This could prove to be an important step towards raising the status and profile of early years work.

Conclusion

Looking back over the past 30 years we can see that, contrary to first impressions, there has been change, and in some areas significant progress. Attitudes have been transformed, for example to working mothers, the role of fathers, and the educational and social importance of the earliest years of life. The rigid barriers which used to divide professionals in different sectors of early years work begin at last to look permeable, though it would be over-optimistic to see them disappearing in the immediate future. New forms of provision have emerged which give more attention to the needs and wishes of parents. Determined efforts are being made to tackle discrimination on grounds of gender, race or disability.

There is a new emphasis on quality in early years provision, a disposition to look closely at how what is provided for very young children contributes to their overall wellbeing and opportunities for learning. The importance of context in children's emotional, social and cognitive development is increasingly recognised, and with it the inadequacy of current forms of training for early years work. In all these developments the National Children's Bureau, and especially the Under Fives/Early Childhood Unit, has taken a active part.

Why then has the gap between what we know about the needs of young children and their parents and what we provide for them grown ever wider? Why have early years services for children in Britain, in contrast to every other European country, failed to respond to changing social conditions and expectations? Why have we still not succeeded in finding any place for children on our political agenda, as was only too evident in the 1991 General Election campaign?

The National Children's Bureau is in a difficult position here. With its core funding coming from the Department of Health, it cannot afford to alienate a government which has shown itself quick to take revenge on those who offend it. This has not prevented the Early

Childhood Unit from arguing the case for improved and more widely available services, as Gillian Pugh did so cogently in her TES/Greenwich lecture (Pugh, 1992). But it does tend to limit the extent to which the Unit can take on an advocacy role, and prevents it from operating directly as a campaigning organisation.

The Unit has succeeded in focusing the interests and concerns of a wide constituency of early years workers. The next step must be to raise general public awareness that these are issues not just for professionals or for parents of young children, but for the population as a whole. The experience of countries like Denmark shows that this is the only way of generating the political will for a major shift of resources in favour of children under school age and their families.

How such a transformation of our national culture might be achieved is beyond the scope of this article. My guess is that we need a three-pronged strategy. On the one hand we should find ways to develop a new type of early years professional: highly educated, articulate and assertive, and no longer exclusively female. Secondly we need a much stronger political voice for children, which will probably not be achieved until there is a Minister to speak for them in the government. Most important, because it underpins all the rest, we need to harness the immense power of the media, the tabloid press, television, popular magazines to create a national demand for better policies for children and families. Otherwise those who are around to look back in the year 2023 may find that under fives are still bottom of the pile.

References

Aspinwall, K. (1984) *What Are Little Boys Made Of / What Are Little Girls Made Of. A Discussion Paper for Student Nursery Nurses*. London: National Nursery Examination Board

Bain, A. and Barnett, L. (1980) *The Design of a Day Care System in a Nursery Setting for Children Under Five*. Occasional Paper No 8. London: Tavistock Institute of Human Relations

Bone, M. (1977) *Day Care for Pre-School Children*. London: Office of Population Censuses and Surveys

Bowlby, J. (1951) *Maternal Care and Mental Health*. Geneva: World Health Organisation

Brannen, J. and Moss, P. (1988) *New Mothers at Work: Employment and*

Child Care. London: Unwin Hyman

Brannen, J. and Moss, P. (1991) *Managing Mothers: Dual Earner Households After Maternity Leave*. London: Unwin Hyman

Bryant, B., Harris, M. and Newton, D. (1980) *Children and Minders*. London: Grant McIntyre

Cannan, C. (1992) *Changing Families, Changing Welfare*. London: Harvester Wheatsheaf

Central Advisory Council for Education (1967) *Children and Their Primary Schools*. Plowden Report. London: HMSO

Curtis, A. and Hevey, D. (1992) 'Training to work in the early years' in Pugh, G. (ed.) *Contemporary Issues in the Early Years: Working Collaboratively for Children*. Paul Chapman in Association with the National Children's Bureau

David, T. (1990) *Under Five - Under Educated*. Buckingham: Open University Press

Davie, R., Butler, N. and Goldstein, H. (1972) *From Birth to Seven*. London: Longman

Department of Education and Science (1990) *Starting with Quality: Report of the Committee of Enquiry into the Educational Experiences Offered to Three and Four Year Olds*. Rumbold Report. London: HMSO

Department of Health (1991) *The Children Act 1989 Guidance and Regulations, Volume Two Family Support, Day Care and Educational Provision for Young Children*

Edwards, R. (1992) *Beginnings: The Department of Health's New Under Fives Initiative 1989-1992*. London: National Children's Bureau

European Commission (1988) *Childcare and Equality of Opportunity*. Brussels: European Commission

European Commission, (1990) *Childcare in the European Communities, 1985-1990*. Brussels: European Commission

Fanshawe, P. (1993) *Young Children in Town and Country*. Bristol Papers in Applied Social Studies, University of Bristol (in press)

Ferri, E. (1981) *Combined Nursery Centres*. London: Macmillan

Ferri, E. (1992) *What Makes Childminding Work? A Study of Training for Childminders*. London: National Children's Bureau

Goldschmied, E. and Jackson, S. (1993) *People Under Three: Young Children in Day Care*. London: Routledge

Hochschild, A. (1990) *The Second Shift: Working Parents and the Revolution at Home*. London: Piatkus

Holman, B. (1988) *Putting Families First. Prevention and Child Care: A Study of Prevention by Voluntary and Statutory Agencies*. Basingstoke: Macmillan

Holtermann, S. (1992) *Investing in Young Children: Costing an Education and Day Care Service*. London: National Children's Bureau

Hood, C., Oppe, T.E., Pless, I.B. and Apte, E. (1970) *Children of West Indian Immigrants*. London: Institute of Race Relations

House of Commons *Educational Provision for the Under Fives*. Education, Science and Arts Commmittee, Session 1988/89 First Report. HMSO

Jackson, B. (1973) 'The childminders', *New Society*, 29 November

Jackson, B. and Jackson, S. (1979) *Childminder: A Study in Action Research*.

Jackson, S. and Allen, D. (1976) *Other Peoples Children*. London: BBC

Jackson, S. (1992) 'Benign or sinister? Parental responsibility and state intervention in Britain' in Close, P. (ed.) *The State and Caring*. Basingstoke: Macmillan

Lamb, M. (1986) *The Father's Role: Cross-Cultural Perspectives*. New Jersey: Lawrence Erlbaum

Leach, P. (1979) *Who Cares? A New Deal for Mothers and their Small Children*. London: Penguin

McCrae, S. (1986) *Cross-Class Families: A Study of Wives Occupational Superiority*. Oxford Clarendon Press

Marshall, T. (1982) 'Infant care: a day nursery under the microscope', *Social Work Service*, 32, pp.15-32

Mayall, B. and Petrie, P. (1977) *Minder, Mother and Child*. London: University of London Institute of Education

Moss, P. and Melhuish, E. (1991) *Current Issues in Day Care for Young Children: Research and Policy Implications*. London: HMSO

Moss, P. (1992) 'Perspectives from Europe' in Pugh, G. (ed,) *Contemporary Issues in the Early Years*. Paul Chapman in association with National Children's Bureau

National Child Development Study (1966) *11,000 Seven-Year-Olds*. London: Longman

National Children's Bureau (1990) *Under Fives Unit Fourth Annual Report*. London: National Children's Bureau

New, C. and David, M. (1985) *For the Childrens Sake*. Harmondsworth: Penguin

Parton, C. and Parton, N. (1988/89) 'Women, the family and child protection', *Critical Social Policy*, 24, pp.38-49

Parton, N. (1991) *Governing the Family: Child Care, Child Protection and the State*. Basingstoke: Macmillan

Penn, H. and Riley, K. (1992) *Managing Services for the Under Fives*. London: Longman

Pringle, M.K. (1979) 'Putting children first', *Concern*, 33, Autumn. National Children's Bureau

Pugh, G. and De'Ath, E. (1984) *The Needs of Parents: Practice and Policy in Parent Education*. London: National Childrens Bureau

Pugh, G. (1992) *An Equal Start For All Our Children?* (TES/Greenwich Lecture, 1992). London: The Times Educational Supplement

Rouse, D. and Griffin, S. (1992) 'Quality for the under threes' in Pugh, G. (ed.) *Contemporary Issues in the Early Years*. London: Paul Chapman/National Children's Bureau

Smith, T. (1980) *Parents and Preschool*. London: Grant McIntyre

Statham, J. (1990) *Playgroups in a Changing World*. London: HMSO

Sylva, K. and Moss, P. (1992) *Learning Before School*. National Commission on Education Briefing. No. 8. London: National Commission on Education

The Times Educational Supplement (1992) 'Editorial', 13 November

Tytler, D. (1993) 'Under- fives in the firing line', *Guardian Education*, 23 February

Walker, H. (1991) 'Family centres' in *Social Work and Social Welfare Yearbook*

Warren, C. (1989) 'Family Centre Survey', *Family Centre Network Newsletter*, 2, pp.7-10

Whalley, M. (1992) 'Working as a team' in Pugh, G. (ed.) *Contemporary Issues in the Early Years*. London: Paul Chapman/National Children's Bureau

7. Understanding adolescence today: a review

John C. Coleman, Trust for the Study of Adolescence

What is adolescence?

While this is an important question to ask, the answer is not a simple one. In the first place no one is entirely sure when the stage begins. For some it may be at 13, the first 'teen' year, while for others it may be at the start of secondary school. For those who prefer a physical marker the commencement of puberty is the obvious moment, yet puberty itself is a very complex phenomenon, with different elements - the growth spurt, menarche, and so on - occurring at different times. The picture is further confused by the fact that, during the 20th century in western industrialised countries, puberty has occurred approximately one month earlier every decade of the century - the so called secular trend (Coleman and Hendry, 1990). Today a proportion of girls in the top class of any primary school will have started puberty - are these 10 or 11-year-olds adolescent?

The situation is even more confused at the upper end of the age range. If legal definitions are to be relied upon, you are adult in some respects at 16, in other respects at 17, and yet others at 18. Continued education and training after 16 for many in our society lead to prolonged dependence on the family. Adulthood is postponed, and more and more young people remain at home until their early 20s. A startling statistic is that in Britain the average age for leaving home in 1979 was 19. In 1990 it was 23! (Social Trends, 1992).

This confusion is an important feature of adolescence. It reflects uncertainty and ambiguity in respect of a wide range of issues, and it is a subject to which I shall return below. While there is, I would suggest, less clarity today than there was 30 years ago about the boundaries of adolescence, the opposite is true concerning the dimensions of race and gender. Considerable advances have been made in encouraging a recognition that the experience of adolescence will not be the same for boys and girls (see for example Archer, 1992), nor will it be the same for Asian, Afro-Caribbean or White teenagers (Phinney and Rosenthal, 1992). While we still urgently need more research in these areas, both practitioners and researchers are now sensitised to such domains, and more balanced views may be found in recent writings (Bosma and Jackson, 1992; Hill, 1993),

Theories of adolescence

There is general agreement by all who have written about adolescence that it makes sense to describe the stage as being one of transition. The transition, it is believed, results from the operation of a number of pressures. Some of these, in particular the physiological and emotional pressures, are internal; while other pressures, which originate from peers, parents, teachers, and society at large, are external to the young person. Sometimes these external pressures carry the individual towards maturity at a faster rate than he or she would prefer, while on other occasions they act as a break, holding the adolescent back from the freedom and independence which he or she believes to be a legitimate right. It is the interplay of these forces which, in the final analysis, contributes more than anything to the success or failure of the transition from childhood to maturity.

So far two classical types of explanation concerning the transitional process have been advanced (for fuller explanation see Coleman, 1992). The psychoanalytic approach concentrates on the psychosexual development of the individual, and looks particularly at the psychological factors which underlie the young person's movement away from childhood behaviour and emotional involvement. In brief, three particular ideas characterise the psychoanalytic position. In the first place adolescence is seen as being a period during which there is a marked vulnerability of personality, resulting primarily from the upsurge of instincts at puberty. Second, emphasis is laid on the likelihood of maladaptive behaviour, stemming from the inadequacy of the psychological defences to cope with inner conflicts and tension. Examples of such behaviour include extreme fluctuations of mood, inconsistency in relationships, depression, and non-conformity. Third, the process of disengagement from parents is given special prominence. This is perceived as a necessity if mature emotional and sexual relationships are to be established outside the home.

The second type of explanation, the sociological, represents a very different perspective. In brief, this approach sees the cause of adolescent transition as lying primarily in the social setting of the individual and concentrates on the nature of roles and role conflict, the pressures of social expectations, and on the relative influence of different agents of socialisation. Both views represent adolescence as being dominated by stresses and tensions. For the psychoanalysts these originate from inner emotional instability, whilst for the sociologists the turmoil comes as a result of conflicting forces within society acting upon the individual.

The research evidence

Broadly speaking, research provides little support for these traditional theories, and fails to substantiate much of what both psychoanalysts and sociologists appear to believe. To take some examples, while there is certainly some change in self-concept, there is no evidence to show that any but a small minority experience a serious identity crisis (Hill, 1993). In most cases, relationships with parents are positive and constructive, and young people do not in large part reject adult values in favour of those espoused by the peer group (Fogelman, 1976). In fact, in most situations, peer group values appear to be consistent with those of important adults rather than in conflict with them (Coleman and Hendry, 1990). Fears of promiscuity among the young are not borne out by the research findings, nor do studies support the belief that the peer group encourages anti-social behaviour, unless other factors are also present. Lastly there is no evidence to suggest that during the adolescent years there is a higher level of psychopathology than at any other time (Offer and Schonert-Reichl, 1992). While a lot still needs to be learnt about the mental health of young people, almost all the results that have become available so far indicate that, although a minority may show disturbance, the great majority of teenagers seem to cope well, and to show no undue signs of turmoil or stress.

Since beliefs about adolescence that stem from traditional theories do not in general accord with the results of research, we need to consider some of the reasons for this state of affairs. Firstly, as many writers have pointed out, psychoanalysts and psychiatrists see a selected population. Their experience of adolescence is based primarily upon the individuals they meet in clinics or hospitals. Such experience is bound to encourage a somewhat one-sided perspective in which turmoil or disturbance is over-represented. For sociologists, on the other hand, the problem is often to disentangle concepts of 'youth' or 'the youth movement' from notions about young people themselves. As a number of commentators have observed, youth is frequently seen by sociologists as being in the forefront of social change. Youth is, as it were, the advance party where innovation or alteration in the values of society are concerned. From this position it is but a short step to use youth as a metaphor for social change, and thus to confuse radical forces in society with the beliefs of ordinary young people (Brake, 1985).

Another possible reason for the divergence of viewpoint is that certain adolescent behaviours, such as vandalism, drug-taking, and hooliganism, are extremely threatening to adults. The few who are involved in such activities therefore attain undue prominence in the public eye. The mass media play an important part in this process by publicising sensational behaviour, thus making it appear very much more common than it is in reality. One only has to consider critically the image of the teenager portrayed week after week on the television to understand how, for many adults, the minority comes to be representative of all young people. All three tendencies mentioned so far lead to an exaggerated view of the amount of turmoil that may be expected during adolescence, and thus serve to widen the gap between research and theory.

Obviously the two traditional theories contain much of value, and it would be wrong to leave the impression that neither is any longer relevant. Perhaps the most important contribution made by these theories is that they have provided the foundation for an understanding of young people with serious problems and a greater knowledge of those who belong to particular groups within society. Thus, for example Coffield and other's book *Growing up at the Margins* (1986) represents an important milestone in our awareness of what it means for adolescents to live in poverty and deprivation in the Britain of the 1980s.

In many respects the two traditional theories have much to offer. However, it must be recognised that today they are inadequate as a basis for an understanding of the development of the great majority of young people. The fact is that adolescence needs a theory, not of abnormality, but of normality. Any viable theoretical viewpoint put forward today must not only incorporate the results of empirical studies, but must also acknowledge the fact that, although for some young people adolescence may be a difficult time, for the majority it is a period of relative stability.

In recent years psychologists have turned away from the question 'Is adolescence inevitably a period of stress and turmoil?', and directed their attention towards issues of coping and adjustment. This current focus is undoubtedly a more productive one, leading to an interest in why some young people run into difficulties while others do not, and a concentration on the characteristics of those who do experience undue stress during the teenage years. Unfortunately research still has some way to go before clear answers can be given to these questions, but at least the questions are being asked. One example of exciting work in this field comes in the book *Coping and Self Concept in Adolescence* by Bosma and Jackson (1990), where a variety of adaptive coping strategies are outlined, and initial attempts are made to relate these strategies to behavioural outcomes.

As Hill (1993) points out, while the results of empirical research have, over the last decades, enabled us to see that the majority cope reasonably well, this increased awareness of normal adolescent development has gone hand-in-hand with a heightened level of concern about problem behaviour. Adolescent suicide and self-harm, drug and alcohol abuse, delinquency, teenage pregnancy - all these phenomena pose pressing problems not only for parents, teachers and other professionals, but for society at large. Here important advances have been made. In Britain, work in all these areas has made possible a greater understanding of the context in which problem behaviour occurs. The advances outlined by Farrington (1992), for example, in the field of delinquency provides one such example. Ann Phoenix's (1991) study of teenage mothers is another. Hawton (1986) and Liebling (1992) have written about adolescent suicide, while Davies and Coggans (1991) and Sharp and Lowe (1989) have provided important insights into drug and alcohol abuse.

Status ambiguity

A major concern for sociologists writing about adolescence has been the impact upon young people of not having a clearly defined status in society. It may well be that this is an issue not unrelated to the problem behaviours we have been discussing. Status ambiguity has a number of implications. First, it is intensely frustrating for adolescents. The feeling of not knowing where you stand, of not knowing exactly how you are going to be treated - as a child or as an adult - can be very difficult to cope with. If society does not have a framework and clear benchmarks to tell you when you have reached adulthood, how can the individual young person work it out for himself or herself? The second implication of status ambiguity is that adults feel confused about adolescence. Not just parents, but adults generally have to play a game in which the rules are being made up as they go along. In this game the institutional framework, such as the law, school rules, and so on, are of little help. Third, the uncertainty of status often serves to place young people in positions where they have very little power, and where damaging stereotypes can flourish easily.

Sexuality may be taken as one example of this, for here stereotypes of 'promiscuity' and 'permissiveness' interfere in the way adults perceive young people, and reduce the chances that boys and girls will receive the support, the education, and the medical care that they need. Sexuality is a particularly good illustration of status ambiguity in the United Kingdom because of what has come to be known as the Gillick case. In 1969 the Family Law Reform Act set the age of medical majority at 16, thus indicating that a person of 16 or over is regarded as medically adult, having the right of confidentiality and being able to decide what information, if any, should be passed to his or her parents. As far as teenagers under 16 are concerned, it had been up to the individual doctor to decide whether to provide contraceptive advice and treatment.

These principles were set out in 1980 in a Department of Health and Social Security statement. Mrs Gillick, a mother of ten, challenged the statement on the grounds that it deprived her of her parental rights. She sought an assurance from her local health authority that no contraceptive advice or treatment would be given to her daughters without her knowledge and consent. The health authority would not give such an assurance, and the case went all the way to the House of Lords. Judgement was finally given in October, 1985. By a three to two majority the Law Lords ruled that a girl under 16 of sufficient understanding and intelligence may have the legal capacity to give valid consent to contraceptive advice and treatment including necessary medical examination, and that giving such advice and treatment to a girl under 16 without parental consent does not necessarily infringe parental rights.

At first sight it may appear that this judgement left the situation unchanged, the individual doctor still having the right to treat someone under 16 without necessarily informing the parents. For at least two reasons, however, the Gillick case has made the position of the under 16s worse rather than better. First, the complexity of the case, and the legal wrangles surrounding it, have left teenagers confused and uncertain where they stand. Second, the publicity accorded to Mrs Gillick, as well as the tightening up of definitions, has left doctors with less room to manoeuvre and has caused almost all medical practitioners to exercise greater caution than before.

While we cannot be certain exactly how the Gillick case has affected adolescent sexual behaviour, what little research there is (for example, Ford, 1992) seems to indicate that young people have experienced increased uncertainty about their rights in relation to medical treatment. Such uncertainty has repercussions far beyond the issue of contraception. Here is something that really matters to adolescents, and yet it must appear to them that the adult world is unable to assist them or to give them clear guidance in a sensible way. Such a message cannot be the right one to be sending to those growing to maturity in the 1990s.

Of course status ambiguity is reflected in many areas apart from sexuality. The dramatic change during the 1980s in the way young people make the transition from school to work is an indication also of the difficulty of assuming an adult status. Whereas in earlier decades well over half of all adolescents in Britain left school to go to work, today virtually no one does so. The setting up of a wide range of training schemes for the 16-19 year age group may possibly have reduced youth unemployment but it has also had the effect of creating an occupational twilight zone where young people are neither pupils nor working - a poor preparation for adulthood.

The Children Act 1989 and the Criminal Justice Act 1991

In Britain there have recently been two major pieces of legislation which are having a profound effect on the lives of young people. It will not be possible here to enter into any comprehensive discussion about either of these two acts of parliament. However, some brief comments are in order. As has been made clear elsewhere (Coleman and Warren Adamson, 1992), when looking at the history of youth policy in this country it seems patently evident that what policy there is has been constructed to meet the needs of adults rather than of young people. This is a point perfectly exemplified by the Children Act and the Criminal Justice Act. Here, within the span of two years, two pieces of legislation have been introduced, both by a Conservative government, which incorporate principles which are diametrically opposed to each other. While the Children Act reflects the view that children and young people should - at last - have a voice of their own, and be treated as individuals with rights and responsibilities, the Criminal Justice Act sees their behaviour - and by implication, themselves - as being the responsibility of their parents. Let us deal with each of the Acts in turn.

Among its many reforms the Children Act has undoubtedly altered the way children and young people are perceived in law. A concept of the rights of parents has been altered to one of responsibilities. The wishes of young people have to be taken into account. Boys and girls under the age of 16 can choose their own religion, change their name, give consent to surgery, seek confidential counselling, and so on, so long as *they have the maturity to understand the implications of the decision or request*. This is obviously an important step forward in recognising the rights of young people. It may in practice, however, prove extremely difficult to define 'maturity to understand', and only time will tell how the courts will interpret this. Some reservations on this score are already being expressed (Wolkind, 1993).

One limitation inherent in the Children Act is that, sadly, no attempt has been made to clear up the ambiguities relating to other aspects of civil status. Thus, for example, can it be right that an adolescent of 17 can join the army and be killed fighting in war, and yet does not have the vote? To take some further illustrations, at 16 you can marry, join a trade union, and live in a brothel, yet you cannot be tattooed, own a house or a flat, or use a porn shop. At 17 you can drive most vehicles, buy a firearm, and hold a pilot's licence, yet you cannot vote, you cannot serve on a jury, or make a will. The law illustrates only too clearly our overall confusions about the status of young people. We do not know how to define adulthood, nor do we see it as a priority to clarify the situation for the sake of this group in society. Adult ambivalence is reflected in legislative ambiguity.

As far as the Criminal Justice Act is concerned, the Act strengthens already existing legislation by:

- requiring a parent or guardian to attend court with a young person;
- creating powers to make the parent or guardian responsible for financial penalties imposed by the court;
- enabling the court to bind over the parent or guardian as a result of offences committed by the young person.

In an excellent paper entitled 'Punishing the parents', Allen (1990) sets out some of the pitfalls implicit in this legislation. He mentions the fact that many parents of young offenders may themselves be struggling to cope. They may be lone parents, they may be unemployed, with inadequate housing, or with disrupted family relationships. The likelihood that they are going to 'mend their ways', and suddenly start to teach their children morality and good behaviour seems improbable. Even more important is the effect on such parents of forcing them to attend court, and thereby bringing them within the criminal justice system. Recent research already indicates that such an outcome is viewed with great anxiety by parents. It seems clear that few would have the resources to cope and to exercise greater 'control' over their youngsters.

This Act reflects an unfortunate attitude among politicians and the judiciary to issues concerning the status of young people. Surely we want our 15, 16 and 17-year-olds to be more responsible, not less responsible for themselves? The message of this legislation is that young people are dependent, and continue to be the 'property' and responsibility of their parents. Nothing could be more designed to ensure a delay in the development of mature adult behaviour in our adolescents.

Conclusion

In bringing this article to a conclusion one has to reflect that while progress has been made - in increased knowledge through empirical research, and as a result of the Children Act 1989 - much ground has been lost. Young people face a harsher world today than they did thirty years ago. Poorer job prospects, more limited housing, and fewer resources in education are just some of the social changes which have occurred and which will have had a direct effect on adolescents. Status ambiguity continues to be a major issue for all youngsters as they move through the teenage years. As we look forward to the 1990s and beyond, it seems important to spell out some of the most obvious needs of young people, so that there may be an agenda for policy makers when they come to address this most pressing of issues - 'how can we best prepare our young people for adulthood?'

The first area to which attention should be drawn is the young person's need for respect. One of the most common complaints of adolescents is that they are simply not taken seriously by the adults around them. They believe their views are rejected as immature even before they have had a chance to express them, and that there is a general attitude among adults which does not allow proper weight to be given to the opinions and ideas which stem from young people. This issue is very much bound up with status. If young people retain the status of children, then they are not taken seriously, and adults can retain power and decision-making responsibilities. It is true that to give up these things and to be willing to share power with young people requires courage and openness. Yet unless this can be achieved, teenagers will continue in an unsatisfactory state of limbo, feeling resentful and hostile because they are not accorded the status they deserve.

The second need is for both information and support. One of the more damaging stereotypes of youth is that because they are seeking independence, they have no further need of the adults around them. Nothing could be further from the truth. All teenagers need support, not only from their parents but from other adults as well. Of course if this is not available, adolescents will turn to the peer group, but it has to be remembered that this only occurs when relationships with adults are poor, or are seen to be damaging. Furthermore, young people need information, and they need to have this provided in a responsible manner. Information about sexuality is a good example. It is only the adult world that can provide the comprehensive sexual information that young people need, but if this information is mixed up with value-laden messages, or is presented in an 'adult knows best' container, it will be of little help. Once again adults can be of most use if they can accept that they do not have all the power, and if they can come to terms with the fact that young people need gradually increasing autonomy in order to become adult.

I have already mentioned the problems associated with ambiguous civil status. The contradictory definitions of adulthood exemplified by current legislation, and the confusion generated by the problem of medical confidentiality for under-16s, are both reflections of an unsatisfactory state of affairs. Young people need to have their civil status clarified and properly defined. We owe it to youth to provide such clarity. In addition to this, however, one has to conclude that the adult world gets the adolescents it deserves. If status is ambiguous, and the messages about maturity are mixed, the behaviour of young people will reflect this confusion. Can anyone be surprised that adolescent behaviour is sometimes childish and sometimes mature, at times caring and at times hostile, both responsible and irresponsible, if the legal framework has exactly these confusions within it? I think not.

Another central need for the most vulnerable young people is the need for protection. Whilst most adolescents will be living in family settings where they are well cared for, a minority will be exposed to risk or danger. It has seemed, particularly over the last decade, that this group - those in care, the runaways, and homeless - have been poorly served by society. Indeed, it is clear that some aspects of social security legislation have led to an increased number who are at risk. This should not be allowed to happen in a civilised society, and it is profoundly to be hoped that the 1990s will see a more caring and protective attitude on the part of our legislators towards the most vulnerable young people.

From what has been said already it will be clear that gradually increasing independence is not only a need, but should be a right for all adolescents. However hard it is, adults have to recognise that with adolescence comes an urgent necessity for a re-evaluation of the balance of the relationship between young and old, or at least between young and middle-aged. Decision-making has to be shared, responsibilities have to be more evenly apportioned, and greater and greater freedom has to be allowed. Some adults will give total independence too early, while others may hang on, inevitably leading to conflict in the end. The task of adults is not easy, but unless the need for increasing autonomy is met, relationships will deteriorate and the opportunities for adults to remain influential in the lives of their youngsters will diminish.

Finally, there is, without doubt, a need for adults to be better informed about adolescents. In large part adults find this stage a puzzling and confusing one. Many talk of 'dreading the teenage years', and it is in this sort of atmosphere that stereotypes take hold. The situation is not made any easier by a marked paucity of good-quality information about adolescence. While much attention is given to babyhood and early childhood, those who want to learn about the adolescent stage of development have to hunt far and wide for the right book or set of training materials. Professionals in the youth field could undoubtedly do more to provide better training and assistance to enable adults to understand this stage more clearly. Ignorance breeds anxiety, but it also leads to poor parenting and relationship skills. Young people need adults to be better informed about adolescence because it is only in that way that their parents, as well as teachers, social workers, and others can given them the most effective support.

References
Allen, R. (1990) 'Punishing the parents', *Youth and Policy*, 31, pp.17-20
Archer, S.L. (1992) 'Gender role learning' in Coleman, J.C. (ed.) *The School Years*. London: Routledge
Bosma, H. and Jackson, S. (1990) *Coping and Self-Concept in Adolescence*. Berlin: Springer Verlag

Brake, M. (1985) *Comparative Youth Subculture*. London: Routledge & Kegan Paul

Central Statistical Office (1992) *Social Trends*. No 22. London: HMSO

Coffield, F., Borrill, C. and Marshall, S. (1986) *Growing up at the Margins*. Milton Keynes: Open University Press

Coleman, J.C. (1992) (ed) *The School Years*. Routledge: London

Coleman, J.C. and Hendry, L. (1990) *The Nature of Adolescence*. Second Edition. London and New York: Routledge

Coleman, J.C. and Warren Adamson, C. (1992) *Youth Policy in the 1990s: The Way Forward*. London: Routledge

Davies, J. and Coggans, N. (1991) *Adolescent Drug Abuse*. London: Cassell

Farrington, D.P. (1992) 'Juvenile delinquency' in Coleman, J.C. (ed.) *The School Years*. London: Routledge

Fogelman, K. (1976) *Britain's 16-Year-Olds*. London: National Children's Bureau

Ford, N. (1992) 'The AIDS awareness and sexual behaviour of young people in the south west of England', *Journal of Adolescence*, 15, pp.393-414

Hawton, K. (1986) *Suicide and Attempted Suicide Among Children and Adolescents*. London: Sage

Hill, P. (1993) 'Recent advances in selected aspects of adolescent development', *Journal of Child Psychology and Psychiatry*, 34, pp.69-100.

Liebling, A. (1992) *Suicides in Prison*. London: Routledge

Offer, D. and Schonert-Reichl, K. (1992) 'Debunking the myths of adolescence': findings from recent research', *Journal of the American Academy of Child and Adolescent Psychiatry*, 31, pp.1003-1014

Phinney, J. and Rosenthal, D. (1992) 'Ethnic identity in adolescence' in Adams, G., Gullotta, T. and Montemayor, R. (eds.) *Adolescent Identity Formation*. London: Sage

Phoenix, A. (1991) *Young Mothers?*. Cambridge: Polity Press

Sharp, D. and Lowe, G. (1989) 'Adolescents and alcohol - a review of the recent British research', *Journal of Adolescence*, 12, pp.295-308

Wolkind, S. (1993) 'The 1989 Children Act: a cynical view from an ivory tower', *ACPP Review and Newsletter*, 15, pp.40-42

8. What role has the law played in getting rid of racism in the lives of children?

Jane Lane
Commission for Racial Equality[1]

Britain's history of colonialism and slavery, exploiting the labour and resources of non-European peoples for its own economic benefit and profit, has left its mark on present-day society. Notions of racial superiority, based on skin colour, culture and language were used to justify such detrimental treatment. Until recently little was done to address its consequences - all those practices and procedures that historically and in the present have the effect of disadvantaging and discriminating against Black and minority ethnic people, that is racism.

Although laws themselves are unlikely to change attitudes in the short term they can, within specific limits, change behaviour. Britain is the only European country to have comprehensive legislation about racial discrimination. As such it is important in having the capacity to remove some of the more obvious forms of racism.

So far, with regard to children, the Race Relations Act 1976 has largely been used in the field of education and rarely in the more interpersonal situations of social services and voluntary/private sector provision. The more recent Children Act 1989, however, does address some aspects of racism in the care of children. While clearly much more than laws are needed to eliminate racism, the way these two Acts are used is some measure of our commitment, as a society, to rectify past and present discrimination and disadvantage. This paper attempts to identify the role of legislation to date and suggests how detailed knowledge of its implications can be effective in getting rid of some aspects of racism in children's lives.

For hundred of years racism has flourished in Britain. Although the Public Order Act 1936 included an offence of incitement to racial hatred it is only very recently that legislation has taken account of specific aspects of its manifest evil by attempting to define how, and in what circumstances, racism could be deemed unlawful, to provide a framework to counter the effects of past discrimination and to ensure that due consideration is given to issues of racial equality in the education and care of children.

Although there were two early Race Relations Acts (in 1965 and 1968) which made certain more obvious forms of racial discrimination unlawful in limited circumstances, it was only with the Race Relations Act 1976 that some of the more insidious forms of racism were addressed by the introduction of the concept of 'indirect discrimination' and areas covered by the legislation were extended.

More recently the Children Act 1989 has required, among other things, those agencies responsible for making decisions about children to give due consideration to a child's 'religious persuasion, racial origin and cultural and linguistic background'. Although other legislation affecting children may have particular implications for Black[2] children and their families (for example, the Child Support Act 1992, because of the disproportionate number of African/Caribbean one-parent families) these are the only Acts that refer specifically to 'race' or racial issues.

How far have these two Acts improved the life experiences and chances of young children with regard to racism? The short answer is likely to be that we don't know - but that, if anything, it's not much (certainly in terms of case law), yet. There are still laws that themselves discriminate against Black children and their families, for example on nationality, immigration and asylum. And the laws relating to discrimination and the field of childcare may never be useful tools for dealing with the historical and structural inequalities of society, unwitnessed situations between an adult and a child or between children themselves. But, by using legislation effectively, it is possible to identify and clarify some of those practices and procedures that are likely to discriminate against and disadvantage children and to establish a framework of non-discrimination, that is by identifying what's 'wrong' we can begin to think about what might be right. By teasing out how discrimination works in practice, and by not only recognising the damage done to children subjected to racism but also addressing the need to counter the learning of racist attitudes at an early age, it is possible to determine what needs to be done in order to comply with both the letter and the spirit of the legislation. More is now known about what exactly is going on. How far, if at all, has this 'unpeeling of the onion' benefited the every day lives of children at home, in nurseries and at school and what is needed to ensure that laws are used to their maximum effect in the future? Laws can (and should) be used to eliminate what they define as unlawful and to ensure that what they define as required, is actually implemented.

Although Black people have migrated to and lived in Britain for centuries it is only since the late fifties and early sixties that their numbers have increased significantly. Until the late eighties, while there were individuals and groups who recognised the need to address the underlying factor of racism as it affected children's (and their own) lives, the majority response of policy makers, teachers and others concerned with the children's education and care was to attempt to address their perceived needs, by providing for the learning of English, where necessary, and by trying to implement policies concerned with assimilation, integration or equality and defined in various ways such as multicultural, intercultural or multiracial education or education for (racial) equality. In social services, voluntary and private sector childcare and day care provision, because of the underlying philosophy of 'treating all the children the same', the general response, with a few exceptions, was to continue existing practice.

Some of these practices were critical and some, but by no means all, of the work with children achieved limited success in countering the effects of racism. However, throughout the sixties, seventies and eighties, the concerns of Black parents about their children in care and in schools and nurseries remained well articulated (to those who wished to listen) and the same - including concerns about levels of attainment/achievement, suspensions and exclusions, racial harassment, admissions and assessment (examinations, tests and assessment for special education). Throughout, issues about valuing and acknowledging all cultures, religions and languages remained on-going.

Although in the late sixties and early seventies the Department of Education and Science (DES) collected data on 'immigrant pupils' (DES 1967-73 - Statistical Return No 63) and suggested that a percentage greater than 30 per cent caused 'serious strains' which might be resolved by dispersal, (that is, bussing - a practice which would have been unlawful under the Race Relations Act 1976), there was no universal statistical basis on the ethnic backgrounds of pupils on which to identify and analyse what was actually happening. It was only from 1990 that the DES required ethnic data to be collected on pupils (DES Circular 16/89), but only on their entry to school, and a little later that it asked for data on those excluded from school (DFE/NERS 1990-91). In the absence of a factual basis on which to compare pupils by ethnic origin, it was easy to dismiss suggestions of racial discrimination as exaggerated and to categorise individual complaints as exceptions to a system delivering equality to all.

Throughout the seventies and eighties there were a few studies undertaken into the achievement/attainment levels of pupils in school, by ethnic origin, but they were largely limited in scope, small scale, localised and seldom controlled for sex or social class variables. They did, however, indicate the low levels of attainment of some racial groups of pupils. In 1985 the Commission for Racial Equality (established under the Race Relations Act 1976) published its response to the Swann Report (DES, 1985), the report of a Committee set up in 1979 as a result of concerns of Black communities and the teaching profession about the apparent 'under-achievement' of their children. The Commission's response (CRE, 1985) drew attention to the fact that the notion of 'institutional racism' (not a legal term) did not inform the Report and had not been used to analyse such structures and procedures as selection, streaming, assessment, admissions, staff appointments, subject choice or careers advice.

By the mid to late eighties some local education and social services departmental policies were incorporating anti-racism (a socio-political policy and practice which sees racism at cultural, institutional and structural levels as the major obstacle to racial equality and seeks to challenge and eradicate all forms of racism - including anti-semitism). This was particularly important in addressing the causes of racism, the racial hierarchies of cultures and languages and dealing with racial harassment. A few were approaching oppressions and inequalities holistically. But, despite the fact that the Race Relations Act 1976 had been statutory for nearly a decade, there was very little acknowledgement of its existence in these policies - or, indeed, in research or other written documents. With a few exceptions they were addressing 'good practice' (clearly an important objective) but not drawing attention to the role of legislation (and in particular the identification of discrimination) in attaining this objective. The Commission for Racial Equality itself must take some responsibility for this. In the field of educational and childcare provision it was believed that the policies put forward by local authorities and others were the best way to promote equality of opportunity (and thereby, eliminate discrimination): and that the role of the Commission was to encourage the setting up of such policies.

It was thought that the field of education and childcare was in some way different from other fields (such as, employment, services or housing) in that 'professionals' would see the good sense of such policies and would, by persuasion rather than law enforcement, address discrimination and disadvantage. There were those who believed classroom situations and the education and care system generally were not susceptible to law enforcement. In any case, the exact blockages or barriers to equality of opportunity had not been identified. In some measure this ambivalence was understandable. The law, as it stands, does not provide immediate remedies for parents, children or students who make complaints under the Race Relations Act 1976. Except for a few individual complaints that had reached the county courts (to provide case law) and formal investigations undertaken by the Commission, very little was widely known, at that stage, about what practices and procedures might be discriminatory and unlawful. The law appeared to be largely irrelevant to the reality of the situation.

In the early eighties the importance of the pre-school years for providing equality of opportunity and for countering the learning of racism by young White children began to be seriously addressed. Inequalities of access to various forms of provision were determining which children went where. The disproportionately long hours and low paid work of parents of young Black children limited their choice of pre-school care/education. The diversity of provision was compounded by their differences in curriculum, opening hours, staff qualifications, experiences and conditions of service and although the DES and the Department of Health had long urged coordination/ integration, there usually remained a division between 'education' and 'care' - a division in which it was difficult to identify racial inequalities in the service overall. There was however, a growing awareness of the early age that young children learn to recognise racial differences and place values on them (see Milner, 1983) and that 'treating all children in the same way' was likely to mean denying the real and important differences between them rather than encouraging all children to learn to respect and value those different from as well as those similar to themselves. But there were (and still are) many multiracial nurseries where all the staff were White, where African/ Caribbean boys in particular were stereotyped as being unable to concentrate and where opportunities to develop learning skills were limited. Black parents and others concerned about the effects of racism felt existing legislation (the Nurseries and Child-minders Regulation Act 1948), determining who was a 'fit person' to look after young children, ignored what they perceived as significant issues in the registration process of day care providers.

In the field of childcare generally (residential care, adoption and fostering) serious concerns about inappropriate placements that took little or no account of racial and cultural differences were raised by Black communities (and others) and by children themselves. This accumulation of concerns, from those involved in day care and residential care, led to a groundswell of support in both statutory and voluntary sectors for changes in legislation which would empower social services and voluntary/private sector staff (responsible for the registration of children's day care and the placement of children) to implement a racial equality dimension in their procedures. In the event the Children Act 1989, for the first time, took account of the needs of children regarding religious, racial, cultural and linguistic issues.

In 1989 the Commission published two documents which describe how the Race Relations Act 1976 works. *The Code of Practice; for the Elimination of Racial Discrimination in Education*, while not statutory, was endorsed by the Secretary of State, and is strictly concerned with the identification of discrimination in the education system. *From Cradle to School; A Practical Guide to Race Equality and Childcare* includes not only information on the implications of the Race Relations Act 1976 but also suggestions for good practice. Both have been important in raising the profile of the Race Relations Act 1976. Everyone concerned with education and childcare now has access to the opportunity to consider, in detail, those practices and procedures that might result in discrimination. The concept of discrimination is on the national agenda - information is available.

What have the Race Relations Act 1976 and the Children Act 1989 contributed to getting rid of racism in children's lives?

The Race Relations Act 1976

The Act defines racial discrimination in four ways: direct and indirect discrimination, segregation and victimisation - this latter applies only to those involved in taking proceedings under the Act.

Direct discrimination

This means treating a person less favourably than another person is or would be treated in the same or similar circumstances, on racial grounds. For example, refusing to admit a child to a school because she or he is White or Black. (Racial grounds are those of 'race', colour, nationality - including citizenship - or ethnic or national origins. Mandla v Dowell Lee [House of Lords, 1983] extended this definition to include groups with a 'long shared history' and a 'cultural tradition' of their own, among other factors. Sikhs, Jews and Gypsies constitute racial groups but neither Muslims nor Christians have been so defined in law).

Indirect discrimination

This is defined in five parts:

- a *requirement or condition* is applied equally to everyone;
- it has a *disproportionate impact* on a particular racial group;
- such that a smaller proportion of that racial group *can comply* with the requirement than other groups;
- the impact of the requirement is to the *detriment* of that group;
- and the requirement cannot be shown to be *justified* irrespective of colour, 'race', nationality (including citizenship) or ethnic or national origins of the person to whom it is applied.

For example, requiring an applicant for a job to have a qualification from a British university would disproportionately affect non-British university graduates. Unless such a requirement could be justified on non-racial grounds, it would be unlawful.

Segregation

Segregating a person from others on racial grounds is defined as less favourable treatment and constitutes direct discrimination. For example, requiring Asian employees to eat in a separate canteen away from other employees.

By far the most important of these forms of discrimination is that of *indirect discrimination*, because it reveals examples of customs, practices and procedures, that may have been in place for some time but were not, necessarily, ever intended to discriminate. Nevertheless they have the effect of discriminating against a particular racial group or groups. The concept of justifiability is important - it means objectively justifiable - weighing up the detrimental effect of the requirement against the reasons for it in the particular circumstances pertaining at the time. It is this form of discrimination in particular that few of those responsible for devising policies have acknowledged. So it has been easy to claim that what was being done was not 'racist', because, in particular, there was no intention to discriminate. Neither direct nor indirect discrimination is concerned with intention or with attitudes. It should therefore be possible to take it out of the 'political' arena and engage everyone in a straightforward matter of a child's right - a right to equal treatment, untainted with accusations or motivations deriving from 'being racist'. What is needed is an analysis of every educational and other decision that has consequences for a child's life - from access to education and care and through all the processes that determine eventual outcomes.

All forms of discrimination must be read together with (and covered by) the relevant section of the Act. Individuals who believe that they may have been discriminated against unlawfully may seek redress through the courts. In employment cases they may file a case to an industrial tribunal and in non-employment cases they may initiate proceedings in a county court or in Scotland, the Sheriff courts. The Commission has powers to conduct formal investigations for any purpose connected with the carrying out of its duties.

Both case law (by individual complaints) and formal investigations have contributed to the identification of unlawful discrimination.

Neither method provides an immediate remedy and both have to be proved - through a court and/or by statistical or other evidence. Individual complaints about discrimination in the public sector of education (LEA-maintained, grant-maintained schools and city technology colleges) should, in the first instance be made to the Secretary of State for Education. He has powers to act where he considers the relevant sections of the Act have not been complied with. In practice there have been very few education or childcare cases brought to court.

In formal investigations evidence for the grounds for belief that discrimination has occurred or is occurring has to be provided and the terms of reference of the investigation issued. The respondent has to be named and has to be given an opportunity to make representations on the grounds for belief and the Commission than considers them. If it is decided to proceed, evidence is collected and analysed and the findings put to the respondent, for comments. The Commission, on the basis of all the information, then decides whether to make a finding of unlawful discrimination and issue a non-discrimination notice to the respondent - except in cases of public sector education bodies where only the Secretary of State has such powers.

In considering the educational and childcare concerns of Black parents, what have individual complaints and formal investigations revealed? And what other issues have been identified as potential discrimination under the Race Relations Act 1976.

Admissions

The case of Mandla v Dowell Lee, concerned a Sikh father who tried to enrol his son at a private school in Birmingham in 1978. The headteacher refused to admit him unless he complied with the school's uniform rules by removing his turban and cutting his hair. With the Commission's assistance the father brought the case to the county court on the grounds that the 'no turban' rule constituted unlawful indirect discrimination. The court dismissed the claim and held that his son could physically comply with the requirement to remove his turban and that the rule was justifiable in terms of the purposes of the uniform rules. They also held that Sikhs were a religious group and not a racial group as defined under the Race Relations Act 1976. After

THE LAW AND GETTING RID OF RACISM IN CHILDREN'S LIVES

an unsuccessful appeal to the Court of Appeal, the case was upheld in the House of Lords in 1983. The Lords ruled that the term 'can comply' should not be interpreted literally but should be construed as 'can in practice comply' consistent with the customs and cultural norms of the racial group. They further ruled that Sikhs were a racial group under the Act and that the 'no turbans' rule could not be justified on educational grounds.

This case is important because it means that conditions or requirements that have a disproportionate effect for cultural reasons may be covered by the legal concept of indirect discrimination. Although there has yet been no case law, the Commission has, on several occasions, been involved with issues of Muslim girls being refused admission to school because of school uniform rules.

A formal investigation, *Secondary School Admissions* in Hertfordshire County Council (CRE, 1992) revealed that Asian applicants (identified by their names) had a lesser chance of being offered a place at either of the two Watford Grammar Schools (a boys' school and a girls' school - both all-ability (non-selective) comprehensive schools, though retaining their traditional names), than non-Asian applicants. There were two explanations for this. The first was that priority places were given to those applicants who had a current sibling at the school. This discriminated against Asian applicants because they were less likely to have a sibling already at the school, perhaps because of their relatively recent arrival in Britain and of past discrimination. The Commission found that, although giving such priority indirectly discriminated against Asian applicants it was, in the circumstances then prevailing, justifiable and therefore not unlawful. The justification given by the Council included such reasons as the following: in general parents wished it, there were advantages in forging strong links between school and parents and, in practice, children could travel to school together, uniforms could be re-used and parents could maintain links with just one school.

The second explanation concerned the reasons that parents gave for their school preference on the application form. Applications were sorted into three categories: strong, medium and weak, based on the case which the parents made as a whole to support their application. In practice, the Commission found that they had to give a minimum number of reasons to be eligible for an offer of a place at the schools: in

1988 it was six and four reasons for the Watford Boys' and Girls' School respectively. As many Asian parents were unfamiliar with the British educational system and had difficulties with the English language, they were less likely than non-Asian parents to be able to meet this 'requirement'.

Unlike the sibling rule the Commission found that this requirement could not be justified and that it constituted unlawful indirect discrimination. The findings were sent to the Secretary of State in May 1992 with recommendations that he uphold the findings, require the LEA and the schools to cease discriminating and require them, and all other LEA's and schools responsible for admissions in the country, to set up systems of monitoring and analysis to identify and eliminate any discrimination. At the time of writing (April 1993) the Commission has received no response but Hertfordshire LEA is now monitoring applications and admissions to oversubscribed schools..

Since the investigation both Hertfordshire County Council and the (by then) grant-maintained Watford Grammar Schools have changed their admission criteria to include giving priority to applicants who can demonstrate a family connection with the school they want because they have siblings or parents who attended the school in the past. It is likely that this will have an even greater disproportionate effect than that of current siblings. The Commission believes that it is unlikely that such a extension could be justified on non-racial grounds.

A formal investigation into a private residential children's home (CRE, 1979) found that the proprietors had applied an unjustifiable requirement that the children submitted for placement should not be 'coloured' and had induced or attempted to induce local authorities and childcare officers to discriminate on racial grounds by deliberately omitting to propose 'coloured' children for admission to the Home. The Commission issued a non-discrimination notice to the proprietors.

Admissions are critical to equality of opportunity for all children. Although there has as yet been no case law on any of the following admission arrangements they may have an unlawful indirectly or directly discriminatory impact on particular racial groups of children:

- culturally biased assessment tests in general and assessing children in English whose home language is not English;
- interviews (of applicants, parents or both), where the possibility of cultural and/or racial stereotyping may influence the situation

unfairly, where there is no common language of communication and where body language (for example, eye contact) may vary between different cultural groups;
- being required to demonstrate a 'commitment' to or 'suitability' for a school;
- quotas based on racial grounds or attempting to have a 'racial balance';
- the operation of waiting lists;
- allocation between nursery/playgroup sessions (for example, morning and afternoon) on racial grounds or using parental reasons;
- using 'word of mouth' recruitment for playgroup/nursery places;
- failing to take account of possible late applications from children who are homeless, travellers, asylum seekers or refugees.

In order to ensure that admissions are not discriminatory, applications and admissions need to be monitored, using ethnic data, as each criterion is applied (CRE, 1993).

Transfers/segregation

A formal investigation into Cleveland Education Authority, *Racial Segregation in Education* (CRE, 1989), found that a parental request for a child to be transferred from a multi-racial school to a largely White school on racial grounds constituted segregation and was therefore unlawful under the Race Relations Act 1976. Cleveland LEA, while not wishing to accept such a request, believing it to be due to racial prejudice, nevertheless felt obliged to do so under education law (Education Act 1980, Section 6). This requires an LEA to make arrangements to enable parents to express a choice of school and places a duty on it to comply with such a preference. The Commission took the opposite view and contended that, under the Race Relations Act 1976 (Section 18), an LEA could not carry out any of its functions if they involved unlawful discrimination.

This amounted to a difference of legal opinion as to which piece of legislation is paramount. The Secretary of State rejected the findings of the investigation. The Commission sought a judicial review of that decision in the High Court (1991) but failed. A subsequent appeal to the Court of Appeal also failed. The issue, however, remains one of concern because the Commission believes that allowing legislation to be paramount over the Race Relations Act 1976 frustrates what Parliament intended at the time of drafting.

Another case, resolved informally, was where Asian pupils, regardless of their competence in English, were allocated to a separate nursery class from all other pupils - a clear case of segregation.

Exclusions/suspensions

A formal investigation into referrals and suspensions of pupils in Birmingham LEA and schools (CRE, 1985) found that black pupils were four times more likely to be suspended (for similar offences), were three times more likely to be placed in suspension units, were more likely to be suspended or referred after shorter periods of 'disruptive' behaviour and six times more likely to be suspended under the age of fourteen than white pupils. Forty-three percent of pupils in special units were of 'Afro-Caribbean' origin (compared with ten per cent of the school population in Birmingham). The Commission concluded that a racial factor (rather than a social factor) was significant in the differential suspensions and referral rates.

Very recently the Department for Education published the results of its exclusions survey (NERS, 1990/91) which stated that 'Afro-Caribbean' pupils appeared to be disproportionately represented within the excluded pupil population (8.1 per cent of the overall total). This confirms evidence from Wolverhampton Racial Equality Council, Nottinghamshire LEA and many other authorities.

While the Commission has been involved in a few cases of Muslim girls being excluded from school because they wished to wear hijab (headscarf/veil) or shalwar kameez, rather than a skirt - likely to be unlawful indirectly discriminatory requirements - the majority of cases concern pupils (usually African/Caribbean boys) who claim they have been discriminated against in the exclusion process. There are two parts of the exclusion process: the informal process leading up to the formal exclusion and the formal exclusion procedure itself. There are many examples where pupils claim they have been racially abused continuously and when they suddenly can take no more and lash out physically, they have been excluded. While the incident itself may fit into the categories of exclusion, it is clear that provocation can play a part. It is therefore essential to monitor all incidents of racial harassment as part of the whole exclusion process. Another present issue of concern is unofficial exclusions where parents are encouraged to withdraw their child from school voluntarily, thereby allegedly making it easier for them to apply to another school without an official exclusion record. It also benefits the 'excluding' school in not having to record the incident under education legislation requirements. Exclusions and racial harassment are of major concern to Black parents and the very recent significant increases overall in exclusions rates, if they include a disproportionate number of Black pupils (as evidence seems to indicate) require careful analysis for any unlawful discrimination.

Separate provision

A formal investigation into *Teaching English as a Second Language* in Calderdale LEA (CRE, 1986) found that the arrangements made for the teaching of English as a second language (ESL) constituted unlawful indirect discrimination. All children newly arrived or recently returned from the Indian sub-continent and all those born in the United Kingdom whose first language was not English, had to take a language test, to see if they needed special ESL tuition. Children who did not pass the test were placed in a separate language class or centre. The effects of these arrangements included issues such as:

- nearly all the children taking the language test were of Asian origin;
- up to 80 per cent of the Asian children in Calderdale schools had spent some time in a language unit;
- because half the language units were away from areas where Asians lived, children had to be bussed and therefore lost school time;
- the curriculum in the language units was often more limited than mainstream schools and, at secondary levels, lacked specialist teachers;
- the parents of children in the language units could not express school preferences, could not appeal against their child's placement or assessment and, in some cases, could not take part in governing body elections, whereas mainstream parents could.

The LEA argued that these arrangements were justified because, at the time they were established, language withdrawal was considered to be educationally sound. The Commission found that, on current theory and research on second language learning (see Appendix 7 of the report), children learn best in mainstream classrooms and that therefore, the requirement (to pass a language test) was unlawful indirect discrimination. The Secretary of State upheld the Commission's findings and instructed the LEA to organise different arrangements for ESL. Calderdale LEA has now done this.

This investigation reveals the discrimination of a system - the teachers' attitudes and intentions were irrelevant.

Allocation to sets and bands

A study by the Commission (CRE, 1992) indicated that the allocation of Asian pupils to sets (teaching groups) might not be based on ability and that, as a result, they were less eligible to sit the public examinations than non-Asian pupils. Two main barriers to equality of opportunity were identified; the school had difficulty in identifying pupils who needed ESL support and found it almost impossible to identify those Asian pupils with learning difficulties who required special needs support. Consequently teachers decided that many pupils for whom English was not a first language were not able to learn successfully in higher ability groups, so they were placed in non-examination sets. Furthermore, once pupils were allocated to low ability sets, it was difficult for Asian pupils to move into higher-ability examination sets because of the inflexibility of the system. As far as optional GCSE subjects were concerned, the school required pupils to take at least five subjects. As Asians, disproportionately, did not achieve a high enough academic standard in all five subjects but would have been able to take two or three if allowed, they were not able to take any and so had to do lower status non-GCSE vocational courses instead.

The findings indicated that the way the setting and banding operated may have been discriminatory (either directly or indirectly according to the particular example). But it demonstrates concerns that other factors than ability may come into play when deciding who to allocate to teaching groups - both formally and informally.

Work experience

A county court case (CRE v Fearn and British Electrical Repairs 1987) concerning two 'West Indian' boys, who were not accepted for their Certificate in Pre-Vocational Education (CPVE) work experience placement because of their racial origin, found that the manager was in breach of the Race Relations Act 1976 (Section 31) because he had tried to persuade their teacher not to place them at his factory, that is, he had attempted to induce the teacher to discriminate. Furthermore the judge found that the firm was in breach of Section 32 of the Act, which makes an employer liable for an act of discrimination by an employee unless he (the employer) has taken reasonable steps to prevent the employee from discriminating. Although the firm had an equal opportunities policy it was not being monitored.

Positive action

Positive discrimination (that is, giving favourable treatment on racial grounds alone) is unlawful under the Race Relations Act 1976. There are, however, a few specifically circumscribed actions which can be taken, under the Act, to begin to counter the effects of past discrimination or to take account of specific circumstances where being a member of a particular racial group is relevant. One such action (usually termed a genuine occupational qualification - Section 5 (2) (d)) permits recruitment of a person from a particular racial group where the jobholder provides persons of that racial group with personal services promoting their welfare (and those services can most effectively be provided by a person of that racial group). It does not apply when there are employees of the racial group in question who are capable of fulfilling the duties and cannot be used to compensate for the under-representation of a racial group in the work-force. An employment case (EAT - Gary Marshall v Tottenham Green Under Fives' Centre - 1991) clarified the legislation regarding a nursery with 84 per cent 'Afro-Caribbean' children wishing to appoint an 'Afro-Caribbean' worker to replace another. A White man applied for the post and was refused an interview because he was not 'Afro-Caribbean'. The tribunal found that this refusal was not contrary to the employment sections of the Act because there was one personal service (that of reading and talking in dialect) which only an 'Afro-

Caribbean' person could have done. This is important because it established that the needs of young children to receive such a service can be satisfied in these circumstances and are covered by this section of the Act.

Racial harassment

One of the most damaging experiences for children is that of racial harassment - ranging from name-calling and ridicule to terrifying, full-blown racial attacks - of themselves alone or of their families (see CRE, 1988; Troyna and Hatcher,1992; Wright, 1992). The Race Relations Act 1976 does not mention racial harassment specifically and it is only likely to be covered if it constitutes 'less favourable treatment' read with section 17 (for example, by a teacher of a pupil), whereas the vast majority of incidents are by other children or out of school by other perpetrators. While the Public Order Act 1986 covers the more obscene forms of incitement to racial hatred, legal and other restraints on prosecution remain. Until the law is changed, policies and enforcement strategies throughout local authorities, schools and other educational and childcare practice remain the only way to counter harassment. They need to be set up in a way that everyone is seen to be accountable to them and, once established, rigorously enforced and monitored.

As a result of the above court cases and formal investigations a few children have ceased to be discriminated against, although some have not themselves benefited from the identification of discrimination. But these examples, together with an analysis of practices and procedures generally, have revealed far more about its operation than was known, even ten years ago. A little of the racism affecting children's lives has been removed.

In a time of rising racial hostility in Europe (including Britain), cutbacks in training and resources addressing inequalities, frequent media ridicule of attempts to establish anti-racism in education and childcare, together with recent education legislation that leaves most decisions in the hands of governors, maximum use of the law is essential. The neutrality of the Act can be a positive asset. It must not be allowed to become impotent. But the fact remains that, under the Act, discrimination has to be proved - it is unlikely to disappear unaided. This means collecting ethnic data at all levels.

The Race Relations Act 1976 does not require anyone to take up specific measures, such as the collection of ethnic data to identify and eliminate discrimination. The Commission's document *Ethnic Monitoring in Education* (CRE, 1992) sets out the arguments for collecting and analysing data. So far, however, hardly any LEA's, social services departments, governing bodies or management committees have set up systems of ethnic monitoring. Systems should reveal, in particular, incidents of indirect discrimination which, so far, have only been identified by a few court cases and formal investigations in a relatively ad hoc way - discrimination in attainment levels, access, exclusions and assessment (including for special education) - the long-existing concerns of Black parents. It is equally important to collect data on boys and girls to identify whether Black boys and Black girls are being treated (or behave) differently. Discrepancies do not necessarily mean that discrimination has occurred but provide evidence on which to ask questions and seek explanations. Similarly, unless detailed information is collected at every stage, discrimination may remain unidentified. Systems of ethnic monitoring are unlikely to reveal subtle, differential ways of treating children in one-to-one situations or in the privacy of a classroom, childcare situation or nursery (see Wright 1992 for ethnographic study of schools/nurseries). This is where the importance of training, commitment and implementation of anti-racist practice is crucial.

There have been many examples where practices have been changed because the likelihood of being in breach of the Race Relations Act 1976 has been demonstrated. While case law and formal investigations do have the effect of setting precedents and are therefore extremely valuable and important, their operation is both cumbersome and time-consuming. (The Commission has recently made proposals for improving the effectiveness of the legislation[CRE, 1992]). But the more that parents, children, teachers/carers, governors and others know about the application of the law to the experiences of children at home, in schools, nurseries and elsewhere particularly in a time of changing education legislation, the more likely that discrimination will be recognised, challenged and eliminated. They can empower themselves to recognise and identify discrimination, to bring it to the attention of those responsible and, should no resolution be forthcoming, if necessary proceed to use the law to implement their rights. Going pro-active on this discrete form of racism - discrimination - might then begin to reach the level of the child - a level where it can be said that the law really is working to get rid of racism in children's lives.

The Children Act 1989

The Children Act 1989 is much newer than the Race Relations Act. Amongst many other issues, it requires local authorities and voluntary organisations to take account of a child's religious persuasion, racial origin and cultural and linguistic background when making a decision about a child for whom they are responsible and when considering whether to cancel the registration of a day care provider because the care provided is seriously inadequate with regard to the needs of a child. And it places a duty on local authorities to conduct a three-yearly review of all their day care taking account of education provision and, in providing day care and foster care, to have regard to the different racial groups to which the children within their area who are 'in need' belong.

The accompanying Guidance (Department of Health, 1991) on family support, day care and educational provision for young children, draws attention throughout the text to the need to address issues pertaining to racial equality. It refers to the need for those working with young children to value and respect the different racial origins, religions, cultures and languages, free of racial stereotyping. It draws attention to the early age that children learn about such differences and their capacity to assign different values to them and identifies the need to have equal opportunities policies with monitoring and reviewing arrangements, using ethnic data, to assess how far the day care and educational services are operating in a non-discriminatory way. It cites the right of children to be free of discrimination such as racism, to be cared for as part of a community which values their diversity - to facilitate their development and to foster a sense of identity. With regard to whether a person is fit to look after children aged under eight it requires local authorities to consider that person's 'knowledge of and attitude to multicultural issues and people of different racial origins' and 'commitment and knowledge to treat all children as individuals and with equal concern'. In conducting the Review, social services departments and LEAs (in consultation with health authorities, other departments and agencies and all local communities) are required to collect basic data on all day care provision and on nursery schools/classes and reception classes in primary schools so that they can analyse the information, including policy objectives, the curriculum and 'multi-cultural and equal opportunities aspects'. This provides a comprehensive framework for promoting equality of opportunity and for countering the learning of racism among young White children, wherever they live.

It is too early to say whether this legislation, in practice, is helping to get rid of racism in the lives of children. This depends on the knowledge and commitment of those implementing the legislation and how it is put into operation. But, like the Race Relations Act 1976, the more that is known about it, the greater the likelihood of its implementation, by those responsible for placements and for conducting the review of day care, and by registration and inspection officers. Many local authorities have developed criteria for registration and inspection that attempt to evaluate the racial equality dimension of care. This is not only to establish a baseline below which registration will be refused but also to identify training and support needs. The collection of ethnic data should provide, for the first time, information across all early years provision that will enable any discrimination to be identified as well as indicating how far issues about racial equality in service delivery are being addressed. But it is already obvious that the requirements of the law are revealing significant gaps in the knowledge and experience of many staff regarding racism and the Race Relations Act 1976, especially in county areas (see Cowley, 1993). At the same time there are severe cutbacks in local authority spending leaving officers isolated, frustrated and with little opportunity for access to training and support.

As a direct result of the Children Act 1989 and its accompanying Guidance, issues of racial equality are now being considered throughout the country where, formerly, many areas would have seen them as irrelevant. Providers, too, have to address the issues if they are to be registered. As racism affects the lives of both Black and White children, considering how it is manifested should benefit all children. Unlike discrimination which, once identified, can be eliminated, tackling the way racism is perpetrated and perpetuated in the lives of children is an infinitely more difficult task. Four hundred years of colonialism, imperialism and slavery have left racism deeply entrenched in our society.

Many organisations, (including the National Children's Bureau - particularly in its recent publications and seminars), have played their part both in ensuring the Children Act 1989 incorporated these issues and in providing support and training materials to facilitate its implementation. Specific organisations such as the Early Years Trainers Anti-Racist Network and the Working Group Against Racism in Children's Resources have, over the last decade, made great strides in providing effective practical advice, resources and training. The climate is changing. A recent European conference on challenging racism in childcare/education demonstrated that Britain, despite having one of the least amounts of provision, almost alone recognises and attempts to address the role that it plays in children's lives (European Commission, in press).

Unfortunately, any progress made by using these two Acts is partly counteracted by recent education legislation, in particular the Education Reform Act 1988 and the proposals under the present Education Bill. With local management of schools and the setting up of grant-maintained schools and city technology colleges, powers to make many decisions are transferred from LEAs to governing bodies. In the absence of requirements from the DFE this magnifies the task of persuading schools to collect, monitor and analyse ethnic data, develop racial harassment strategies and implement anti-racist practice. It also diminishes the likelihood of the powers given to LEA's, under the Children Act 1989, being realised to the extent that was originally envisaged. Once again the vision of integrated early years provision recedes, leaving a fragmented service where the education sector may be untouched by the Children Act 1989.

Legislation, however good, has its limitations. Government, courts and those implementing it can make it effective or frustrate its intentions. But without it we would be relying on commitment and goodwill to remove racism - factors that are not widely accepted in our society. The law has tempered the edges of racism by removing some of its effects on children. And it provides a climate within a framework, for those who wish to use it, to ensure as wide an implementation as knowledge and commitment to anti-racism will allow.

But there is no room for complacency. The fact that the Race Relations Act has so far not been used, or not been able to be used, to address some of the most personally damaging and hurtful forms of racism is of acute concern. There is hope that the implementation of the Children Act will result in some of these more inaccessible forms of racism being addressed. Certainly a more comprehensive understanding of the causes and consequences of racism by those responsible for institutional and personal practice would greatly facilitate change. Passive acceptance of legislation is likely to have little effect on children's lives. To remove racism from their lives two things are needed: a dispassionate determination to use legislation to ensure the right of every child to equal treatment and a passionate personal commitment to challenge racism wherever its exists. And that means *all* of us.

Notes
1. Jane Lane works at the Commission for Racial Equality but writes here in her own capacity.
2. In this text the term 'Black' is used to define those who are likely to be discriminated against on grounds of skin colour, culture and ethnicity.

References
Commission for Racial Equality (1979) *Barlavington Manor Children's Home: Report of a Formal Investigation*
Commission for Racial Equality (1985) *Birmingham LEA and Schools: Referral and Suspensions of Pupils*
Commission for Racial Equality (1985) *Swann: A Response from the Commission for Racial Equality*
Commission for Racial Equality (1986) *Teaching English as a Second Language: Report of a Formal Investigation in Calderdale LEA*
Commission for Racial Equality (1988) *Learning in Terror: A Survey of Racial Harassment in Schools and Colleges*
Commission for Racial Equality (1989) *Racial Segregation in Education: Report of a Formal Investigation into Cleveland LEA*
Commission for Racial Equality (1989) *Code of Practice for the Elimination of Racial Discrimination in Education*
Commission for Racial Equality (1989) *From Cradle to School: A Practical Guide to Race Equality and Childcare*
Commission for Racial Equality (1991) *Code of Practice for the Elimination of Racial Discrimination in Education (Scotland)*
Commission for Racial Equality (1991) *The Lessons of the Law: A Casebook*

of Racial Discrimination in Education

Commission for Racial Equality (1992) *Secondary School Admissions: Report of a Formal Investigation into Hertfordshire County Council*

Commission for Racial Equality (1992) *Set to Fail: Ethnic Minority Pupils in Secondary Education*

Commission for Racial Equality (1992) *Ethnic Monitoring in Education*

Commission for Racial Equality (1992) *Second Review of the Race Relations Act 1976*

Commission for Racial Equality (1993) *Comments on DFE Draft Circular on Admission Arrangements*

Cowley, L. (1993) *Registration and Inspection of Day Care for Young Children*. National Children's Bureau

Department of Education and Science (1967-73) *Statistical Return No.63*

Department of Education and Science (1985) *Education for All: report of the Committee of Inquiry into the Education of Children from Ethnic Minority Groups*

Department of Education and Science (1989) *Ethnically-based Statistics on School Pupils, Circular No.16/89*

Department for Education (1991) *National Exclusions Reporting System* (NERS). Initiated by DFE letter of 12 February 1990 to Chief Education Offices and the Chairmen of Governors of Grant-Maintained Schools. Preliminary analysis, based on returns to the Department in the first year of NERS

Department of Health (1991) *The Children Act 1989, Guidance and Regulations. Volume 2, Family Support, Day Care and Educational Provision for Young Children*. HMSO

Early Years Trainers Anti-Racist Network, PO Box 1870, London N12 8JQ

European Commission (in press) *Challenging Racism in European Childcare Provision*. Brussels

Milner, D. (1983) *Children and Race: Ten Years On*. Ward Lock Educational

Troyna, B. and Hatcher, R. (1992) *Racism in Children's Lives: A Study of Mainly-White Primary Schools*. Routledge in association with the National Children's Bureau

Working Group Against Racism in Children's Resources, 460 Wandsworth Rd, London SW8 3LX

Wright, C. (1992) *Race Relations in the Primary School*. David Fulton Publishers

9. Education: thirty years of change - for better or for worse?

Vivienne Little and John Tomlinson
Department of Education, University of Warwick

Context and organisation of the education service

Let us start by looking at some of the aspects of change. The 1944 Education Act had set a target of 'Secondary Education for All'. It was achieved so far as the law was concerned in two stages: the minimum school-leaving age was raised to 15 in 1947 and to 16 in 1972. More significantly still, the meaning of secondary education changed. The tri- or bi- partite system envisaged in 1944 had become comprehensive for 96 per cent of pupils in maintained schools by 1988. It betokened another radical change: the attempt to open access and opportunity. Primary schools followed the same odyssey but in a different way. 'All-age' (5-15) schools finally disappeared in the 1960s and the Plowden Report (1967) declared that 'at the heart of the educational process lies the child'. This much misunderstood phrase was declaring that in creating the curriculum and organisation of primary schools it was necessary to understand how children grow and learn. It was a short step from having more regard for the child as an individual to considering also the family and giving parents (now acknowledged as the prime educators of their children) opportunities for partnership. The white lines on the playground and the notices 'no parents beyond this point', became anachronisms. By the end of the period parents had designated places on Governing Bodies that had trenchant new powers. Within a generation, parents had been cast successively in the roles of pariahs, partners, then police.

While these changes in purpose, attitude and organisation were being carried forward the primary and secondary education system rode a demographic roller coaster. Rapid expansion to provide for the children born in the two peak years for the birth rate (1947 and 1964) was followed by painful contraction as the birthrate began to fall and continued at an historically low level. The number of pupils in England and Wales was 7.7 million in 1965, rose to 9.7 million in 1975 and by 1985 had fallen back to 7.9 million. The numbers of teachers changed in consequence as, at first, strenuous efforts were made to recruit students to an expanded training system and then numbers were cut back. In 1965 there were 350,000 teachers, in 1975, 500,000 and in 1985, 405,000. In 1963 the numbers entering teacher training had been 27,000; by 1973 this had been increased to 50,000 and as soon as 1982 had been cut back to less than 20,000. By 1992, in England, there were 6.8 million pupils, 394,000 teachers and fewer than 14,000 students completing courses of teacher training.[1]

Table 1
England and Wales

	Pupils	Teachers	Teacher Training Entrants
1965	7.7 m	350,000	27,000
1975	9.7 m	500,000	50,000
1985	7.9 m	405,000	20,000

For those working in the system during these years this pattern was much less clear, and corrective policies were often brought in at breakneck pace. The Annual Report of the Ministry of Education in 1963 made this confident forecast:

Although the birth-rate has still not returned to the 1947 peak it has risen every year since 1955 and is expected to set a new sixty-year record early in the 1970s.

In fact the birth rate fell steadily every year from 1964 to 1977 and numbers in primary schools did not begin to rise again until 1986, albeit slowly.

The high-water mark of the period was, without doubt, the government's White Paper of December 1972. It was boldly entitled *A Framework for Expansion* and proposed imaginative changes to expand the in-service training of teachers, the school building programme, higher education opportunities and, most significantly, nursery education. 'The nursery programme' it proclaimed, 'extends the boundaries of the education service to include children aged three and four' (HMSO, 1972, para 6). All parents of three or four- year-olds who wanted nursery education for children would be entitled to it. The following year the oil-crisis struck, followed by severe economic difficulties. It all came to nothing. Most notably of all, nursery education has never been reinstated as a prime object of government policy, despite all the evidence for its efficacy for children and efficiency in saving remedial expenditure later.

Thus our period opens with a confident sense of continued expansion as the high birth rate groups of 1946, 1947 and 1948 finished their term of compulsory schooling and those following belonged to historically large age groups which would feed into the schools until the late 1970s. As we now know, the decline in the birth-rate continued and the population has moved into long term decline as birth-rate falls below replacement level. The effect on schools was more than proportionate, for at least two reasons. The contraction of the late 1970s and onwards coincided with stringent financial policies so that the service suffered 'double cuts'. At the same time, political attention moved away from the declining age group of young people to the rising age groups of older people who were living longer and making greater demands on welfare services and health care. Just as children became a scarcer resource and we might have decided to pay even more attention to their nurture and education, political concern moved elsewhere.

Yet despite these dramatic experiences within the schools and local education authorities the level of qualification required of teachers was raised step by step and examination results at 16 plus showed steady improvement. In the 1960s most teachers had either received two years of higher education and training or were untrained graduates. The three-year course was introduced in 1960; the BEd honours course in the 1970s and the requirement for all graduate entrants to be trained as teachers was in place by the early eighties. In

1967 25 per cent of men teachers and 11 per cent of women teachers were graduates; in 1990 the corresponding figures were 64 per cent and 45 per cent. The proportion of pupils gaining an 'O' level/GCSE qualification rose from about 20 per cent in 1960 to over 80 per cent in 1988. Among these, the proportion of school leavers gaining five or more GCE/GCSE passes at grades A-C (a proxy for the old School Certificate) rose from about 7 per cent in 1965 to 38 per cent in 1990. And this fed through to 18 plus and higher education. In 1960 the proportion of the age group gaining two 'A' levels (the minimum required for a mandatory higher education award) was 6.5 per cent; in 1970 it had doubled to nearly 13 per cent; by the mid-1980s it was 16 per cent and by 1990, 22 per cent. More than 25 per cent of the age group are entering higher education courses of one kind or another in the early 1990s.

The organisation and control of the education system across the board - schools, further education and the universities - also underwent dramatic change. The 1944 Education Act had given the role of maintaining schools and further or higher education colleges to the local education authorities under the general direction of the minister. This was the system that supported post-war reconstruction, the elimination of all-age schools, the raising of the 'school leaving age' in 1947 and 1972, the expansion of schooling and teacher training to meet rising numbers and subsequently their contraction. At a more significant level it was also the system that initiated and carried through innovation in school building design, in-service training and the education of those with special needs, new forms of curriculum and school organisation (including the Schools Council, the first major national agency for developing curriculum), considerable expansion of further education and the development of the polytechnics. Now it has been almost entirely swept away. The polytechnics have been designated universities and drawn into the direct funding arrangements of the separate Higher Education Funding Councils for England and Wales. Likewise the colleges of further education and sixth form colleges have been removed from the responsibility of the LEA and placed under the Further Education Funding Council. In both sectors the power-relationship will now be based upon the individual governing body of the institution working directly to a government-appointed agency. In schools a parallel process was set in train, but its outcome is still uncertain in 1993. During the 1980s school governing bodies were strengthened in constitution and progressively given additional powers so that by the early 1990s they are responsible for hiring and firing staff, managing a delegated budget determined by national formula, the delivery of the national curriculum and assessment arrangements and for giving account of their stewardship to parents, LEA and central government. A new form of school organisation and funding, the grant-maintained school, appeared in the 1988 Education Act and is being strongly promoted by government in the early 1990s. In effect this removes the role of the LEA and in 1992 government proposed a Schools Funding Agency (to complete the trio of central agencies with Higher and Further Education). These developments underscore the general trend of transferring control to institutions on the one hand and central government on the other. By the 1990s Britain has, arguably, the most centrally controlled education system visible in the developed world. Funding is entirely in the control of central government because LEAs have virtually lost the power of local taxation to meet locally perceived needs while schools, further and higher education have only the power to earn additional funds by the extraneous use of buildings or staff. Beyond this, in the schools sector, curriculum, assessment, examinations, teacher appraisal, the curriculum of teacher training and the powers and duties of governors are all directly and in detail controlled by central government. The 1993 Education Act proposes to push the process even further by writing out the duties of the LEA and making the Secretary of State all-powerful.

There can be little doubt therefore that in the thirty years 1963-93 the whole education system experienced dramatic change physically, politically and, as we shall now see, in its underlying value system.

Inside the schools

A public system of education must, like Janus, look two ways, at individuals and at their social role. The physical, organisational and political changes outlined above reflect, through the thirty year period, changing adult aspirations for children stemming from new understandings of the nature of childhood and varied conceptions of the needs of society. Examining what went on inside primary and secondary schools and classrooms during the thirty years under review, and thus more directly what happened for pupils, reveals differing, sometimes antipathetic, views of both childhood and the social purposes of education.

Since at least the eighteenth century, in discussions about education, the vision, born essentially of religion, of children and indeed human beings as fallen or flawed, with instincts and desires which must be curbed and refined by the disciplines of family, work or school had contended with that of the child/individual as capable of moral and intellectual growth, even perfectibility, but corrupted or restrained by social pressures and in need of liberation. By the twentieth century the insights of Freud and William James among others, and the emergence of developmental psychology and new child-rearing approaches had reinforced the second view and contributed to the recognition of the experiences of childhood as crucial to, if not totally determinative of, the quality of adult citizens.

This valuing of childhood is perhaps unsurprisingly most visible in the primary schools of the period. As many 'living history' projects bringing to life the elementary school testify, today's primary classrooms are in appearance and emotional climate far removed from those of Victorian times, the thirties and even the fifties. They are full of visual interest, colour and movement. Stacking trays and asymmetrical collections of child-size, lightweight furniture have replaced tiered benches and rows of wooden desks. Ink wells have given way to felt tips and dog-eared plain or paper-covered text-books have been replaced by glossy libraries of reference and delight, while teachers learn to use computers from their pupils. Children are active, demanding, cared about and for the most part content to learn and few now go 'unwillingly to school'. A classroom-based research project found that 'Children in the ORACLE classrooms were, for the most part, well-behaved, highly-motivated and contented'... 'all our observers commented favourably on the contrast between the atmosphere in today's classrooms and those where they were pupils' (Galton and Willcocks (eds.), 1983). This is a fact rarely celebrated or even recognised. It can be attributed to the influence of progressivism, that, ill-understood set of ideas some of which were expounded in the Hadow Report of 1931 and reflected, not invented, in the now notorious Plowden Report (1967). It is a legacy perhaps at risk whose loss would not go unlamented or without consequence for the quality of our society.

Methods of teaching: progressive or traditional?

The period from the sixties to the eighties in primary education was characterised in curriculum terms by a dialogue, at times a war of words, between progressive and traditional methods of teaching. The aim of the former, briefly stated, was to simulate and refine, in school, the ideal learning environment of babyhood and the pre-school years, in which children, a central concern of their loving and intelligent parents, explored and discovered and learned what they wished to know, when they wished to know it, helped at appropriate moments and generously praised for the acquisition of each new skill. Teachers as parent-substitutes (later in partnership with parents) provided a similar but richer environment beyond the home and children's natural curiosity and need to make sense of the world would lead them to want to learn to read and write, observe and calculate, so long as paper, implements and guidance were to hand, and to paint and draw and model and dance, driven by a categorical imperative to express themselves. Faced with competition from peers and gently persuaded from fight or flight they would learn that nature's path to survival was via recognition and respect of the equal rights of others and thus would emerge balanced, fulfilled and cooperative adults with unbounded talents and skills freely to contribute to the functioning and evaluation of a democratic society, whose undetermined pattern could be only dimly discerned. In contrast, the traditional way to produce useful and productive citizens was to turn their attention as early as possible to acquisition of those skills essential to functioning in contemporary society, to provide them with such information about its history, geography and natural history as might enable them to begin to understand it, to teach them the manners and mores which would equip them to live comfortably and peaceably within it and to cope also with its dangers and difficulties and to discover and foster what academic or artistic talents they might muster for its service.

Child-centred primary schools - the revolution that never was

These very different philosophies issued in different curricula. Indeed at the extreme, progressive teachers eschewed the concept of teaching - teachers 'facilitated' what children wished to learn and children were their own curriculum builders. The class dissolved. Internal classroom walls were removed. Children took individual responsibility for their learning and progressed at their own pace. In the sixties, primary schools all over Britain, but notably in the West Riding of Yorkshire, in Leicestershire and Oxfordshire, influenced by charismatic directors of education like Alec Clegg, energetic HMI like Christian Schiller and Robin Tanner and inspirational teachers like Sybil Marshall of Cambridgeshire developed 'facilitating' techniques of intense subtlety and deep structure with encouraging results, and became international showcases of a primary education revolution. Meanwhile many primary schools in England and Wales had a more familiar air. Blackboards and chalk turned to white-boards and spirit markers, desks became tables; but teachers still taught. They asked most of the questions and did most of the talking. (See, for example, Perrott, 1982). Text books were colourful and there was a great variety of equipment, but teachers still decided what children should be set to learn, when they should learn it and what was to be done if they did not or could not. In fact, given the undoubted change in emotional climate and despite the deleterious effect on standards currently claimed for it, except for some aspects of education in the earliest years, the British primary education revolution was shown in the 1980s to have been largely a myth (Simon and Willcocks, 1981). Eleven years after *Children and their Primary Schools* (1967), *Primary Education* (1978) and *Education 5-9* (1982) (the titles themselves are telling) - a couple of HMI surveys - claimed that the problem with primary education was not too little concentration on the basics, as some politicians and some parents feared, but too much. The primary school curriculum, even where freed from the constraints of the eleven-plus entrance examination for selective secondary education, had not changed very much, especially in the junior years. Most of children's time at school was spent on language and mathematics exercises set or directed by teachers. Art, music and physical education were usually taught as separate subjects and the rest were approached intermittently by means of topic work, an impoverished and virtually science-less version of progressivist ideals of a child-centred, integrated curriculum and one which HMI (1978) judged unsatisfactory in many schools in its nature and level of challenge. The child might indeed be held to be at the heart of the educational process and primary teachers might vociferously defend their claim to teach 'children not subjects', to 'start from children's interests' but in most children's experience, apart perhaps from a steady increase in learning from first-hand experience and by doing, their practice belied them (Alexander, 1984, esp. p.40)

Teaching style and pupil progress

Critical consideration of these competing philosophies (not, we insist, mindless advocacy of progressivism) undoubtedly characterised establishments of teacher education in the '60s and '70s and ideas based in progressivism were, for a time, the orthodoxy of the leaders of professional opinion. In 1976, however, a research project (Bennett 1976) neatly but perhaps ironically coincident with Callaghan's Ruskin speech, was attempting to see whether any hard evidence could be found in classrooms to justify different teaching styles. The results of this study of a small number of primary teachers were hailed as vindicating formal or traditional methods. Actually they were less clear-cut and more fruitful. They indicated that some formal methods might be more successful for some subject-matter and for some children, but that informal methods were often the more successful for others. The most successful teacher overall was a devotee of informal methods. The findings implied that mixed methods were most appropriate and they were confirmed and extended by a more complex study, the Oracle project published in a series of volumes from 1980 onwards. Its findings, which were securely based in extensive classroom observation, suggested that in the real world, teaching styles could not be simply categorised as traditional or progressive. Six different styles were discernible and, moreover, they were linked to recognisably different, but relatively consistent, forms of pupil behaviour, another dimension which needed to be considered. Oracle confirmed the HMI 1978 survey findings that primary schools were orderly places, with teachers well in control of behaviour and learning, and that there was no evidence of a drop in standards of attainment in the basics. There was over-concentration on the latter, an excess of managerial over intellectual interactions between teachers and pupils, quite a lot of subject-based teaching, insufficient skill in developing integrated curricula and very little teaching of science. The Oracle team also claimed that the virtues of whole-class teaching and group work by children were under exploited (Galton and others, 1980).

These classroom-based studies convinced many teachers that the relationship between the ways they chose to teach and the effectiveness of their children's learning was worthy of study and resulted in much further work which informed and encouraged dispassionate reflection on practice, in a profession always dedicated to the welfare and advance of its charges. Their influence on policy was less productive, however, since they were quarried by press and politicians in support of polarised points of view and selectively used as 'objective' evidence for or against ideological constructs, which bore little relationship to the ways children were actually being taught. As we write, government agencies and ministers still stalk straw men in primary schools, and children and teachers, already exhausted by their efforts to absorb the national curriculum, suffer the slings and arrows of the outrageous 'back to basics' brigade. It is as though the 'Black Paper' movement, which had called as early as 1969 for a 'return' to traditional methods, had sustained its life independent of the findings of either research or HMI. The real advances of the period, in understanding about how individual children learn and how to plan and manage the curriculum to facilitate the progress of all of them, are thus obscured or denied and endangered.

Secondary education: the comprehensive approach

At the secondary level, the lives of young people were similarly conditioned by the evolving and competing goals of their elders. With comprehensive schools, there was an attempt to link the idea of secondary education for all with that of equality of treatment and therefore of opportunity. The tripartite approach of the '44 Act had tried to offer education for all according to ability, but it had foundered on the rock of the relentless social cachet and funding magnetism of the academic curriculum. Thus had technical schools burgeoned, only to decay or be captured by grammar schools, and secondary modern schools striven officiously to be 'as good as the grammar'. In the sixties and seventies the curriculum of comprehensive schools had further challenges to meet. It had to provide 'under one roof' for a very wide range of attainment and social background, with staff who came for the most part from the aspiring lower middle class. It had to come to terms with increasing ethnic diversity as well as social class difference among pupils, with a teaching force almost entirely drawn from one ethnic group. It had to cope, in a context of adolescence, with the emergence of the youth culture and pressure for pupil autonomy, when teachers might not be authoritarian, must justify their exercise of authority and could be authorities only on a small part of what there was to know (see R.S. Peters, 1959). It had to wrestle with inordinate problems of selection posed by the knowledge explosion and to respond to its concomitant, the march of technology. And it had to do all this in the period of demographic fluctuation described above which was also one of increasing dislocation of family life, discussed elsewhere in this issue, and during a short-lived boom followed by insistent economic decline.

Developing the secondary curriculum

Small wonder, then, that the secondary curriculum was problematic throughout the period, and debated (like the primary) in terms of the progressive and traditional paradigms. Attempts at mixed-ability teaching were among the earliest efforts to provide access to the same curriculum for disparate groups and individuals. Some techniques were borrowed and adapted from primary progressive practice and increasingly sophisticated reprographic and other teaching aids were pressed into service. But since children, both as they turn into adolescents and as they grow older, must learn more, so the effects of their social background upon their attainments and aspirations have ever greater effect; and the task for one teacher, even a subject specialist, to manage the learning of thirty-plus diverse pupils grows too much for all but the most resourceful. Nevertheless, much useful experimentation was done. The Humanities Curriculum Project (Schools Council, 1970) explored the now ambivalent role of the teacher, especially in dealing with controversial issues, and encouraged children to study what was common across the disciplines it embraced, as a basis for later specialisation. In a complementary way, the so-called 'new history' (*History 13-16* Project, Schools Council, 1972) and Nuffield science were not, in the minds of teachers, about destroying traditional disciplines, but about helping young people to cope in an age when education would mean less the storage of information in the mind, more the ability to gain access to it, to analyse, synthesise, manage and deploy it. The curriculum developers and theorists of the sixties and seventies recognised that schools would soon be preparing pupils for the 21st century when the effects of a communications revolution vastly more profound than the invention of printing would work themselves out. It is scarcely surprising that, when so much was attempted, some efforts were less than successful or appeared so in comparison with the more familiar achievements of the age that had its roots in the 19th century.

As understanding grew of the crucial importance of environmental experiences, especially early ones, to success at school and the virtual impossibility therefore of providing access to the same curriculum for all, so different approaches to the goal of equality of opportunity were tried. Community schools, where efforts were made to ground learning in children's experience and to draw on the resources of the community to enhance the relevance and utility of the curriculum, became more common. Educational Priority Areas were established, where above-norm staffing and additional resources were provided and attempts made to compensate for the disadvantage in the education stakes thought to spring from 'cultural deprivation' and linguistic divergence.

These efforts had little success and research continued to show that significant elements of both the majority and minority populations were virtually untouched by the education system, remaining at school only because legally forced and leaving with little they could turn to material or other advantage. Teachers who had striven with vigour, ingenuity and sincerity had reluctantly to accept, it seemed, that there was little they alone could do. Schools could not change the world, they only reflected it.

Community education and other efforts to provide a curriculum relevant to real needs came to be seen as compounding rather than compensating disadvantage, as making 'ugly clothes for the poor'. But like all educational experiments they had some successes. They enriched the lives of some individuals, if they could not change statistical patterns and they provided ammunition for those who argued that the fault might, partly at least, lie in the curriculum itself.

Parallel with the HMI survey of primary education (1978) had come a survey of secondary education in 1979. It showed how much had been achieved in the attempt to provide secondary education for all since 1944. It revealed, however, that from the age of fourteen, pupils in different schools were offered very different kinds and quality of choice, and 'some are deprived of important areas of experience .... both the more able and less able pupils .... Others are not readily able to relate to what they learn in different subjects or to see applications in new contexts' (DES, 1979, p.266). These findings intensified the debate about the secondary curriculum. Granted there should be access for all to the curriculum, but to what curriculum? Was it self-evident that an academic curriculum was right for all, or necessary for all? There was a need for more whole curriculum planning and above all more coherence and less complexity in the curriculum post-14. Curriculum theorists had been working on different ways of organising the curriculum, dividing it into areas of experience rather than subjects and seeking a pattern which would give pupils a foundation in all, with opportunities later to specialise in some, but in more breadth and less haphazardly than the cafeteria system of GCE and CSE allowed. They had been working towards a common examination at 16 plus and new forms of assessment. Above all they had been working to change the balance between academic and vocational elements in the secondary curriculum. They aimed at increasing the status accorded the latter and the occupations into which they led by developing closer links between education and industry.

Towards opportunities for all: the reckoning

As a result of all this thought and experimentation at primary and secondary levels, several hopeful things were happening in schools by the early '80s. First, the concept of special needs had developed, behind which research and resources were being directed at helping schools cope with the effects of social class and ethnic differences, and with new understandings of the significance of gender and the needs of the disabled, while pursuing the ideals of a pluralist rather than mono-cultural society. Second, in the Technical and Vocational Education

Initiative (TVEI), the financial resources of the Manpower Services Commission and the skill and ingenuity of teachers had combined, after initial mutual hostility, to show that a change of focus, a planned and monitored programme of more active and participatory learning methods and a curriculum related to the needs of the twentieth rather than the 19th century could set more young people on the path to significant achievement. Thirdly, the school effectiveness movement was showing that, while undoubtedly the worst effects of poverty and its attendant social ills could only be offset by social and economic rather than educational change, individual schools not only could but did make a difference to the life chances of significant numbers of individuals and salient characteristics of these schools could be described and analysed for emulation (see, for example, Rutter and others, 1979; Mortimore and others, 1988).

Enormous progress had been made in understanding the nature of the school curriculum and how it could best be planned and managed for the benefit of all pupils. A major curriculum development project *Curriculum 11-16* published significant analyses of the curriculum and organisation of schools (DES, 1977; 1979; 1983). It showed that the curriculum was coming to be seen as organic, unitary and embracing the compulsory years of schooling. It encompassed the structures of knowledge, defined as areas of learning and experience; the elements of knowledge - information, concepts, skills and attitudes - and the scope of what should be learned conceived in terms of breadth, balance, coherence, differentiation and progression. It also embraced methods of teaching and the processes of evaluation and assessment which were integral to learning. It should not be forgotten that the notion of a common or core curriculum, the first signs of a rationale for which had emerged in the Ruskin speech of 1976, together with more sophisticated and more inclusive forms of assessment, was the brain-child of maligned 'education professionals'. Much of the powerful content and method, though not the cumbersome and obsolete structure, of the National Curriculum was drawn from the ideas and dedicated work, over more than a decade, of what a very senior civil servant recently described, in our hearing, 'as the most intelligent and best qualified work-force in the country'. HMI *Curriculum 5-16* and *Better Schools* (DES), both published in 1985, when the National Curriculum still lay in the future, reflected and celebrated these achievements of collective thought and development.

Thus, in the first two decades of our period the public education service had been steadily developing its understanding of both the constant and the changing needs of learners, mobilising social resources in their support and contributing to ambitious social goals. Until the mid-'80s, the education service and most of its political masters had struggled through a period of unprecedented social and global change, to widen opportunities for all pupils. Their efforts should not be rated against the narrower goals of the past. The furore over falling standards is a smoke screen and a diversion from the real problem, which is that the levels of education and skill required for a modern economy and modern life are high and expensive and the impediments to their attainment in Britain today are manifold and intractable. There has, however, been much solid achievement, as we have tried to show and, a good deal more still working itself out in individual lives, that cannot be measured or recorded. The scapegoating of the service, touched off by the oil crisis of 1973, compounded by the nation's understandable dismay at its loss of international status, should not be allowed to obscure that strong endeavour and its real legacy.

The system - purposes, principles and prospects

We have seen, in the period 1963-93, fundamental questions playing themselves out in the classroom and the system at large. One of the underlying assumptions of any education system is whether the 'pool of human ability' is deemed, by and large, to be fixed, or whether 'ability' is seen at least partly as a function of educational opportunity. The dominant mood of the first half of the period 1963-93 was a dynamic version of the second view. The 'strong' theory of equality of educational opportunity held that it is not enough merely to open opportunity through processes of selection at various points in the educational process. That would always disadvantage those whose backgrounds limited their patterns of speech, richness of vocabulary and expectations of life compared with those having the advantages of articulate parents, supportive homes and varied social experience. Children's ability actually develops according to the opportunities they are offered. Hence arose programmes of positive discrimination and social priority. Most importantly, this idea was captured within the Left-Right political consensus of that time. Edward Boyle as Conservative minister accepted it as much as did the socialist Anthony Crosland (Kogan, 1971). It was Edward Boyle who ended his striking Foreword to the Newsom Report in 1963 with the sentence:

The essential point is that all children should have an equal opportunity of *acquiring* intelligence, and of developing their talents and abilities to the full (our emphasis) (Newsom, 1963).

This spirit also informed the recommendations of the Plowden Report (1967) for educational priority areas and was made yet more explicit in the action research and report *Educational Priority* of 1972.

This consensus was one of the casualties of the concerns about education in the 1970s and which were notably expressed by James Callaghan as Prime Minister in his speech at Ruskin College, Oxford in October 1976. Callaghan questioned whether the basic subjects were being taught well enough, and whether school leavers had been given the basic tools for a working life. He regretted the vacancies in science courses in higher education when those in humanities were over-full, and lamented that so few girls took up science and engineering. He called for 'a basic curriculum with universal standards'. He also argued that parents and employers should have more say in determining the purposes of schools and their government.

This speech and the 'Great Debate' which followed it set the agenda until the mid-1980s: essentially the same issues were being addressed in Sir Keith Joseph's White Paper *Better Schools* in 1985. Moreover, although Government had asserted far more control and direction by this time, the reforms of curriculum, teaching quality and school governance proposed in *Better Schools* were all set in the context of a continued partnership of central government, LEAs and the schools.

The radical break came with the election of the third consecutive Conservative government in 1987. The 1988 Education Reform Act had two different and contrasting aspects. On the one hand it set up the National Curriculum and assessment arrangements and on the other it created the conditions for a market in schooling. It was the notion of the market that reversed any continuing trend in government policy based on the strong theory of equality of opportunity. To create the market new kinds of school were created (grant maintained and city technology colleges) and parents were given much greater freedom of choice through open enrolment applying to all schools. Instead of differentiation of curriculum being provided within schools it is to be provided between schools. Behind the rhetoric of the market as a way of increasing parental choice lies the desire to reintroduce selective schools. And it is proving to be the case that as schools become popular they choose which pupils to admit rather than expanding rapidly to meet demand and hence satisfy 'parental choice'. The values of the New Right political philosophies of the 1980s and early 1990s are individualistic, competitive, non-statist and market based. Parental choice, competition between schools and market forces rather than planning are to determine the nature and distribution of educational provision. This approach, together with increased reliance on private funding, when applied to schooling cannot sustain the principles of access, entitlement, social justice and public service that were embodied in the education service of the 1960s and 1970s. Access is to be as consumer, not citizen. Distortions in provision of schooling, caused by parental choice affected by considerations of ethnic background, class, sex or religion will get built into the system and institutionalised. In this way, parental choice, in the sense of what schools are actually available, will come to depend on a mixture of prejudice and affluence.

At a deeper level, this reversal accurately reflects the underlying change in political philosophy.

There are only two ways of constituting civil society: either upon the basis of person or upon property. By a civil society based upon person is meant one in which the right of access to whatever that society provides collectively is gained solely through membership of the society. The projects to offer equality before the law, or freedom of speech or the right to vote would lie within this philosophical context. So pre-eminently, would the National Health Service, the social benefits system, and 'education for all' in the period of the British Welfare State. The notion of constituting civil society upon the basis of property adopts a wholly different starting point. By 'property' is meant not only physical possessions, but also what an economist would call 'positional goods', those possessions and attributes which confer advantages (or otherwise) in the market place and social milieu. Among them would be genetic endowment, class, ethnicity, gender, inherited wealth and, of course, education. Each of these, and especially their combined effect, confer advantages or disadvantages in the market place. Societies of this kind have been more common and include aristocracies, feudal societies, or Victorian England for example. The neo-liberal project of the 1980s was to return British society to a basis of 'property' after the attempt to base it upon 'person'.

By the 1990s, therefore, children and their parents had become subject to a more competitive and differentiated regime both in the system as a whole and within schools than in the 1960s. However, as we have shown, understanding of children's needs and how to meet them had also developed significantly. It may prove that teachers will be able to meet both the wider requirements of the curriculum and the social and personal needs of children while working within this changed ethic. The remarkable achievements of teachers between 1963 and 1993, briefly chronicled here, which progressively raised educational standards against a background of increasing family and social disruption, demographic expansion and contraction, radical structural change, and a general loss of respect for authority figures which directly affected teachers, arouse gratitude for their resilience and inspiration and a sense of optimism about future possibilities of the profession. But society itself must decide, and decide soon, whether its schools are to remain instruments of personal and social concern for children or be reduced to being chiefly instruments of academic and vocational training. It if is to be the latter, then, as A.H. Halsey argues elsewhere in this book, as yet un-thought-of social mechanisms for the nurture of families and children will be required.

Note
1. Figures for UK 1970-1990 are: teachers in maintained schools 1970 : 402,000; 1980 : 503,000; 1990 : 444,000.

References
Alexander, R.J. (1984) *Primary Teaching*. London: Holt, Rhinehart & Winston

Bennett, N. (1976) *Teaching Styles and Pupil Progress*. London: Open Books Ltd

DES (1972) *Educational Priority. Volume One, EPA Problems and Policies* in Halsey, A.H. (ed.). London: HMSO

DES (1978) *Primary Education in England: A Survey by HMI*. HMSO

DES (1979) *Aspects of Secondary Education in England. A Survey by HMI*. HMSO

DES (1982) *Education 5 to 9: An Illustrative Survey of 80 First Schools in England*. HMSO

DES (1983) *Curriculum 11-16: Towards a Statement of Entitlement. Curricular Reappraisal in Action*. DES

DES (1985a) *Better Schools White*. Paper. Cmnd. 9469

DES (1985b) *The Curriculum for 5-16*. Curriculum Matters 2. An HMI Series. HMSO

DES (1991) *School Examinations Survey 1988-89*

DES (1992) 'Teachers in service and teacher vacancies in January 1991', *Statistical Bulletin 1/92*, January 1992

DFE (1992) School exam results improve', Press Release 249/92

DFE (1993) 'Education statistics for UK 1992', *Statistical Bulletin 2/93*, January 1993

Galton, M., Simon, B. and Cross, P. (1980) *Inside the Primary Classroom*. London: RKP

Galton, M.and Willcocks J. (eds.) (1983) *Moving from the Primary Classroom*. London: RKP

HMSO (1972) *A Framework for Expansion*. Cmnd. 5174

HMSO (1975) *Education Statistics for the U.K.*

Marshall, S. (1963) *An Experiment in Education*. CUP

Mortimore, P., Sammons, P., Stoll, L., Lewis, D. and Ecob, R. (1988) *School Matters: The Junior Years*. London: Open Books

Perrott, E. (1982) *Effective Teaching*. London: Longman

Peters, R.S. (1959) *Authority, Responsibility and Education*. New York: George Allen & Unwin

Putting the Record Straight (1992). Various Authors. Network Educational Press Ltd

Rutter, H., Maughan, B., Mortimore, P. and Ouston J. (1979) *Fifteen Thousand Hours*. Open Books

Schools Council (1972) *History 13-16*

Schools Council/Nuffield Foundation (1970) *The Humanities Curriculum Project*

Simon, B. (1981) 'The primary school revolution: myth or reality?' in Simon, B. and Willcocks J. (eds.) *Research and Practice in the Primary Classroom*. London: RKP

Williams M., Daugherty, R. and Banks, F. (eds.) (1992) *Continuing the Education Debate*. Cassell

10. Thirty years of change: children with special educational needs

Sheila Wolfendale
Psychology Department, University of East london

Preamble

Thirty years of change in the area known and referred to as 'special educational needs' just happens to co-incide with the period of time that I have spent working in education, for a short while as a teacher, with stints as a remedial teacher, but mostly working as an educational psychologist and latterly as one who trains educational psychologists. It seems quite legitimate, therefore, for this review to be an amalgam of a personal/professional perspective and a documented account of change and development.

This account is juxtaposed at a time when we can look back over 30 years and name specific government reports, surveys, pieces of legislation as being influential and pivotal to (then) future events; at the same time we are positioned in anticipation of further change within education which renders uncertain future directions in the area of special educational needs.

We want to believe that, on the whole, the notion of 'change' in the realms of education and childcare is in positive directions, whereby provision and practitioner expertise 'improve' and thus are manifestly superior to what went before.

In the area of special educational needs workers and researchers are aware of a paradox - we have advanced conceptually; there is an increased range of educational and curriculum techniques; there is more manifest expertise on the part of teachers who themselves are supported by co-professionals from other services and non-teaching personnel - and in theory vulnerable children ought not to 'slip through the net', their needs unrecognised and unacknowledged.

The paradoxical element is that 'needs' are apparently not finite, whilst resources are; that the structure, organisation, funding of schools now and in the future may militate against best efforts to maintain guaranteed sound and effective identification and intervention systems on behalf of those children, who collectively are labelled 'SEN', and who individually comprise pupils with rights and entitlements.

A conceptual excursion into changing terminology is essential at the outset of this review for the very term 'special educational needs' has not been a constant over time, nor does it have the same connotations for all involved, nor has a consensus over its meaning been achieved despite the universality of its use and its legal currency.

The nature and notion of 'need'

Three terms have been extant for around 20 years, and each has generated a specific literature, whilst concurrently, at times, each has been used interchangeably with one of the others. The three related terms are: needs, special educational needs, and special needs. Some attention will be given to each, with emphasis on the first two.

The concept of needs

The first Director of the Bureau, Mia Kellmer Pringle, was influential in propagating the universality of children's needs. In *The Needs of Children* (1974) she posited a four-fold classification of *needs*: for love and security; for new experiences; for praise and recognition; for responsibility, perceiving these as constancies throughout life, adding 'of course, their relative importance changes during the different developmental stages as do the ways in which they are met' (p.34).

A critical scrutiny of this conception of 'need' has been undertaken by Woodhead (1991) who cites innumerable government and other official reports on child welfare provision for children of the last twenty years, each of which invoke the fundamental premise that children have these basic needs. Each report then posits a number of requisites, distinctive to particular settings (home, nursery, care facility, and so on) essential to ensure that these needs are met.

Woodhead's particular criticism is that, whilst the notion of 'need' may be seen to be a benign starting point to secure an eventual match between 'need' and provision to meet it, nevertheless each 'need' is presented as immutable, proven, 'timeless and universal' (p.40). He asserts that at worst, the conception is value-laden, an *a priori* construct and blunts a person-specific appraisal precluding a sensitive account of an individual child in his/her domestic cultural local, community contexts. 'Need' becomes a politicised issue when the construct is invoked to argue for or against certain types of provision, for example expansion of day care.

Thus, the construct is seen to be flawed in a number of ways, yet it is powerful enough to have influenced policy-setting. Woodhead sets out the main danger thus:

...the inadequacy of making simplistic inferences about children's needs from such complex and often context-specific processes is already abundantly clear (p.46)

and

...the challenge ..... is to recognise the plurality of pathways to maturity (p.50).

From the universality of needs we have come to a definition of children *in need* in the 1989 Children Act which acknowledges adult and societal responsibility (a and b below) whilst at the same time making *need* child-specific, as in c below.

In the Children Act:

A child is in need if:
a) s/he is unlikely to achieve or maintain, or to have the opportunity of achieving or maintaining a reasonable standard of health or development without the provision for him/her of services by the local authority;
b) his/her health or development is likely to be significantly impaired or further impaired without the provision for him/her of such services, or;
c) s/he is disabled

Thus the use of 'need' over time shows that it is a malleable term; perhaps its very imprecision makes it amenable for administrators, policy-makers, practitioners to use to provide or to restrict resources.

The concept of 'special educational needs'

This term has generated tremendous discussion and debate. Many welcomed its advent as it obviated the need for an invidious system of official categories of handicaps; others have believed that 'SEN' is a global replacement label that serves to perpetuate the marginalisation of a minority of children from their peers.

Looking at the origins of the term 'special educational needs' (SEN) we see that it appears in the Younghusband Report (1970), a report from a working party under the auspices of the National Children's Bureau. Although the Report itself does not make the connection, we could surmise that the working party members, who included the Bureau Director, Mia Kellmer Pringle, defined SEN as those *needs* which are different, extra, special *and* which can be met in educational settings (special and/or mainstream). In other words there was seen to be a relationship between the universality of the needs of all children and those deemed to be 'special' on a number of criteria. The Younghusband Report paved the way for the Warnock Report 1978, which explicitly adopted the SEN term and made it 'official'.

This article is not the place to become embroiled in the wrangle on definition and terminology - other authors have thoughtfully and critically dissected and analysed the term (Hegarty, 1987; Norwich, 1990); also see Cameron and Sturge-Moore (1990) for their discussion on the relativity of the term and World Health Organisation definitions of associated descriptors such as disability, handicap, impairment; and see Roaf and Bines (1989) for a conceptualisation of SEN within broader contextual 'rights' issues - which is consistent with the Articles in the United Nations Convention on The Rights of the Child which refers to the 'mentally or physically disabled child' (Article 23).

Notwithstanding controversies, the SEN term over the years has become common currency, enshrined into law since the Education Act 1981, re-affirmed in the Education Bill published on 30 October 1992 and recent reports such as the Audit Commission (1992a).

A postscript to terminology: it has become quite common to use the term 'special needs' as a shorthand, synonymous term to SEN in educational circles. Yet around the time when the Education Act 1981 came into force (1 April 83) the 'purist' approach was to differentiate SEN and *special needs*: SEN by definition referred to educational contexts as mentioned above whereas 'special needs' could encompass non-educational provision. The Children Act 1989 'in need' conception referred to earlier rather resembles the global 'special needs' in its earlier conception. 'Special needs' has become the least precise of these terms, partly because it is not anchored in law, as are SEN and the 'in need' conceptions.

Having attempted a brief dissection of core concepts, the article will move on to review change and development in key areas against the backcloth of reports and legislation. It would not be feasible to be all-inclusive, so these significant areas have been selected which epitomise initiatives and denote change over the last 20 to 30 years. The emphasis is on developments within education, but not exclusively so, as can be seen from those examples which embrace multidisciplinary endeavours.

The impact of reports on special educational needs policy and provision

As cited above, the Younghusband Report paved the way to the Warnock Report, but prior to 1970 the distinction between 'remedial' and 'special' education was still adhered to and the major criterion for entry into separate special education was still psychometric assessment that yielded an intelligence quotient. In other words children were assigned a score which determined their placement.

The Warnock Report, by postulating a continuum of special educational needs, contributed to the just-beginning debate on the appropriateness of standardised testing (Gilham, 1978). In other ways the Report was both a stimulus for new thinking and a reflector of emerging practice - for example Portage had then recently arrived in the UK and the Warnock Report drew attention to and commended this early intervention programme. The Report has been regarded as seminal in that the Education Act 1981 philosophy and some of its provisions are based on Warnock thinking and recommendations.

Indeed 'Warnock' thinking has been pervasive ever since the

publication of the Report since special educational needs as a defined 'area' has had higher profile and greater attention than hitherto. Some examples of this assertion include: explicit reference to special educational needs in the Education Reform Act 1988 (for example with provision to 'modify' or 'disapply' the National Curriculum and the revision of Circular 1/83 into Circular 22/89 to take account of the Educational Reform Act); a whole spate of books appearing during the 1980s on SEN (especially see the 'Special Needs in Ordinary Schools' series edited by Mittler, published by Cassell); whole tiers of LEA administrators and related bureaucracy to deal with Education Act 1981 procedures; the evolution of erstwhile 'remedial' teaching staff into SEN coordinators and learning support teachers.

Warnock acknowledged the influence of the Court Report (1976) which, although focusing on child health services, nevertheless took the view that early identification and intervention prevents or at least reduces educational failure and that inter-disciplinary cooperation as well as parental involvement enhances the effectiveness of educational strategies.

Other reports on aspects of children have contributed to the broad area of SEN, such as the Underwood Report on maladjustment which was published in 1955 and the recent Elton Report (1989) on Discipline in Schools. Underwood focused attention on services, such as psychological and child guidance services, and the Elton Report has influenced inservice training on behaviour management and the evolution of school policies on discipline.

At the present time, the impact of another government-initiated report reverberates. This is the Audit Commission/DFE Report (1992a) which was charged to review the workings of the Education Act 1981 and make recommendations. The major recommendations concerning the length of time it has taken/should take to complete Section 5 formal assessment; the right of parents to express a school preference; the creation of tribunals to replace the present appeals procedure - are all contained in the Education Bill published at the end of October 1992.

These new legal provisions will be paralleled by revision of practice at LEA and school levels along the lines recommended, again by the Audit Commission/DFE, in their *Management Handbook* published in November 1992 (Audit Commission/DFE, 1992b).

Practitioners, researchers and administrators have become familiarised to responding to official reports, acting voluntarily and selectively on a number of recommendations and at the same time operating within legal frameworks. Thus there is strong evidence of the reverberating impact of Reports upon policy and practice, yet their effects are double-edged. It can be argued that within the SEN sphere, the Reports cited have been benevolent and enabling in intent, designed to further the best interests of children with SEN. Yet by their existence, presentation of facts, commendations of emerging good practice, informed opinion, and their recommendations, they also raise expectations as to levels of provision, staffing, and other material resources. Hence, recent debates about 'resource-worthiness' (Dessent, 1987), and about concerns in the rise of numbers of children referred for 'statementing' (1981 Education Act Section 5 Assessment) so that they may be guaranteed extra resources. *The Management Handbook*, referred to just above is an attempt to create a consensus over the means of identifying, assessing, and providing for children with SEN within realistic budgetary frameworks of the LEA and schools which now have such significantly increased control over their own finances.

This review now goes on to examine two key SEN areas, which are characterised by change and innovation over the last 30 years.

Towards the empowerment of parents

The path towards parent-professional partnership and the full inclusion into decision-making and placement is turning out to be a long one. The Plowden Report (1967) firmly reiterated the rationale that came to underlie so many of the subsequent parental involvement projects in these words: 'by involving the parents, the children may be helped' and the Younghusband Report appearing three years later, used direct parental testimony as a cornerstone of the Report. This parental 'evidence' of the stresses and anxieties of bringing up children with handicapping conditions, and parents feeling unsupported by professionals provided a graphic account and has been echoed, down the years, by many other books and reports which likewise have attested to: parental grief, which needs understanding before comfort is offered; parental ignorance which needs redressing with information;

and parents being excluded from decision-making. Calls to ensure that these anomalies were addressed came later from the Warnock Report which called explicitly for partnership (see Wolfendale, 1983; Pugh, 1989; Wolfendale 1992 for definitions).

Established 'good' practice has included Portage, initially described by Pugh (1981), and subsequently, in the spate of Portage Conference books and their reports published by NFER-Nelson (for example, Cameron, 1986). Despite the withdrawal of government funds for local Portage programmes, many continue to flourish, funded by education, or social services or joint funded. This is a testimony to the robustness of the theory-base (behavioural psychologies/theories of instruction), of the methodology (operational structures at every level) and to the efficacy of parents-as-educators within a multidisciplinary framework. As Hanvey and Russell summarise (1990):

Portage is an important example of involving all consumers in a programme which teaches success, which is sensitive to social, personal and cultural variables, and which can be utilized in a wide range of care settings (p.23)

Another notable innovation of the 1980s has been the rise of parents' groups at local and national level, acting as parent support as well as lobbying groups, pressing local education authorities as well as central government to make adequate provision for SEN and to provide for progression towards integrated education (see Wolfendale, 1989, Chapter 8). Parent-to-parent support has been demonstrated in a variety of other ways, too, such as books written by parents for parents (Kimpton, 1990), the telephone help line described by Hornby (1988), also see Elfer and Gatiss (1990, Section 4).

The 1981 Education Act created a framework for closer cooperative working with parents, since it conferred these rights upon parents/carers:

- to request an assessment of their child;
- to be consulted regarding referral and assessment;
- to be in receipt of the draft and final statement;
- to contribute to assessment (advice) and annual review;
- to be present at assessment (unless classroom-based);
- to be represented and to have a representation;
- to appeal, locally and to Secretary of State.

Surveys carried out periodically during the last few years have revealed wide geographical variation, in the extent to which local education authorities responded during the 1980s to these various provisions in the Act concerning parents. Such cumulative evidence, combined with the most recent data, contained within the Audit Commission/DFE report (1992a) and a Spastics Society Report (1992) confirm this patchy picture, and led to proposals which form the basis for a number of provisions contained in the Education Bill (30 October 92). See earlier in this article for the key areas.

The government explains that the proposed strengthening of parents' rights is a logical extension of principles contained in the Parents' Charter 'Children with Special Needs' published early in 1992 (DES, 1992). The new proposals have to be considered within the broader context of the Government's plan (as outlined in the Education Bill) to introduce a Funding Agency for Schools, which as (it is envisaged) more and more schools become grant-maintained will progressively take responsibility for funding away from LEA's. Parents will want to know of the funding and resourcing arrangements for special educational needs in this scenario, where the new funding Funding Agency is directly answerable to and therefore under the control of, central government. Parents, as well as practitioners and administrators currently still working for the LEA, will want to know what accountability there will be under the new system and commensurately what means of redress there will be.

We have seen over the last few years, steady progression towards inclusion of parents in a number of key SEN areas and a corresponding 'flexing of parental muscle'. The National Children's Bureau, and within it, The Council for Disabled Children (which was known as the Voluntary Council for Handicapped Children until 1992) has played an influential part in endorsing and promoting parent-professional initiatives, of which one of the most recent has been the DES funded project 'Partnership in Assessment'.

Thus, proven, established practice provides the momentum for sustaining and extending it. Drawing upon such solid achievement, the Centre for the Study of Comprehensive Schools and the National Association for Primary Education, in association with other organisations have published a leaflet reiterating ten key *Principles in Partnership* which it is hoped will inform practice in the future (CSCS, 1992).

Towards inclusive education

The towering SEN issue of the past 30 years is undoubtedly that of *integration*. It is an influential and pervading issue of attitude, philosophy, educational theory and practice and it impinges upon educationalists, parents, children alike.

The nature of the debate first explored in some depth in the Younghusband Report (1970) echoes to this day, but has become a more conceptually and educationally complex issue. For example, the Younghusband Report sets out an aspiration that today reads simplistically even though surely it was not intended to deny the very controversies the members themselves identify:

Ideally, we should provide each child with the kinds of special help he needs and do so with the minimum degree of separation from his normal fellows and the minimum disturbance of normal family life. This concept makes unnecessary such controversies as to whether handicapped children should be educated in special or ordinary schools (p.23).

Yet the committee members make their fundamental position clear: 'we start from the assertion that wherever possible they should be educated in an ordinary school' (p.223).

They go on to consider the implication of their own caveat 'wherever possible' - it turns out that these are a foretaste of the caveats which were later to be outlined in Section 2 of the Education Act 1981, namely the provision of resources, and concern that the needs of 'handicapped children' can be fully met in ordinary schools, as against merely containing them.

As we know, the Warnock Committee went further in proposing an explicit model of integration, but which still, in its conception, allowed a degree of 'mix and match' - full time/part time attendance in an ordinary school, pupils on roll jointly at a special and mainstream school, cross-links between special and mainstream special unit provision within ordinary schools operating degrees and variations of social, locational, functional integration.

During the 1980s case studies were carried out which demonstrated the efficacy of such working links (Hegarty and others, 1982; Hodgson and others, 1984; and the Centre for Studies on Integration in Education [CSIE], 1992 published individual school case integration studies from time to time). In their book, Booth and Potts (1983) and their contributors explore the practice and issues and provide a selected 'Bibliography of Integration Schemes' as an Appendix.

Ostensibly, the Education Act 1981 espoused a policy of integration, subject to the caveats referred to above but the statistics confirm that the pace towards integration has been extremely gradual, with a few local education authorities prepared to make a commitment and move systematically towards the dismantling of segregated provision and an unified 'education for all'.

Ever since the Education Reform Act 1988 came onto the statute book there has been concern that Local Management of Schools and increased numbers of Grant Maintained Schools could put at risk such moves towards integration, especially since the government has never pronounced unequivocally that it intends that full integration should proceed apace. Indeed a dual attitude is evident on the part of the current government. Taking heed of the findings the Audit Commission Report (1992a) that a majority of parents (in the sample) of children with special educational needs preferred their children to be educated within mainstream school, there is a section within the Education Bill (30 October 92) which stated parents' right to express a preference of school for their child, that this wish should be recorded on the child's statements and that a school so named must admit that child, unless (and here follow the famous caveat clauses of resources, and so on). But this does represent an advance, for many parents will cite a mainstream school. The Government also plans that Local Management of Schools will also be extended to special schools, thus allowing them the same financial freedom from the LEA.

That the Government is driven by fiscal rather than philosophical considerations is also evident from the advice to LEAs contained in the Audit Commission/DFE Handbook (1992b) to rationalise special schools wherever possible. True, there is certainly a case to be made for 'efficient use of resources', to match need and provision to streamline the system, but the recommendation is not accompanied by a clarion call to integration.

Yet there is a strong and articulate lobby of educationalists, parents, other professionals arguing on equal opportunities/human rights grounds for integration (Rieser and Mason, 1990). Campaigners have continued to press their cause, as case study and other evidence has accumulated over the years. Inspired by evidence of successful integration in other countries such as Canada (Shaw, 1990) and frustrated by official inertia, the Integration Alliance published in 1992 *A National Policy for Fully Integrated Education*. Not only does this booklet contain an implementation plan, but it proposes a draft 'Inclusive Education Act', closely modelled on the existing Education Act 1981 but containing explicit commitment to integration.

The current dedicated view is that the term 'inclusive education' should replace 'integrated education' and that this betokens far more than a semantic name-change. It is a profound acknowledgement that it is all children's right to be fully included and valued, from the outset of education. The conception goes further than accommodating children with SEN into the mainstream - it is about full involvement in all social and learning activities.

John Hall (1992) has referred to the 'integration salad', the pot pourri of provision characteristic of the contemporary UK scene, and has criticised the location/social/functional model of integration proposed by the Warnock Committee as 'primitive'. He offers a view of 'inclusion':

The term inclusion has a very specific meaning implying that the child should attend his/her local school or college on a full-time basis in an age-appropriate group and be supported to function as an active member of the learning community such that it matters if he or she is not present (p.12).

Elsewhere the Canadian Inclusive Education experts (Forest and Pierpoint, 1992) have described Inclusive Education as:

...it means being with another and caring for one another .... it means inviting parents, students and community members to be part of a new culture (p.10).

The rhetoric is matched by the realities of cooperative classroom learning and social interaction, though more such evidence is needed in UK settings.

'Inclusive education' is a logical sequitur to the integration momentum which has been building up over recent years. Whether the momentum will be sustained or whether such progress that has been made will dissipate as a result of a fragmenting national education service remains to be seen.

Special needs: a shared responsibility

Time and again in the last 30 years we have witnessed enduring themes and concerns recurring in reports and in the literature. In fact there have been significant and substantial changes and developments, in SEN provision, in staff expertise, in the knowledge base. But whilst practice has developed, tensions remain. Differences in ideology and increasingly scarce resources ensure the maintenance of professional unease and parental anxiety.

At a number of levels the notion of shared responsibility for Special Educational Needs is propagated. At the international level, a number of Articles in the United Nations Convention on the Rights of the Child specifically refer to the rights of the 'disabled child' whilst another Article urged 'states parties' to assist parents in their task of raising children.

At the national level the government can point to the legislation (Education Act 1981 particularly) and the Parents' Charter for Special Educational Needs as a demonstration of shared commitment, whilst at local and school levels models of practice to enact shared responsibility have been put forward (Wolfendale, 1992).

Also, now, at national level, one consequence of so much change in the education system has been the emergence of a new solidarity between all the stakeholders in the special needs field. The Special Educational Consortium (established under the auspices of the Council for Disabled Children) has brought together a wide range of professional, voluntary and statutory agencies, parent organisations and groups - in order to respond to the many challenges to special needs presented in the Education Bill. Members of the SEC share common concerns about the consequences of major structural changes in the organisation of the education system as a whole and their implications for the importance of ensuring that schools take a broad view of their responsibilities to all their children in the community which they serve. The implementation of the Children Act has also had considerable impact on the special educational needs field - with new awareness of the importance of a corporate responsibility between health, education and social services for children with special educational needs.

There are no easy solutions - but the Consortium's contribution to a sharing of concerns, perceptions and possible solutions with regard to the shape of special educational provision over the coming years has reiterated the National Children's Bureau's foundation principle of 'cooperation in childcare'.

Sharing responsibilities in practice may or may not allay anxieties and disquiet. But, as we have seen, it can imbue the enterprise with common purpose. Thirty years after the birth of the National Children's Bureau, special educational needs have never been higher on the education agenda. It is now an imperative that when schools are inspected, every four years, by a team of registered inspectors as specified in the Education (Schools) Act 1992 schools' policy and provision for children with SEN should be one of the key performance indicators for determining the effectiveness of the school. Furthermore, the government has now indicated that all schools will be required, under the Education Bill, to have and to publish SEN policies, and to inform parents of the SEN provision within their school.

Despite the legitimate concerns already covered in this review, let us recognise that this requirement confers an opportunity upon schools to demonstrate the quality of their provision and the nature of their commitment to meeting the educational, learning and social needs of their children.

References

Audit Commission/HMI (DFE, 1992a) *Getting in on the Act, Provision for Pupils with Special Educational Needs: The National Picture*. London: HMSO

Audit Commission/HMI (DFE 1992b) *Getting the Act Together: Provision for Pupils with Special Educational Needs, A Management Handbook for Schools and Local Education Authorities*. London: HMSO

Booth, J. and Potts, P. (eds.) (1983) *Integrating Special Education*. Oxford: Blackwell

Cameron, R.J. (1986) *Working Together: Portage in the UK*. Windsor: NFER-Nelson

Cameron, J. and Sturge-Moore, L. (1990) *Ordinary, Everyday Families: A Human Rights Issue*. Mencap, 115 Golden Lane, London EC1 OTJ

Centre for the Study of Comprehensive Schools (1992) *Principles in Partnership*. Leicester University

Court Report (1976) *Fit for the Future*. London: HMSO

C.S.I.E. (1992) *Bishopswood, Good Practice Transferred*. C.S.I.E. 415

Edgware Road, London NW2 6NB

DES (1992) *Parents' Charter: Children with Special Educational Needs*. DES

Dessent, T. (1987) *Making Ordinary Schools Special*. Lewes: Falmer Press

Elfer, P. and Gatiss, S. (1990) *Charting Child Health Services*. London: National Children's Bureau

Elton Report (1989) *Discipline in Schools*. London: HMSO

Forest, M. and Pearpoint, J. (1992) 'Inclusion - the bigger picture', *Learning Together Magazine*, I, January, pp.10-11

Gilham, B. (ed.) (1978) *Reconstructing Educational Psychology*. London: Croom Helm

Hall, J. (1992) 'Token integration: How else can we explain such odd practices?', *Learning Together Magazine*, 3, October, pp.9-13

Hanvey, C. and Russell, P. (1990) *Children with Special Needs*. Workbook Four, K254. Milton Keynes: Open University

Hegarty, S. and Pocklington, K. (1982) *Integration in Action*. Windsor: NFER-Nelson

Hodgson, L., Clunies-Ross, L. and Hegarty, S. (1984) *Learning Together, Teaching Pupils with Special Educational Needs in the Ordinary School*. Windsor: NFER-Nelson

Hornby, G. (1988) 'Launching parent to parent schemes', *British Journal of Special Education*, 15(2), June

Kellmer-Pringle, M. (1974) *The Needs of Children*. London: Hutchinson

Kimpton, D. (1990) *A Special Child in the Family*. London: Sheldon Press

Integration Alliance (1992) *The Inclusive Education System: A National Policy for Fully Integrated Education*. 34a, Dafforne Road, London SW17 8TZ

Norwich, B. (1990) *Re-appraising Special Needs Education*. London: Cassell

Plowden Report (1968) *Children and their Primary Schools*. London: HMSO

Pugh, G. (1981) *Parents as Partners*. London: National Children's Bureau

Pugh, G. (1989) 'Parents and Professional in pre-school services: is partnership possible?' in Wolfendale, S. (ed.) *Parental Involvement Developing Networks Between School, Home and Community*. London: Cassell

Rieser, R. and Mason, M. (1990) *Disability, Equality in the Classroom: A Human Rights Issue*. London: ILEA

Roaf, C. and Bines, H. (eds.) (1990) *Needs, Rights and Opportunities*. Lewes: Falmer Press

Shaw, L. (1990) *Each Belongs, Integrated Educational in Canada*. CSIE, 415 Edgware Road, London NW2 6NB

Leonard, A. *(1992) A Hard Act to Follow: A Study of the Experience of Parents and Children under the 1981 Education Act*. Spastics Society 12 Park Crescent, London W1N 4EQ

Underwood Report (1955) *Report of the Committee on Maladjusted Children*. London: HMSO

United National Convention on the Rights of the Child. Children's Rights Development Unit, 235 Shaftesbury Avenue, London EC2H 8EL

Warnock Report (1978) *Special Educational Needs*. London: HMSO

Wolfendale, S. (1983) *Parental Participation in Children's Development and Education*. London: Gordon and Breach

Wolfendale, S. (Ed) (1989) *Parental Involvement: Developing Networks between School, Home and Community*. London: Cassell

Wolfendale, S. (1992) *Primary Schools and Special Needs Policy, Planning, Provision*. Second Edition. London: Cassell

Woodhead, M. (1990) 'Psychology and the cultural construction of children's needs' in Woodhead, M., Light, P. and Carr, R. (eds.) *Growing Up in a Changing Society*. Milton Keynes: Open University

Younghusband Report (1970) *Living with Handicap*. London: National Children's Bureau

11. Trends in child health

Caroline Woodroffe and Myer Glickman
Wolfson Child Health Monitoring Unit, Institute of Child Health,
University of London

Introduction

Over the last 30 years the National Children's Bureau has provided a unique focus on children and all aspects of their lives. Such a unified approach is essential for child health, as it is widely recognised that the health of the child population depends more on their standard of living than on health services. The lifetime of the Bureau has witnessed impressive technical and scientific advances in medical knowledge; but at the same time homelessness, long-term unemployment and poverty have increased. Thirty years after the founding of the Bureau we have reached a position where some seriously ill children receive expensive organ transplants while other children die in house fires because their parents, unable to afford electricity, use candles to light their home.

Overview of child health

The overview of child health covers the UK, Great Britain, or England and Wales, depending on the coverage and timeliness of available data. The children of Northern Ireland are missing, for example, from the major population surveys conducted in Great Britain by the Office of Population Censuses and Surveys (OPCS). Although time trends are indicated for some data (where possible for the period since the

opening of the Bureau), priority is given to describing the prese
the first part of the overview health outcomes are presented mair
age, including the 15 to 19-year-old age group, often invisible w
information for older adults. Gender differences are given where they
are important, for example in injuries. The second part of the overview
describes children's health in relation to their socio-economic
characteristics.

In the period since the founding of the Bureau the remarkable
success in reducing infant mortality in the first half of the century has
continued. In the years 1963-91 infant mortality (deaths under one
year per 1000 live births) fell by 65 per cent (OPCS DH1). However,
despite this success, in 1990 UK infant mortality (7.9 per 1000 live
births) was higher than in France, West Germany or the Netherlands,
although lower than in Ireland or Italy (WHO, 1992).

Of all children and teenagers under age 20, infants are by far the
most vulnerable. Over half of deaths under 20 occur in infancy - a third
in the first month of life. In 1991 of the 8,900 deaths under age 20 in
England and Wales, 5,200 were infants and 3,100 of these were
neonates (less than a month old). The number of stillbirths (3,300) was
similar to the number of neonatal deaths (OPCS DH2, DH6)

The main causes of neonatal death in the UK are congenital
anomaly and prematurity, each contributing nearly a third of the total
(OPCS DH6/4; RG Scotland, 1990; RG N Ireland, 1991).

Birthweight is the strongest predictor of infant mortality. Babies
weighing under 2500g (5.5 lbs) at birth are twice as likely to die in their
first year as those born over this weight. Of all live births 6.5 per cent
weigh under 2500g (OPCS DH3/24). Recent advances in neonatal
intensive care have succeeded in keeping a higher proportion of low
birthweight newborns alive, making a major contribution to the
reduction in neonatal mortality. There has been much less success,
however, in reducing the proportion of low weight births (Alberman,
1991).

A steep decline in the number of children born with a congenital
anomaly of the central nervous system has contributed to the fall in
infant mortality. Between 1979 and 1990 the proportion of live and
still births diagnosed (within seven days of birth) as having spina
bifida fell from 13 per 1000 to 2 per 1000 while the proportion with
anencephalus fell from 7 per 1000 to less than 1 per 1000. The

reduction in prevalence at birth is partly accounted for by the provision of antenatal screening and termination of pregnancy and partly by a decrease in incidence attributed to improved nutrition (OPCS MB3/5).

Death in the remaining eleven months of infancy (the postneonatal period) is dominated by Sudden Infant Death (SID) of which the cause is, by definition, unknown. Of postneonatal deaths in the UK in 1990, 44 per cent were classified as SID, while congenital anomaly, the second largest category, was the cause of 16 per cent (OPCS DH2/17; RG Scotland, 1990; RG N Ireland, 1991).

There has been a recent reduction in the number of Sudden Infant Deaths. The long-term increase appears to have been reversed since a peak in 1988 with SID mortality in England and Wales falling from 2.3 per 1000 live births in 1988 to 1.3 per 1000 in 1991 (OPCS DH3). This reduction has been closely linked to a fall in the proportion of infants sleeping on their fronts (Wigfield, 1992).

Deaths from injuries contribute only 2 per cent of the 6,300 deaths to infants, but 29 per cent of these injury deaths are either known or suspected to be non-accidental (OPCS DH3).

There has been less success in reducing mortality among older children, and least among 15 to 19-year-olds. In the period 1963-91 deaths to older teenagers fell by only 18 per cent. Figure 1 shows the trends in mortality for age groups after infancy. At the beginning of the period mortality was higher among 1 to 4-year-olds than among 15 to 19-year-olds; thirty years later this order had been reversed. Mortality is twice as high among pre-school children and older teenagers as among children at school (OPCS DH1, DH2).

Injuries (including poisoning) cause almost half of all deaths age 1 to 19 in the UK. In this age group the main causes of death are injuries (47 per cent), cancer (14 per cent), diseases of the nervous system (10 per cent), congenital anomaly (9 per cent), and respiratory illness (7 per cent). Injury increases in importance from 24 per cent of deaths aged 1 to 4 to 60 per cent of deaths aged 15-19 (OPCS DH2/17; RG Scotland, 1990; RG N Ireland, 1991). Four fifths of injury deaths are known to be accidental. The remainder are suicide (among older teenagers), homicide, or are recorded as an open verdict. In every age group the risk of death from injury is higher for boys than for girls, young men aged 15 to 19 being at 3.5 times the risk of young women. Suicide and death from solvent abuse are increasing among young men (OPCS DH2).

Figure 1
Trends in mortality by age group 1963-1991, England and Wales

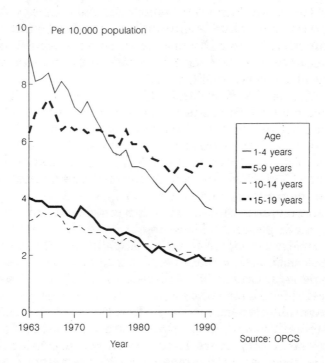

Source: OPCS

Death is the extreme end of the spectrum of health. Morbidity (illness and disability) affects a much larger number of children with varying degrees of severity and length of illness.

National levels of childhood morbidity are estimated from population surveys, notifications of infectious diseases (for example, measles and whooping cough), registers of children with specific conditions (for example cancer and cerebral palsy), and hospital admission data. The data presented here are from population surveys conducted by the OPCS and from hospital admissions.

The population surveys indicate that the prevalence of chronic illness in childhood increases with age (after infancy), and is greater in boys than girls. The 1991 General Household Survey (GHS) found 'long-standing illness, disability or infirmity' reported in 12 per cent of

0 to 4-year-olds, 16 per cent of 5 to 15-year-olds, and 20 per cent of 16 to 19-year-olds in Great Britain. More severe chronic illness, described as 'limiting activity', was reported for between 4 per cent and 7 per cent of these age groups (OPCS GHS; Woodroffe and others, 1993).

Respiratory illness, usually asthma, is the most commonly reported chronic illness, with a rate of 8 per cent of children aged 0 to 15. Skin problems (eczema) and ear complaints, each at 2 per cent, are the next most frequently reported (OPCS GHS).

Since 1972, the first year of the GHS, the reported levels of chronic illness have doubled. This may partly be the result of changes in expectations, but an increase, particularly in respiratory disease and diabetes, has been confirmed by other research (Anderson and Strachan, 1991; Strachan and Anderson, 1992; Nabarro, 1988). Improved survival of the small number of children with previously fatal conditions including some cancers, congenital heart disease, and cystic fibrosis has contributed to the increase in morbidity.

The improved survival of low weight births has led to increased levels of morbidity throughout childhood. Children born at low weights have an increased risk, for example, of sensorineural deafness (Oxford Region Register of Early Childhood Impairments, 1992). They are also at increased risk of cerebral palsy. In births weighing 2500g or more cerebral palsy has not increased in the last 30 years, but among lighter births there has been a marked rise (Pharoah and others, 1990). The poor quality of life achieved by some survivors of premature birth has become a major problem of modern paediatrics (Court and Alberman, 1988)

The prevalence of disability in Great Britain was separately estimated in the OPCS Disability Survey conducted (once only) in 1985-8. Disabilities were divided into functional categories, such as mobility, vision and hearing. Behavioural disability was the most common and probably the most difficult to interpret. Parents reported that 2.5 per cent of 10 to 15-year-olds had a behavioural disability. Nearly two thirds of disabled children under 16 were restricted in more than one function (Bone and Meltzer, 1989). In contrast to the GHS, lower levels of disability were reported for 16 to 19-year-olds than for 10 to 15-year-olds for all functions except vision (Martin and others, 1988). In both surveys parents responded for children and younger teenagers while the older teenagers replied on their own behalf.

An estimate of the incidence of short-term illness, defined as illness or injury in the last fortnight which restricted normal activity, is available from the GHS. The proportion of children and teenagers who were ill in the last fortnight is constant at 11-12 per cent for each of the age groups 0-4, 5-15, and 16-19 years. According to the GHS data, short term illness has increased in recent years (OPCS GHS; Woodroffe and others, 1993).

Hospital admissions are used as an indicator of the amount and type of serious illness in the child population. These data, however, are designed to measure workload, and are only an indirect measure of morbidity. Changes over time and place may reflect changes in the supply of services or in medical policy. Some children are now treated as outpatients, day cases, or in paediatric home nursing schemes, who would previously have been admitted to hospital overnight. Others are kept in hospital for shorter periods before planned readmission, and few computer systems so far link the admissions and readmissions of an individual child. Thus while the average length of stay in hospital has fallen, the number of admissions recorded has risen (DoH Statistical Bulletins).

National information on hospital admissions by diagnosis has not been available for England since 1985, a highly unfortunate interruption in the Department of Health's system of data collection. Any national trend since 1985 in the number of neonates requiring treatment has been concealed so far by their inclusion in the total figures of all babies born in hospital whether sick or well (DH Statistical Bulletins).

Despite these limitations, hospital admission data give some indication of the relative importance of serious childhood conditions. Recent (1990) data for Scotland show that respiratory disease and injury are the most important causes of childhood hospital admission. Respiratory disease accounted for 25 per cent of admissions of children aged 0 to 4 and 19 per cent of those aged 5 to 14 while injury was the cause of 13 per cent of admissions aged 0 to 4 and 22 per cent of those aged 5 to 14 (CSA, 1991).

Data linking the admissions of an individual child are available for the Oxford Region. Children aged 1 to 14 who spent a total of five or more days in hospital in one year were characterised by diagnosis. Congenital anomaly, asthma and appendicitis were the most common conditions, each causing hospitalisation of this length of 5 to 6 per 1000 children in the population (Henderson and others, 1992).

The population-based GHS estimates the proportion of children admitted to hospital at least once in the past year as 10 per cent of 0 to 4-year-olds, 7 per cent of 5 to 15-year-olds (OPCS GHS 21) and 8 per cent of 16 to 19-year-olds (Woodroffeand others, 1993).

Child health and poverty

Poverty is strongly associated with increased risk to child health. The strength of the link has been widely acknowledged since the publication of the 'Black Report' (DHSS, 1980; Davey Smith and others, 1990). Direct evidence relating household income to the health of individual children is difficult to obtain but indirect evidence of a correlation is available at population level for small areas or at an individual level using interrelated characteristics closely associated with relative poverty, such as the mother's age and marital status or the social class of the household .

The correlation of income and child health at the level of small geographical areas has been demonstrated in a study of local government wards in Scotland. Each ward was assigned a deprivation score based on overcrowding, male unemployment, low social class, and not having a car. The proportion of births under 2500g, infant mortality, and mortality aged 1 to 4 years all showed clear gradients with this score, with the areas with the most deprivation having the worst health (Carstairs and Morris, 1991).

Low income is an important component of the factors causing increased risk to infants of teenage mothers. The risk of death in infancy is 1.3 times greater for children born to mothers under 20 years of age. In the postneonatal period, when socio-economic circumstances may be more important than in the first month of life, mortality in children of women under 20 is more than twice that in children of mothers aged 25 or more. Infants of younger mothers are more likely to die of respiratory conditions, infectious diseases, injuries and particularly SID (OPCS DH3/24).

Low income is an important component of the increased risk to infants of all unsupported mothers. Although the two groups - young mothers and unsupported mothers - overlap, only a fifth of births outside marriage are to mothers aged under 20. Births are registered within marriage, jointly by parents living at the same address, jointly by parents living at different addresses or solely by the mother. The type of birth registration gives some indication of the degree of support from the father. Infant mortality rises as the mother's economic and social support fall as indicated by the status of the father at registration of the birth. Infant mortality is 7 per 1000 births within marriage, 10 per 1000 jointly registered by parents at the same address, 11 per 1000 births jointly registered from different addresses, and 13 per 1000 solely registered births (OPCS DH3/24).

The most widely used measure of a child's socio-economic circumstances is the occupation of the male 'head' of the household in the Registrar General's scale of five social classes. Social class (as defined by occupation) describes more than income, but income is an important component. A child in the lowest (unskilled manual) social class is twice as likely to die before age 15 years as a child in the highest (professional) social class (OPCS DS8 and DH3/24). One disadvantage of this classification is that an increasing number of children are excluded because their 'head' of household is unemployed, chronically sick, or a lone mother (Cooper and Botting, 1992). Thus the analysis of infant mortality by social class in England and Wales excludes the 8 per cent of infants born outside marriage in 1992 and registered only by their mothers. Of the children aged 1 to 15 who died in the period 1979-83 in England and Wales, 19 per cent could not be assigned a social class (OPCS DS8)

Infant mortality shows steep class gradients for similar birthweights (and the risk of low birthweight is greater in lower social class families). Once again the class gradient is steeper in postneonatal mortality than in the first month of life. Infants in unskilled manual households are three times as likely to die of SID in the postnatal period as infants in professional households (OPCS DH3/24). Children aged 1 to 14 in households whose male 'head' is an unskilled manual worker are almost four times as likely to die from injuries - the most important cause of death in later childhood - as children from professional households. The differences are even greater for pedestrian deaths in traffic accidents and deaths from fires (OPCS DS8). Poorer families are less likely to have a car, a safe play area or safe heating.

Children in manual social classes are more likely to be ill. According to the GHS a higher proportion of children in manual than in non-manual groups suffer long-standing illness limiting their activity (Woodroffe and others, 1993). Further evidence of the link between social class and morbidity comes from the cohort study of children born in Great Britain in 1970. Children in manual social classes were more likely to have had pneumonia by age five (Butler and Golding, 1986). By age 10 they were more likely to cough regularly and to have missed school due to ill health. Behaviour problems at age 10 also showed clear class gradients (Woodroffe and others, 1993).

Children living in poor quality housing are at increased risk of morbidity. In the 1970 birth cohort children living in damp housing were more likely to have bronchitis, to wheeze and to miss school due to ill health, risks that increased with the degree of severity of the dampness of their home (Woodroffe and others, 1993). Some 10 per cent of children live in housing officially classified as damp or unfit (Dept of Environment. Housing Condition Survey 1986, personal communication)

How many children are living in poverty? In the absence of an official UK definition of poverty, the European Community definition is used. This defines relative poverty as half the national mean household income, adjusted for household size and age of children. In the UK in 1990 the poverty line was £134 a week for a family of two parents and two children. By this definition over 3 million children - or 26 per cent of all children in the UK - were living in poverty in 1987, and the proportion had increased from 12 per cent in 1979 (Oppenheim, 1990; DSS, 1990). In Northern Ireland 39 per cent of children live below the UK poverty line compared to 19 per cent in Scotland and 10 per cent in the South East of England (House of Commons Social Services Committee, 1990).

Unemployment is the most important cause of poverty. Most children in poverty (54 per cent) have an unemployed 'head' of household, including 23 per cent who live with an unemployed lone parent. Low pay is the reason for a further 38 per cent of child poverty. The risk of living in poverty is highest (79 per cent) for children with an unemployed 'head' of household (DSS, 1990).

Social security benefits are inadequate to lift these children above the poverty line. The means-tested income support child allowance is less than a third of the average cost of bringing up a child (National Children's Home, 1992). The value of the universal child benefit (for a family with three children) has fallen during the lifetime of the National Children's Bureau from 20 per cent of average male manual earnings to only 9 per cent (DSS, 1991).

The poverty statistics are based on private households and exclude children in homeless families. In England 146,000 households were officially classed as homeless in 1990, more than two and a half times the number when the current system of counting began in 1978 (DOE, 1979-91). These families included an estimated 200,000 dependent children. A quarter of homeless families with children are in bed and breakfast accommodation, typically with increased risk of accidental injury resulting from inadequate cooking facilities and play space (Wilson and Jenkins, 1985; Drennan and Stearn, 1986; Stearn, 1986; HVA and BMA, 1989). In addition there is a growing number of older homeless teenagers who, failing to qualify for rehousing, are not officially counted as homeless (CSO Social Trends 21).

Poverty increases the risk of poor health, and having a disabled child increases the risk of poverty. Families with a disabled child have on average only 78 per cent of the resources of all families with children (Smyth and Robus, 1989).

The overview of child health leads on to questions of policy. Given the pattern of health among the child population, and the current state of knowledge about preventing and treating illness, how should the resources available for child health be allocated? What aspects of child health are most valued by society? Whatever the amount of resources available, some form of rationing will be required. How should the decisions be made? For simplicity we have confined the discussion to the allocation of resources within the health services. The methods discussed apply equally, however, to evaluating the cost-effectiveness of action beyond the health services to improve child health, such as pollution control, accident prevention, or the relief of poverty.

Allocating resources to improve child health

The separation of purchasers and providers in the NHS has provided the opportunity for a rational examination of resource allocation in accordance with the expressed values of society. Hitherto decisions made on the basis of history offered less opportunity for change.

Society's political values are expressed in answers to a hierarchy of questions. The first, which determines the overall level of public expenditure, asks what priority does society place on freedom from taxation as compared to collective responsibility? In broad terms the public answers this question at the general election. The second asks what weight should be given within public expenditure to health as compared, for example, to education. This decision is taken annually by the government in the public spending round. The public used to have a 'second chance' at the ballot box in local government elections for those areas of public expenditure controlled by local authorities. However the powers of elected local authorities to decide priorities in public expenditure have been eroded, and most importantly health is not included.

The third value question assigns relative weights to different health outcomes. Is one healthy year of life gained for a child worth the same as one healthy year of life gained for an adult? How are physical illness, mental illness and mental handicap to be compared? Is the reduction of health inequalities between social classes one of the objectives? Here there is no democratic structure in place. The health of the resident population is the responsibility of the unelected health authority. Moreover the health authority's power to purchase services is now shared with the fund-holding GPs. As the number of fund-holding GPs and the type of health care they may purchase increases, the balance of purchasing power is shifting away from the health authority. GPs may have different values from health authorities, and both may hold different values from the public. A consultation exercise in City and Hackney Health District found that all the groups of doctors (GPs, hospital consultants, and public health medicine specialists) gave higher priority to reducing mental illness than was given by the public (Bowling, 1992).

At what level should the objectives of health care be decided? At the same time as setting national targets for health gain (which inevitably include political judgements), the government is leaving many of the decisions on purchasing to the health authorities and fund-holding GPs, aware that any explicit rationing will be unpopular. Health authorities are busy making their own explicit or implicit value judgements, and some are devising structures for consulting public opinion before doing so. There are advantages in allowing variation in objectives at local level. There are also arguments, however, for setting health service priorities at national level in order to formulate national policy on GP contracts, tertiary care, training, research, public health education, and to provide a consistent service across the country. Most importantly, the politicians deciding on the total size of the health service budget at national level should not be protected from the problem of rationing out a budget which may be inadequate in the first place.

It is essential to separate the question of rationing into two parts: what are society's values, and how may public funds be spent most efficiently, in terms of cost-effectiveness, to promote these goals. The value questions concern outcomes, not inputs, and are matters of political opinion to be agreed by democratic process. The calculation of cost-effectiveness is a matter of fact, and requires expertise, not democracy. It determines how the available resources may be allocated most efficiently to achieve the political goals valued by society.

So far most local attempts at public consultation have failed to make this distinction. The well-known experiment in Oregon, USA, and comparable exercises in the UK, have asked the public for their preferences on treatments (inputs) rather than outcomes in questions which combine opinion and fact, values and efficiency. A comprehensive review of the exercises in public consultation undertaken in the UK is included in the report of consultation in one district (Bowling, 1992). The report raises the dilemma of a health authority which invites the public to rank health service treatments, rather than outcomes, and is then faced with priorities which it would be inefficient, in terms of the implied public values, to implement.

In contrast, the government's strategy document *The Health of the Nation* targets health outcomes, not treatments, starting with the overall target of increasing healthy life expectancy (Secretary of State for Health, 1992). The key disease groups are chosen for their contribution to the total burden of disease, to the number of premature deaths and healthy years of life lost. Remarkably, however, there is no attempt to compare the cost-effectiveness of the different strategies in achieving this goal, and thus no overall strategy on efficient allocation of resources.

Of course - and perhaps this is the government's excuse - much of the information on the effectiveness of interventions, and even more on cost, is missing. Resource allocation cannot wait, and yet it is important to understand the implied process behind the decisions. Comparison of the costs of different ways of obtaining the same health outcome is still rare, while comparison of costs across different outcomes, requiring a common currency for health gain, is rarer still. The best known common currency, the Quality Adjusted Life Year (QALY), has been developed by assigning weightings to different health states described in terms of disability and distress, and accordingly modifying the number of years of life gained. The relative efficiency of different interventions in terms of the cost per QALY gained may then be compared.

An example illustrates the use of QALYS in evaluating paediatric care. The cost per QALY gained by neonatal intensive care of infants weighing 500-999g and infants weighing 1000-1499g was compared (Boyle and others, 1983). The quality weightings were obtained by asking a sample of parents of schoolchildren to rate the desirability of the various health states experienced by the survivors. The scale allowed them to rate some health states as worse than death. When the two groups were compared, the cost per life saved was twice as high in the lighter group, the cost per life year gained was three times higher, and the cost per QALY gained was seven times higher. Subsequent authors were able to compare the cost per QALY gained in Boyle's study with other areas of health care. At that time intensive care of newborns weighing 1000-1499g was found to compare unfavourably, for example, with screening of neonates for phenylketonuria (PKU) (Mugford, 1988). Cost-effectiveness is compared at the margin rather than the average, and changes in different circumstances.

Some clinicians fear that rationing means a health economist will be looking over the doctor's shoulder in the consulting room. They may be reassured that screening for cost-effectiveness will be conducted at two levels: coarse screening by the purchasers of the proposed treatment and fine screening by the clinician of the individual's ability to benefit.

Should our health objectives be limited to increasing healthy life expectancy? Reducing the differences in health between groups by improving the health of the disadvantaged is the first target of the World Health Organisation's European strategy 'Health for All' (WHO, 1985). The striking health inequalities in this country between children of different social classes have already been described. Despite paying tribute to the WHO targets, however, the government's strategy for health rejects equality as a goal. (Secretary of State, 1992).

In this overview of child health in the lifetime of the Bureau we have described encouraging trends in mortality, less encouraging trends in morbidity, and continuing inequality. The socio-economic circumstances which increase the risk of childhood illness require solutions beyond the bounds of health services. The government's strategy for 'The Health of the Nation' has rightly emphasised the impact on health of many areas of policy such as housing and transport. The greatest health gain for the country's children in 1993 would come from a real commitment to tackle poverty and deprivation.

Acknowledgements
Thanks are due to Eva Alberman, Terri Banks, Alison Frater, Philip Graham, Chris Power, and Brent Taylor for their comments on an earlier draft of this chapter, and to the Wolfson Foundation for financial support.

Note
This work was undertaken in the Wolfson Child Health Monitoring Unit, Department of Epidemiology, Institute of Child Health, University of London.

References
Alberman, E. (1991) 'Are our babies becoming bigger?', *Journal of the Royal Society of Medicine,* 84, pp.257-260

Anderson, H.R. and Strachan, D.P. (1991) 'Asthma mortality in England and Wales, 1979-89', *British Medical Journal,* 337, p.1357

Bone, M. and Meltzer, H. (1989) *The Prevalence of Disability Among Children.* OPCS Surveys of Disability in Great Britain, Report 3. London: HMSO

Bowling, A. (1992) *Local Voices in Purchasing Health Care. An Exploratory Exercise in Public Consultation in Priority Setting.* London: St Bartholomew's Hospital Medical College

Boyle, M.H., Torrance, G.W., Sinclair, J.C. and Horwood, S.P. (1983) 'Economic evaluation of neonatal intensive care for very-low-birthweight infants', *New England Journal of Medicine,* 308, pp.1330-1337

Butler, N.R. and Golding, J. (1986) *From Birth to Five*. Oxford: Pergamon Press

Carstairs, V. and Morris, R. (1991) *Deprivation and Health in Scotland*. Aberdeen: Aberdeen University Press

Central Statistical Office. *Social Trends* (annual). London: HMSO

Common Services Agency (1992) *Hospital Statistics, Scotland 1991*. Edinburgh: SHH

Cooper, J. and Botting, B. (1992) 'Analysing fertility and infant mortality by mother's social class as defined by occupation', *Population Trends*, 70, pp.15-21

Court, D. and Alberman, E. (1988) 'Worlds apart' in Forfar, J. (ed.) *Child Health in a Changing Society*. London: British Paediatric Associati

Davey Smith, G., Bartley, M. and Blane, D. (1990) 'The Black Report on socioeconomic inequalities in health 10 years on', *British Medical Journal*, 301, pp.373-377

Department of Health (1992) *Personal Social Services: Local Authority Statistics. Children in Care of Local Authorities, Year Ending 31 March 1991, England (Provisional)*. London: DH

Department of Health and Social Security (1980) *Inequalities in Health: Report of a Research Working Group (The Black Report)*. London: DHS

Department of Health Statistical Bulletins. *NHS Hospital Activity Statistics for England*. DH, London

Department of Social Security (1990) *Households Below Average Income: A Statistical Analysis 1981-87*. London: HMSO

Department of Social Security (1991) *Social Security Statistics 1990*. London: HMSO

Drennan, V. and Stearn, J. (1986) 'Health visitors and homeless families', *Health Visitor,* 59, pp.340-342

Health Visitors Association & British Medical Association (1989) *Homeless Families and Their Health*. London: BMA

Henderson, J., Goldacre, M.J., Fairweather, J.M. and Marcovitch, H. (1992) 'Conditions accounting for substantial time spent in hospital in children aged 1-14 years', *Archives of Disease in Childhood*, 67, pp.83-86

House of Commons Social Services Committee (1990) *Households Below Average Income: A Regional Analysis 1980-85*. London: HMSO

Martin, J., Meltzer, H. and Eliot, D. (1988) *The Prevalence of Disability Among Adults*. OPCS Surveys of Disability in Great Britain, Report 1. London: HMSO

Mugford, M. (1988) 'A review of the economics of care for sick newborn infants', *Community Medicine*, 10(2), pp.99-111

Nabarro, J.D.N. (1988) 'Diabetes in the UK: some facts and figures', *Diabetic Medicine*, 5, pp.816-822

National Children's Home (1992) *The NCH Factfile - Children in Britain 1992*. London: NCH

Office of Population Censuses & Surveys, Series DH1. *Mortality Statistics: Surveillance (Time-Trends)*. London: HMSO

Office of Population Censuses & Surveys, Series DH2. *Mortality Statistics: Cause*. London: HMSO

Office of Population Censuses & Surveys, Series DH3. *Mortality Statistics: Perinatal and Infant*. London: HMSO

Office of Population Censuses & Surveys, Series DH6. *Mortality Statistics: Childhood*. London: HMSO

Office of Population Censuses & Surveys, Series DS No 8. *Occupational Mortality*. London: HMSO

Office of Population Censuses & Surveys, Series GHS. *General Household Survey*. London: HMSO

Office of Population Censuses & Surveys, Series MB3. *Congenital Malformation Statistics*. London: HMSO

Oppenheim, C. (1990) *Poverty: The Facts*. London: Child Poverty Action Group

Oxford Region Register of Early Childhood Impairments. Annual Report for 1991 (1992)

Pharoah, P., Cooke, T., Cooke, R. and Rosenbloom, L. (1990) 'Birthweight-specific trends in cerebral palsy', *Archives of Disease in Childhood*, 65, pp.602-606

Registrar General for Northern Ireland. *Annual Reports*

Registrar General for Scotland. *Annual Reports*

Secretary of State for Health (1992) *The Health of the Nation: A Strategy for Health in England*. London: HMSO

Smyth, M. and Robus, N. (1989) *The Financial Circumstances of Families with Disabled Children Living in Private Households*. OPCS Surveys of Disability in Great Britain, Report 5. London: HMSO

Stearn, J. (1986) 'An expensive way of making children ill', *Roof*, October, pp.11-14

Strachan, D.P. and Anderson, H.R. (1992) 'Trends in hospital admission for asthma in children', *British Medical Journal*, 304, pp.819-820

Thomas, A. and Niner, P. (1989) *Living in Temporary Accommodation: A Survey of Homeless People.* London: HMSO

Wigfield, R.E., Fleming, P.J., Berry, P.J., Rudd, P.T. and Golding, J. (1992) 'Can the fall in Avon's sudden infant death rate be explained by changes in sleeping position?', *British Medical Journal*, 304, pp.282-283

Wilson, T. and Jenkins, S. (1985) *The Health of Homeless Families.* London: Meeting of Community Paediatric Research Group

Woodroffe, C., Glickman, M., Barker, M. and Power, C. (1993) *Children, Teenagers and Health: the Key Data.* Milton Keynes: Open University. In press

World Health Organisation Regional Office for Europe (1992) *Health For All Indicators Eurostat/PC.* Copenhagen: WHO

World Health Organisation Regional Office for Europe (1985) *Targets for Health for All.* Copenhagen: WHO

12. The care of children in hospital

Peg Belson, Vice-Chair, Action for Sick Children

Over the past three decades in Britain the care of children in hospital has been transformed. Thirty years ago children used to face long, lonely admissions to hospital. They were passed over like a parcel, usually to a nurse at the reception desk. They would be visited infrequently or not at all and collected days or even weeks later, physically recovered but sometimes emotionally harmed. Today most children's wards are welcoming, caring and family centred. Many parents have been enabled to participate fully in their children's care, to sleep beside them, to be with them when they go to the operating theatre, to be there to comfort and support them when they 'come round' again, to make them feel secure and safe in this strange place.

Many of these changes have resulted from the work in the previous decade of James Robertson (1952; 1953; 1958) at the Tavistock Institute of Human Relations, the publication in 1959 of the Platt Report *The Welfare of Children in Hospital* and the establishing in 1961 of the National Association for the Welfare of Children in Hospital, now Action for Sick Children. In the fifties a child in hospital might see his parents once a week, once a month or not at all. Indeed it was generally believed that parents of sick children should be restrained as much as possible from visiting. They might bring infection into the ward and their visits 'evidently upset the children', who, left to themselves, 'would soon settle down and forget about home'.

There were a small number of exceptions to this pattern (Robertson, 1962, pp.27-45). It was from these and from the work, done from 1948 onwards, at the Tavistock Institute of Human Relations on maternal deprivation and separation anxiety that a gradual rethinking came about regarding the role of the parents, especially the mother, in the care of the sick child. James Robertson's contrasting documentary films *A Two Year Old Goes to Hospital* released in 1953 and *Going to Hospital with Mother* in 1958 clearly demonstrated that the greatest single cause of distress for the young child is not illness or pain but separation from mother.

The Platt Report

The 1952 Ministry of Health annual report recorded that only 23 per cent of hospitals admitting children allowed daily visits, while 11 per cent prohibited all visiting. By 1954, the proportion with daily visiting had risen to 65 per cent, but these visits rarely lasted more than one hour. By 1956 sufficient concern about the need for change in the care of sick children had been aroused to cause the Department of Health to set up a committee to 'make a special study of the arrangements made in hospitals for the welfare of ill children as distinct from their medical and nursing treatment and to make suggestions which could be passed on to hospital authorities'. This committee's report, *The Welfare of Children in Hospital*, published in 1959 and known as the Platt Report, was prefaced by a general statement recognising the role of parents and the significance of the emotional and mental needs of children in hospital (DHSS, 1959). It made 55 important recommendations for change, including the following:

- children should not be admitted to hospital if it can possibly be avoided;
- children and adolescents should not be nursed on adult wards;
- a children's physician should have a general concern with the care of all children in hospital;
- mothers should be admitted with their children, especially if the child is under five and during the first few days in hospital;
- a child in hospital must be visited frequently to preserve the continuity of his life;
- parents should be allowed to visit whenever they can and to help as much as possible with the care of the child;
- the training of doctors and nurses should include a greater understanding of the emotional and social needs of children and their families.

Opposition to change

These recommendations were passed to the hospitals but the health service itself could not enforce these policies and consequently there was little change nor indeed any appreciation of the need for change. A correspondent in a medical journal could confidently state:

...the great majority of hospitals seemed oblivious to the enormous amount of suffering put upon children and their parents by rules which break important relationships necessary for the maintenance of good mental health.

The truth of this statement could be seen from a study made during the Nuffield Foundation's appraisal of the use of existing accommodation for children in hospital (Duncum, 1963, pp.63-64). A survey of the support of members of the British Paediatric Association (BPA) and the Association of British Paediatric Nurses (ABPN) towards the admission of mothers gave the following results:

Table 1

	BPA %	BPA (n)	ABPN %	ABPN (n)
Generally in favour of admitting the mother with any child	15	(25)	11	(54)
Generally in favour of admitting the mother of any young child, particularly a toddler	42	(62)	27	(138)
Only in exceptional circumstances	24	(68)	16	(81)
Only for established reasons: breastfeeding, critically ill or dying child, or to learn management	10	(17)	21	(106)
Opposed in any circumstances	5	(8)	3	(17)
Attitude not clearly stated	4	(5)	22	(109)
Total	100	(162)	100	(505)

Source: Duncum, 1963, p.66

Community action begins

In 1961 extracts from James Robertson's films were shown on television and in a series of newspaper articles he urged community pressure to implement accepted Department of Health policies for children in hospital (Robertson, 1961). Some Battersea mothers took up his challenge and, under his guidance, set up Mother Care for Children in Hospital, later called the National Association for the Welfare of Children in Hospital (NAWCH), now Action for Sick Children. The group visited the few hospitals where unrestricted visiting and accommodation for mothers was the accepted practice. In most other hospitals they found little recognition being given to the recommendations of the Platt Report. From discussions with nursing, medical and administrative staff to discover the reason for this, a number of important factors emerged. It was considered 'natural' for children to cry in hospital: tears had long been accepted as inevitable. It was believed a child soon forgot what happened in hospital: his memory was very short, so no permanent damage could result. Many children, who cried bitterly when first left, settled down and could even become 'quite happy'. They just 'didn't miss their mothers'. Many seemingly good reasons were given for not changing the traditional arrangements. Most hospitals were old with little space to spare. Cross infection might increase. The routine would be disturbed. Mothers would be 'difficult'. Very few mothers asked for longer visiting hours or beds to be with their children. In any case they all had home commitments which would prevent them being in hospital with their children. Many children far from home would be treated unfairly if others had frequent visitors. Since parents had not sought for change, they were unlikely to make use of extra visiting or living in accommodation. Thus the need for change went unrecognised, and the probable effects of change were exaggerated or mistaken (Belson, 1982).

A postal survey by NAWCH of hospitals in South East England in 1962 showed a wide variation, both in the hours of visiting allowed and the interpretation of unrestricted visiting. Most hospitals had less then three hours visiting and very few welcomed parents throughout the day. Two-fifths had less than two hours visiting, some had half an hour a day and some quite famous hospitals had no visiting at all to some categories of child patients. One regional hospital board advised that almost all its hospitals 'had implemented the Ministry circular' yet the hospitals themselves reported visiting only in the afternoons ranging from half an hour to five hours. One interesting feature in some hospitals was that fathers could visit in the evenings 'usually from 6.00 to 6.30pm'. The hospitals gave various meanings to 'unrestricted'. 'It is our aim to have unrestricted visiting but visiting in the morning is not encouraged'. 'Visiting on this ward is unrestricted, but please do not stay longer than half an hour'. 'Visiting on operation day is at Sister's discretion and is discouraged to save parents any unnecessary distress'. 'Most convenient hours are between two and four' (NAWCH, 1962).

In those early days parents' accommodation was rarely available, visiting before or after operations was negligible, sibling visiting hardly ever considered. Play programmes were in their infancy and few hospitals offered any relevant information to parents prior to admission. Publicity in the media, at conferences and seminars, and contacts with other professional and voluntary bodies helped NAWCH to promote the need for family involvement with children in hospital. With branches in many parts of the country, the Association was able to offer advice and support to those parents who were unable to find the hospital care they knew their child needed (Belson, 1981).

The beginning of family centred care

Change was slow to come, but with an increasing number of professional staff in its ranks the Association was finding it possible to work in constructive and cooperative ways with hospitals to acknowledge the common concern of parents and staff regarding what was best for children and families (McCarthy, 1962). Parliamentary questions to the Minister of Health resulted in a clearer definition of terms. By 1964 'unrestricted visiting meant that visitors were allowed into the ward at any reasonable hour during the day, subject to the discretion of the consultant in charge and the ward sister'. In 1956 'reasonable hour' was explained to mean 'during the hours at which children would not normally be put to bed'. In 1966 the position was further clarified in Hospital Memorandum (66)18, which stated that fixed visiting hours were to be abandoned (DHSS, 1966). There should not be any rule restricting visiting before or after operations or of children who had an infectious disease, and any decision to advise the parent not to visit the child on a particular day should be made only by the consultant in charge. Hospital leaflets and notices should make it clear that parents may visit at any time during the day and mothers of young children should be able to stay in hospital with their children. In 1967 the NAWCH Hospital Admission Leaflet was published to alert parents to the need to be with their children in hospital. Distributed by the hospitals themselves, it has remained a best seller ever since. In 1980 a specialist library and information service was set up offering help to parents, staff, students, tutors and researchers, as well as providing the basis for consultations for government.

A comparison of visiting arrangements and parents' accommodation in one health region from 1962-1979 shows the gradual pace of change (Tables 2, 3 and 4).

Table 2

Visiting hours for children's wards in one health region (1962-1979)

| | Total of visiting hours | | | | | Average |
	0-3	4-6	7-9	10-13	24	no. of hours
	%	%	%	%	%	
1962*	55	25	15	5	0	3
1964**	55	22	14	9	0	3.5
1966***	28	27	27	18	0	5.5
1969	10	34	13	42	0	6
1971	0	18	37	40	5	9.5
1973	0	15	33	40	12	11
1975	0	8	22	42	28	12.75
1979	0	7	10	19	64	18.5

*   42% less than 2 hours
**   18% less than 2 hours. 9% less than half hour.
*** 10% less than half hour.   37% less than 2 hours.

Source: Peg Belson, 1979 Association for the Care of Children's Health Conference, Los Angeles.

Table 3

Visiting on day of operation 1966-1979

	%
1966	44
1969	52
1971	54
1973	57
1975	70
1979	84

Source: Peg Belson, 1979 Association for the Care of Children's Health Conference, Los Angeles.

Table 4

Parents' accommodation 1962-1979

	%
1962	(2 hospitals only)
1966	14
1969	24
1971	25
1973	52
1975	50
1979	83

Source: Peg Belson, 1979 Association for the Care of Children's Health Conference, Los Angeles.

By the early eighties NAWCH could report, from its survey of access and facilities for families, that throughout England, more than three-quarters of the wards could offer some accommodation for parents and almost half had unrestricted visiting throughout the day and night though there were considerable variations between regions (Thornes, 1983).

Since then there has been a steady but patchy improvement. In some wards there are not enough beds for all the parents who would like to stay; in others there are the beds but staff do not encourage their use. Paediatric staff have fully accepted the need for children in hospital to be accompanied by a parent and welcome them as members of the caring team, but there is still a need to improve the training of other nurses and doctors in the basics of child development and parent-child relationships. The recent study of hospital services for children by the Audit Commission in 1992 showed that there were still serious deficiencies in the provision of accommodation for parents (Audit Commission, 1993).

Comprehensive children's units and integrated child health care

The Department of Health has been active in promoting change for the care of children in hospital. The publication of the Platt Report and the welcome ministerial statements on appropriate arrangements have already been noted. In 1971 the Department issued HM(71)22 *Hospital Facilities for Children*. Besides reiterating the recommendations of the Platt Report, this important memorandum asked Regional Hospital Boards to review their services for children to secure their location within a comprehensive children's department, a concept first referred to in the Platt Report. It detailed the requirements of such a department as part of a District General Hospital, under the supervision of a consultant paediatrician and with a registered sick children's nurse (RSCN) in charge of every children's ward. The value of play and education in hospital was recognised. Separate provision for children in outpatients and accident and emergency departments was advocated, as was an extension of day care and day surgery to reduce the necessity to admit children to hospital. The need for separate and appropriate accommodation for adolescents either within or closely associated with the children's department was promoted. For the first time overnight accommodation for fathers would be offered! (DHSS, 1971).

There was reference to what would later come to be known as an integrated child health service. 'Modern child health care requires a service with closely related community and hospital elements'. Recognition of the child as part of his family was yet to come, but HM(71)22 did emphasise the need 'to provide for the child as a whole and not just for the condition for which he requires treatment'. It recognised 'the emotional vulnerability of the young child and the effect which early experiences may have on his later development' and stressed the importance of children being nursed by those with requisite experience and skills. For the first time 'visiting was seen as a preventive and a therapeutic measure and not simply as a social exercise'. In the 22 years since this memorandum was issued, some of its recommendations have been followed, but regrettably not all. The Court Report in 1976 gave further emphasis to the need for a child and family centred service, in which skilled help is available and accessible, which is integrated in as much as it sees the child as a whole and as a continuously developing person and which ensures that paediatric skill and knowledge is applied in the care of every child, whatever his age or disability or wherever he lives. But Court was also to say that 'most children's ward are without a trained children's nurse for some of the time, many are without for much of the time and some at all times' (DHSS, 1976a). In 1991 the Department of Health's Guidelines for the *Welfare of Children and Young People in Hospital* gave as a minimum, 'Two Registered Sick Children's Nurses (RSCNs) on duty 24 hours a day in all hospital children's departments and wards' and a 'RSCN on duty 24 hours a day to advise on the nursing of children in other departments'. In its 1993 study the Audit Commission noted that 'despite having RSCN's on their establishment many wards are at times during the day staffed with only one RSCN or occasionally none at all, with the situation at night being even worse'.

Separate provision for children and adolescents

Despite frequent Department reminders since 1959 against such a practice many children aged 0 to 16 are still being nursed on adult wards. In 1984, the last year for which detailed figures are available, 10 per cent of children aged 0 to 4, 22 per cent aged 5-11 and 62 per cent aged 12 to 16 were in 'wards not designated for children', a total of 26 per cent of all children in hospital (*Caring for Children in the Health Service*, 1987). There has been very little recognition of the need for separate provision for adolescents. In 1985, the BPA report on adolescent care demonstrated that a health district could fully use an adolescent unit of 15 beds. The Audit Commission Report (1993) suggests that the average daily number of adolescents in hospital could be as high as 16. The numbers admitted under paediatricians are increasing as survival rates for adolescents with chronic illness continue to improve and there are already a large number admitted under the care of surgeons. Separate provision for children in outpatient and accident and emergency departments has been very difficult to achieve. There are a number of paediatric accident and emergency departments in children's hospitals, and a few in district general hospitals (Evans, 1988). Some accident and emergency departments have been able to provide a separate waiting area for children but few have as yet made provision for the specialised paediatric medical and nursing care recommended in HM(71)22 and reiterated in the *Welfare of Children and Young People in Hospital* (DH, 1991). Separate provision for outpatient care of children other than for paediatric services is rare. Even when a separate outpatient facility for children is provided, some specialists will only see children in their own departments.

Play in hospital

Independent, personal observation during the early sixties of the aimlessness of children in hospital by Dr David Morris, then consultant paediatrician at the Brook Hospital, and Susan Harvey, an adviser to Save the Children (SCF) community playgroups, led to the setting up in 1963 of the first SCF hospital play scheme in the Brook Hospital. The paid part-time worker was provided with advisory support from a professional in her own specialised field and was clearly identifiable as distinct from the medical and nursing staff. Further play schemes quickly followed and by 1978 Save the Children had play staff in 26 hospitals (SCF, 1989). Some health authorities were setting up their own hospital play schemes. From the late sixties many NAWCH branches established and supported ward play schemes most of which were handed over to the health authorities. The Pre-school Playgroups Association also established play schemes in hospital and in 1971 Charlotte Williamson of PPA and Peg Belson of NAWCH set up the first coordinating body for this work, the Play in Hospital Liaison Committee. In 1972 the Department of Health set up an Expert Group on Play for Children in Hospital. The Report of this Group recognised the importance of play for children in hospital, recommended that 'hospitals should employ play workers to meet children's needs' and that 'play workers should be a separately managed group within the hospital service' (DHSS, 1976).

These recommendations were not fully accepted by the Department, but play schemes continued to be set up, now more usually staffed by trained hospital play specialists, who had completed the training courses available from 1973. Play provision in hospital is now fully supported by the Department of Health, and its value was recognised in the *Guidelines for the Welfare of Children in Hospital*. In 1992 the NHS Management Executive recommended that all hospitals should employ play specialists and that they should be a separately defined occupational group.

Research findings and practical experience support the case for play in hospital provided by an appropriately trained play specialist working as an integral member of the paediatric team (Gaynard, 1990). However there are still many hospital wards without play staff. A survey in 1985, by the Play in Hospital Liaison Committee and Save the Children, found enormous regional variations in provision. Overall only 37 per cent of wards had salaried play workers (Belson, 1988). Besides providing a focus for play on the ward, the play specialist has a major role to play in another area of change for the child in hospital. It is now fully accepted that preparation both for admission to hospital and for the procedures the child will then experience can reduce the trauma experienced by the child in hospital. Play specialists have a particular role in helping to prepare children for these experiences. Some hospitals have been able to institute a home visiting programme to prepare children for complicated clinical procedures, for example renal transplants and bone marrow transplants (Wilson, 1992).

Welcome changes in patient care

Another significant change since the sixties for the child in hospital is undoubtedly the length of stay. Nowadays the majority of children on paediatric medical wards seldom stay more than one night, very few stay longer than one week. There are more admissions every year, at least 50 per cent more than in 1960, but because of the way statistics are collected it is not possible to determine how many of these are re-admissions. Many more children are now treated as day patients, both for medical and surgical procedures (Hill, 1989). The welcome extension in home care services with paediatric community nurses, available at the last count in almost one third of the health districts, has enabled many sick children to be cared for in their own homes, or to be discharged far earlier from hospital (Whiting, 1989).

Travel costs

One area of care for families with a child in hospital which has seen no change over the past 30 years is the assistance many families need with the cost of visiting a child in hospital. Like many other humane improvements this was first recommended by Platt. *The Welfare of Children and Young People in Hospital* (DH, 1991) gives as 'a cardinal principle of hospital services for children, complete ease of access by his or her parent'. Although access to children in hospital has clearly improved through the years, travel problems have continued and with rising costs the situation for families is even bleaker. Recent research carried out by Action for Sick Children shows that many families suffer severe financial hardship as a result of visiting costs. Six per cent went into debt and 12 per cent had nothing left at the end of the week to cover existing costs. One family's costs were £245 per week and several lived over 100 miles from their child's hospital. This is a situation which clearly requires a remedy, with funding provided to enable hospitals to directly reimburse parents at point of need. 'Sick children must be visited according to their emotional needs and not their parents' ability to pay' (Shelley, 1992).

Specifications and contracts

The changes in service provision brought about by the NHS Act could provide the basis for improvement in services for children in hospital if the contract specifications now called for demand the best practice from all units, and commissioners ensure these demands are met. The NAWCH Charter for Children in Hospital, published in 1985, gained endorsement from the Department of Health, the British Medical Association, the British Paediatric Association, the Royal College of Nursing, the National Association of Health Authorities and almost all the many other voluntary and professional organisations involved with children (see Figure 1 on p.215). Many health authorities incorporated the Charter's principles in their first specifications for children's services. In 1989 the Charter was translated into standards to assess the quality of health care for children and published as the

Figure 1

The NAWCH Charter

1

Children shall be admitted to hospital only if the care they require cannot be equally provided at home or on a day basis.

2

Children in hospital shall have the right to have their parents with them at all times provided this is in the best interests of the child. Accommodation should therefore be offered to all parents, and they should be helped and encouraged to stay. In order to share in the care of their child, parents should be fully informed about ward routine and their active participation encouraged.

3

Children and their parents shall have the right to information appropriate to their age and understanding.

4

Children and their parents shall have the right to informed participation in all decisions involving their health care. Every child shall be protected from unnecessary medical treatment, and steps taken to mitigate physical and emotional distress.

5

Children shall be treated with tact and understanding and at all times their privacy shall be respected.

6

Children shall enjoy the care of appropriately trained staff, fully aware of the physical and emotional needs of each age group.

7

Children shall be able to wear their own clothes and have their own personal possessions.

8

Children shall be cared for with other children of the same age group.

9

Children shall be in an environment furnished and equipped to meet their requirements, and which conforms to recognised standards of safety and supervision.

NAWCH Quality Review: Setting Standards for Children in Health Care. This review has been extensively used by health authorities to plan and monitor their services for children. Four other quality review documents followed, setting standards for play in hospital (Hogg, 1990), adolescent services (Action for Sick Children, 1990), mental health care (Action for Sick Children, 1992) and services for Black and minority ethnic children (Action for Sick Children, 1993).

These each list high quality standards and have been recommended by the Department of Health to health authorities to use in developing contract specifications. But to monitor the services being provided, authorities need specific information as well as the right of access to the services to carry out the monitoring process. It would clearly not be possible to specify every detail of care, but authorities do need to ensure that each provider unit has a written policy of care for sick children that follows the principles set out in the Department of Health's guidelines and further detailed in the *Quality Reviews* from Action for Sick Children. At least one purchasing authority has appointed a commissioner with the specific remit to purchase services for children. Some provider units have been able to develop management structures which incorporate all services for children within an integrated system, though as yet with only limited involvement of the general practitioners.

Areas of current concern

Hospital services for children have seen enormous changes over the past thirty years but many areas of concern remain. Children are said still to be inappropriately admitted to hospital, possibly in some cases because they are not seen by paediatric staff. The interface between the hospital and the community services fails to meet the needs of families, whether during admission to hospital or at discharge. There are still areas of disintegration between the services families require to fulfil their total needs, particularly if they have a child with a chronic illness or disability. In such circumstances they may require continuing or episodic care from health services (primary, secondary, tertiary), social services for support, educational services to meet possible educational needs, social security for travel costs and perhaps even the housing authority *(Caring for Children in the Health Services,* 1993).

With the current cost containment required of local education authorities many hospital school services have been considerably reduced, to the detriment of care for sick children especially those with lengthy or repeated admissions. Very few hospitals fully meet the needs of families from Black and minority ethnic families for health care. Few unaccompanied children have the continuing care of one concerned staff member, now recognised as essential to their continued emotional well-being (Jolly, 1981; NAWCH, 1988).

Far too many children and adolescents are still being cared for in adult wards. Surgery is still used as an excuse to limit parental visiting and many parents cannot accompany their child to the anaesthetic room. Adolescent wards are only rarely to be found. Parents can now help to support their children in many hospital wards but few hospitals can offer the support and counselling the parents may need in this unusual and disturbing situation.

Paediatricians and paediatric nurses

Probably the most important change for the care of sick children has been the recognition of paediatrics as an important part of medicine. Paediatricians have trebled in number since the sixties and their influence has extended. There are now paediatricians in every district general hospital where they act as lively advocates for children and families. They have seen their role as spreading good practice for the care of sick children throughout the hospital. They have been effective in influencing government and hospital administration as to the appropriate care of sick children. The care of babies has moved from obstetrics to paediatrics and there are now few areas of child health care where their influence is not being applied. They still have a major part to play to influence and affect care in accident and emergency, in X-ray and in theatres. They look to the time when the care of all sick children is given in comprehensive children's departments with ongoing effective links to the primary and community services, providing the continuity of care within an integrated service promoted in so many reports and government circulars (British Paediatric Association, 1991).

Although many wards still lack sufficient paediatric trained nurses, much credit for the improvement in service provision for sick children must also go to the registered sick children's nurses (RSCNs), whether working on the wards or involved in nursing management and nurse training. Of equal value have been the many high quality articles they have contributed to both the general and the specialised nursing press.

The role of the Department of Health

From the Department of Health has come much careful thought and activity epitomised in the *Welfare of Children and Young People in Hospital*:

We now have far greater knowledge of how children develop both emotionally and physically. With that understanding has come an awareness of the emotional vulnerability of the young child and the effect which early experience can have on later development. This has influenced how we should care for the sick child. A good quality service for children should provide for the child as a whole, for his or her complete physical and emotional well-being and not simply for the condition for which care is required. It must be child and family centred with children, their siblings and their parents or carers experiencing a 'seamless web' of care, treatment and support as they move through the constituent parts of the National Health Service (DoH, 1991).

This leadership role, with its clear understanding of the unique qualities of children should help to keep the needs of sick children at the top of the agenda. A child is no longer a small adult in a smaller sized bed!

References
Action for Sick Children (1984) *The NAWCH Charter*
Action for Sick Children (1989) *NAWCH Quality Review: Setting Standards for Children in Health Care*
Action for Sick Children (1990) *Setting Standards for Adolescents in Hospital.*
Action for Sick Children (1992) *With Health in Mind*
Action for Sick Children (1993) *Health for All Our Children*
Audit Commission (1993) *Children First*. HMSO

Belson, P. (1981) 'Parents' advocacy for parents' in *The Family in Child Health Care*. Wiley

Belson, P. (1988) in *A Policy for Play*. Play in Hospital Liaison Committee

British Paediatric Association (1985) *The Needs and Cares of Adolescents*, p.4

British Paediatric Association (1991) *Towards a Combined Child Health Service*

Caring for Children in the Health Services (1987) *Where Are the Children?* Action for Sick Children

Caring for Children in the Health Services (1993) *Bridging the Gap*. Action for Sick Children

DHSS (1959) *The Welfare of Children in Hospital: The Platt Report*. HMSO

DHSS (1966) *Visiting of Children in Hospital*. HM(66)18 HMSO

DHSS (1972) *Hospital Facilities for Children*. HM(71)22 HMSO

DHSS (1976a) *Fit for the Future: The Court Report*. HMSO

DHSS (1976b) *The Report of the Expert Group in Play in Hospital*. HMSO

Department of Health (1991) *The Welfare of Children and Young People in Hospital*. HMSO

Duncum, B.M. (ed) (1963) *Children in Hospital: Studies in Planning*. The Nuffield Foundation, pp.63-64

Evans, R. (1988) 'Somewhere for the children', *Nursing Times*, 84(22)

Gaynard, L. (1990) *Psychosocial Care of Children in Hospital*. Washington, USA: Association for the Care of Children's Health, pp.115-128

Hill, A.M. (1989) 'Trends in paediatric medical admissions', *British Medical Journal*, 298, pp.1479-83

Hogg, C. (1990) *Quality Management for Children: Play in Hospital*. Play in Hospital Liaison Committee

Jolly, J. (1981) *The Other Side of Paediatrics*. Macmillan

MacCarthy, D. (1962) 'Children in hospital with mothers', *The Lancet*, March 24, pp.603-608

Ministry of Health (1953) *Report for the Year Ended 31st December, 1952*. HMSO, pp.23-24

Ministry of Health (1955) *Report for the Year Ended 31st December, 1954*. HMSO, pp.26-27

National Association for the Welfare of Children in Hospital 91962) *Survey in Visiting* (internal report)

National Association for the Welfare of Children in Hospital (1967 and 4 reprints) *Coming into Hospital: Hospital Admission Leaflet*

National Association for the Welfare of Children in Hospital (1987) *The Child Alone*

Robertson, J. (1952) (film) *A Two Year Old Goes to Hospital*. Tavistock Institute of Human Relations

Robertson, J. (1953) 'Some responses of young children to loss of maternal care', *Nursing Times*, April, pp.382-6

Robertson, J. (1958a) (film) *Going to Hospital with Mother*. Tavistock Institute of Human Relations

Robertson, J. (1958b) *Young Children in Hospital*. Tavistock Publications

Robertson, J. (1961) in *The Observer,* 15, 22, 29 January 1961 and 12 February 1961

Robertson, J. (1962) *Hospitals and Children - A Parent's Eye View*. Gallanz, P

Save the Children Fund (1989) *Hospital: A Deprived Environment for Children? The Case for Hospital Play Schemes*

Shelley, P. (1992) 'Too dear to visit', *Paediatric Nursing*, 4(10)

Thornes, R. (1983) 'Parental access and family facilities in children's wards in England', *British Medical Journal*, 287, 10 July

Whiting, M. (1989) *Community Paediatric Nursing - A Research Report*

Wilson, L. (1992) 'The home visiting programme', *Paediatric Nursing*, July

13. From prevention to partnership: child welfare services across three decades

Jean Packman, Dartington Social Research Unit

Prevention

The National Bureau for Co-operation in Child Care (later to be renamed the National Children's Bureau) was launched at a critical and highly significant stage in the development of public welfare services for children. In 1963, the year of its birth, local authority children's departments were already fifteen years old. As such they shared many of the characteristics of most adolescents - idealistic, acutely critical of both their ancestors and contemporary establishment figures (especially medical ones); optimistic and pushy about their own capacities to do good and ambitious to do more.

One such ambition was to break out of the somewhat narrow confines of their originating legislation - the Children Act, 1948 - which had been concerned with the primary task of laying the Poor Law ghost by raising standards for children who came into local authority care. By the sixties the childcare service had made considerable headway in this regard. With a partially trained and largely enthusiastic staff, the psychological needs of children in care were receiving much more careful attention that in the past and there was a marked shift away from institutional resources towards foster care and the ordinary family life it was presumed to provide. By 1960 the proportion fostered had risen from a third to a half of all children in care and most children's homes had been reduced in size and improved in quality. But within at least some parts of the new service there was a strong desire to go beyond this; to reach out to the families from which the children came in order to forestall or prevent the disruptions and deprivations which had led to their coming into care in the first place. Some departments had endeavoured to undertake such preventive work from the beginning, but they were constrained by lack of legal sanction and accompanying funds and frustrated by the difficulties of coordinating their efforts with other crucial agencies like health, education, income maintenance, housing and numerous voluntary organisations for childcare and family welfare. Coordinating machinery, to facilitate such cooperation, had been set up in the fifties, often convened and chaired by the children's officers who headed the childcare service. But a clear statutory duty to assist families before they broke down was lacking, and departments were boxed in by their own narrow specialisms.

The Children and Young Persons Act of 1963 took the first step in the desired direction, albeit a small and timid one. Its first clause laid a duty on every *local authority* (not just the children's departments) to:

...make available such advice, guidance and assistance as may promote the welfare of children by diminishing the need to receive children into or keep them in care ... or to bring children before a juvenile court.

Thus, in statute, prevention was firmly linked to the avoidance of children coming into public care (or before the courts) and it lacked the more expansive, promotional tone of the Ingleby Report (Home Office, 1960) on which it was based. Ingleby had asserted:

Everything within reason must be done to ensure not only that children are not neglected but that they get the best upbringing possible ... It is the duty of the community to provide through its social and welfare services the advice and support which such parents and children need (Home Office, 1960, para.8).

By comparison the legislation was cautious, but in practice something of Ingleby's positive approach survived and it had a profound effect upon the scale and direction of local authority childcare services, which became involved in an enormous range of preventive activity, tilting the balance of their work in new directions. By 1967, for example, more than three times as many children were being assisted directly or indirectly through section 1 of the Children and Young Persons Act, as were admitted to local authority care.

Preventive work also involved much greater cooperation (and sometimes conflict) with other agencies - in fact, exactly the kind of issues that the Bureau was set up to address. Attempts were made to clear rent arrears, avoid evictions, and, in line with the restrictiveness of the statute, even to give money and goods to families living in poverty - but only 'in exceptional circumstances'. This inevitably drew the childcare service into closer, though not always harmonious relationships with other public bodies - housing, health departments, the National Assistance Board, the probation service and the courts, for example. By breaking through the narrow confines of its initial concern for the small, but highly vulnerable group of children in public care the service was taking a much wider view of its responsibilities to children and their families. Its awareness of the extent of deprivation was heightened, and it was entering a larger and more complex arena of operation and negotiation than it had occupied hitherto.

Part of this wider arena contained the delinquent child or young person - a fresh target for the childcare services' concern. The Ingleby Committee's original brief had concerned delinquency and the juvenile court system and the requirement to focus on prevention had been added, almost as an afterthought. But the subsequent report had reinforced the link, making strong connections between prevention and offending, by asserting that:

If children are to be prevented from becoming delinquent, and if those in trouble are to get the help they need, something more positive is required ... It is the duty of the community to provide through its social and welfare services the advice and support which such parents and children need (Home Office, 1960, para.8).

Amongst other adjustments to the juvenile justice system, it proposed that the age of criminal responsibility be raised by stages to fourteen years, which would have de-criminalised most schoolchildren of that era. In the event the 1963 Act only lifted the threshold from an archaic eight years to ten years, where it has remained ever since.

But enthusiasm for rescuing young offenders from aspects of the criminal justice system was already evident at local authority level.

By the early sixties some pioneers in the childcare service were busily promoting policies based on the assumption that delinquent youngsters were generally victims of neglect or troubled family circumstances. In consequence they should be treated in ways similar to those used for other deprived children. Juvenile court magistrates and their clerks, along with police and probation officers were persuaded that, if offenders needed to be removed from home, admission to care would be a more positive response than consigning them to approved schools or detention centres.

The Labour Party was also travelling along a similar route. After a long period in opposition it was re-furbishing its policies in preparation for the possibility of power. Lord Longford's working party report 'Crime - a challenge to us all', a large part of which was devoted to juvenile delinquency, was published in 1964 (Labour Party, 1984). Here the argument was twofold. Breaking the rules was part of the normal process of growing up and, as such, should not be amplified by the stigma of criminality and the processes and disposals of the formal justice system. On the other hand, it was presumed that youngsters whose waywardness was persistent or serious were likely to be the victims of troubled or deprived family and social circumstances for which punitive sanctions were not the answer. For them, panels of professional experts and concerned laymen and women should replace the courts and, with less formality and without the testing of guilt or innocence they would agree the best means of tackling the offending behaviour with the youngsters and their families. Treatment and care were to be the preferred options.

In the event, and despite the success of the Labour Party in the elections which followed, the road to the decriminalisation of young offenders and their incorporation into the services for their deprived brethren proved stony and full of pitfalls. The 'childcare' view was hotly contested by other opinions and interest groups: police, magistrates, much of the probation service, sociologists of deviance, lawyers and (often one and the same) Conservative MPs in opposition. Original legislative plans had to be severely amended and the Children and Young Persons Act itself was not passed until 1969, nor implemented before the Labour government fell. In the words of Harris and Webb:

(T)he result was compromise: the second White Paper compromised the first; the legislation compromised the second; and the implemented legislation further compromised the Act in its pristine form (Harris and Webb, 1987, p.27).

Nevertheless, by encouraging diversion from the courts, incorporating the old approved schools into the childcare system and offering 'care' to delinquents, it attempted to blur distinctions between the deprived and the depraved. It also assumed that delinquents should be viewed and responded to within their family context and, like prevention, its success rested on a shared understanding and approach amongst a diverse range of professions and agencies involved. The theme of cooperation in childcare was therefore as important in this sphere as in that of prevention.

A third development of the early sixties was also destined to change the face of childcare, though its significance was less obvious at the time. At the end of 1963, following research and publications in the United States, the first home-grown article on the Battered Baby Syndrome appeared in the British Medical Journal (Griffiths and Moynihan, 1963). As Nigel Parton (1985) demonstrates, it was perhaps the first signal that the low-key, post-war perception of and approach to neglect and cruelty to children was about to change. The childcare service already shared responsibility with the NSPCC for investigating and acting in such cases, but they represented a relatively small proportion of its caseload. Also, in reaction against what were seen as the heavy-handed interventions of the pre-war period, intensive preventive work with 'problem families' was a popular approach and 'neglect' rather than 'abuse' was the term most commonly in use. One of the earliest research studies into the working of the new service was, in fact, entitled *The Neglected Child and his Family* (Donnison, 1954).

In contrast, the term 'battered babies' had a much more dramatic and sinister ring and contributed to a rising professional consciousness of a problem that must be taken more seriously. At this stage it appeared to be the radiologists, paediatricians and the NSPCC who took the keenest interest, though at least one Children's Officer immediately convened a meeting of staff from childcare, medicine, education and the police, to discuss and disseminate information on the new phenomenon (Packman, 1981). Indeed, the need for multidisciplinary dialogue and cooperation was to prove as vital in this sphere of childcare as it was in prevention and in tackling delinquency, though another decade was to pass before child abuse became a matter of overwhelming public as well as professional concern.

Thus the childcare service of the sixties was expanding its operations and reframing its responses in at least three directions: preventive work with families; diversionary and remedial work with offenders; and, to a lesser extent, investigative and rescue work with neglected and abused children. Of these, preventive work was the most prominent, accounting for a large proportion of the overall caseload of children's departments and, in some urban authorities, consuming substantial amounts of cash, as well as manpower hours. Lorraine Fox-Harding sees the decade as 'the high point of the emphasis on prevention and the natural family' - a policy she characterises as 'defence of the birth family and parental rights' (Fox-Harding, 1991, pp.134-148).

It was also a period of heightened self-examination, when established aspects of service began to be examined and tested through research. Three studies of foster care (Trasler, 1960; Parker, 1966; George, 1970) spanned the decade and cast a critical eye over the most cherished caring resource of the service. Its stability and efficacy were challenged by the high breakdown rates revealed, and the dissonance between the views of foster carers and those of social work staff. Such gloomy findings reinforced the trend towards working to keep children within their own families.

Both in its original title and in its aspirations, the National Children's Bureau can therefore be seen as a child of its time. Its broad view of child welfare echoed and amplified expansion in the childcare service. Its emphasis on cooperation between agencies and disciplines mirrored and magnified the trends apparent at local authority level. Furthermore, its commitment to research and the early launch of the National Child Development Study promised an invaluable reference point for those dealing with the most deprived children and families in the community.

Protection

For child welfare services, the seventies were years of even greater change. The conviction that better services could be provided by means of re-organisation - re-drawing boundaries between services, and aiming at a new and more rational division of responsibilities - appeared to be at its height as the new decade began. (Appearances can be deceptive. Organisational change has continued unabated, into the nineties, sometimes imposed from without and sometimes self-inflicted (Challis, 1990). Perhaps it should now be regarded as endemic - a chronic condition without hope of cure).

The Seebohm Committee had reported in 1968, recommending a merger of all the small, specialist local authority personal social services into a comprehensive social services department. The sixties theme, stressing the need for services to cooperate and coordinate their responses to personal problems was carried to its logical conclusion. An emphasis on building and operating from a secure and sophisticated knowledge base was also apparent:

...personal social services are large-scale experiments in ways of helping those in need. It is both wasteful and irresponsible to set experiments in motion and omit to record and analyse what happens... however little intended, it indicates a careless attitude towards human welfare' (Seebohm, 1968, para.455).

Institutions, like the Bureau, which engaged in research were clearly in a position to play an important role in future.

The favoured family focus for operation was accepted by Seebohm, but was expanded to embrace the personal service needs of 'everybody'. A more radical notion of prevention was also proposed, stressing the significance of natural communities as definers of need, potential givers of help and essential goads and critics of statutory services. However, it was mainly the voluntary agencies who carried this ideal into practice, as Bob Holman (1981; 1988) has vividly described. For although many social services departments moved gradually to more patch-based forms of organisation in an attempt to respond to local needs, preventive work in childcare was squeezed and distorted during the ensuing decade. On the one hand the issue of child abuse became top priority, through a series of scandals that began with Maria Colwell's death in 1973. On the other, a combination of disillusionment with the parenting record of corporate bodies like social services departments and an increased sensitivity to the benefits of continuity for a child's development cast prevention in a stubbornly defensive mould.

The emergence of child abuse as a prominent social problem of the seventies and eighties is well analysed by Parton (1985). Whether or not its incidence has escalated over this period is unproven, but there is no doubt of the increased awareness of, and anxiety about the phenomenon, amongst both professionals and the public. Sins of professional commission and omission which contributed to failure to protect children stoked anxiety about the workers' lack of skills and attracted public censure. Scandals also contributed to a steady increase in the use of compulsory measures as social workers chose to 'play safe', in order to protect children at risk. Place of Safety Orders were the most telling example, increasing more than threefold within the space of four years. A rarely used emergency measure was transformed into a standard way of removing children from their homes and, by the end of the seventies, at least a quarter of all children entering local authority care were doing so in this dramatic and potentially damaging way (Packman and others, 1985).

The use of voluntary care, with a prepared entry and parental agreement, declined proportionately as court orders and compulsion grew and childcare workers were more often seen as interveners than enablers in family life. Concern with continuity for children in care and the pursuit of 'permanence' compounded this trend in Britain. By concentrating more on achieving permanent substitute placements for children, through adoption and long-term fostering, at the expense of supporting natural families in providing a stable home, social services departments were often cast as antagonists rather than protagonists of the children's birth families. In addition, the time available for the lower key often long-term preventive work with families was squeezed by the immediate demands of the machinery of child protection, involving joint investigations, urgent action, multidisciplinary case conferences and the like.

Disillusion with the benefits of local authority care further affected prevention. A pervading pessimism about the quality of the care experience for most children was evident by the late seventies. The Bureau itself set up an influential working party at this time to consider means of improving standards for children in public care (Parker, 1980). Experience and an increasing body of research noted persistent foster breakdowns, poor quality residential care, grim prognoses for youngsters leaving care and the widely perceived stigma of the care system itself. The pioneering optimism with which the post-war childcare service had started out was, by now, severely dampened.

A jaundiced view of the childcare system was also fuelled by the complaints and criticisms of its users. To oversimplify, the welfare services of the immediate post-war years were characterised by benevolent maternalism, even when they were aiming at family support. (There was an emphasis on care and nurture and the vast majority of the workforce was female!) A shared, participative style of work, which would now be called 'partnership' was only fitfully applied and professionals were more usually champions of the deprived, rather than their collaborators.

A significant development of the seventies was the rise of pressure groups on behalf of children and families involved in the welfare system. Organisations such as the Family Rights Group, The Voice of the Child in Care, the Children's Legal Centre and the National Association of Young People in Care (NAYPIC) all introduced new perspectives and helped to articulate users needs, providing a powerful critique of the services given. NAYPIC was perhaps the most vivid example of service users finding a voice for themselves and using it to considerable effect. It stemmed from the Bureau's *Who Cares?* initiative in 1975, which drew together a group of youngsters to talk about their 'in care' experiences (Page and Clark, 1977), and became a lively and influential body, with some stern messages for local authority services. The problems for social services departments in providing adequate, never mind remedial, parenting were starkly illustrated and added to the gloomy view of the care system that many of its staff already shared. Again, the notion of admission to care as an option of last resort was reinforced.

The seventies were also the years of disillusionment with the 1969 Children and Young Persons Act and retreat from its attempts to draw offenders into the embrace of the childcare system. An emasculated Act was further hampered by the doubts or downright hostility of the courts who passed sentence on the one hand, and the underdeveloped and overwhelmed capacities of social services to cope on the other. In the event, the Act's intentions were turned on their head. Thus, far from replacing custody with care, custodial sentences escalated whilst the care system itself was criticised for drawing the youngest and least deviant into its net of care, intermediate treatment or supervision, thus enhancing the risk of a stigmatised and even criminal career. Local authority care was seen as likely to damage a child's life chances just as much as a custodial sentence and even community based alternatives were likely to push the repeat offender up the 'tariff' and draw him inexorably into the penal system. Diversion from both the penal and the child-care systems therefore increasingly replaced the earlier policy of transferring delinquent children from one to the other.

Thus, to summarise, the positive and idealistic stance of the sixties, in which pride in an improved care service did not dampen optimism about the help that could be offered to families in their own homes, had been superseded by a gloomier analysis, leading to tougher interventions. We can look to Lorraine Fox Harding's typology again (Fox Harding, 1991) which characterises the seventies as a high point of 'state paternalism and child protection'. (Indeed, the widely-read book, *The Needs of Children*, by the then Director of the Bureau (Pringle, 1974) is cited as a key text of this era). The argument for the label is couched in terms of increased intervention in cases of child abuse, combined with the popularity of somewhat lopsided notions of 'permanence' for children, which concentrated heavily on achieving stable substitute homes (preferably through adoption) and much less on struggling to reunite children with their natural families. She also points out that the major piece of legislation in the seventies was the Children Act, 1975, which extended the grounds for assuming parental rights over children in care, introduced custodianship and time-scales to prompt long-term decision making and required parents to give notice of removal of their child from 'voluntary' care after a stay of six months.

But Fox Harding's argument does not embrace policies for young offenders and, coincidentally, the Bureau has not shown a keen interest in this aspect of child welfare. Yet, as we have seen, delinquents were central to developments in the seventies. The decade was remarkable in that it saw first the rise and then the rapid decline and fall of a policy that tried to treat offenders as just another group of deprived children, by sweeping them into the mainstream of child-care. Its failure to take hold and the trenchant criticisms of the injustices and damage that 'care' could perpetrate added to the depressed and defensive posture of the service as a whole.

Partnership

The 1980s offered the childcare services no respite from scrutiny and trenchant criticism. Indeed, research, child abuse enquiries and searching reviews reached a crescendo during the decade and culminated in far reaching legislative change. The outcome was the Children Act 1989.

The genesis of the Children Act and the many influences that shaped it have been thoroughly discussed, most notably by Parton (Parton, 1991), and need only be outlined here. Early influences were the research initiatives of both the DHSS and ESRC. By the start of the decade both bodies had taken the unusual step of funding a set of studies in childcare which overlapped and were complementary. (The Bureau was responsible for one of the DHSS funded projects). By the mid-eighties the strategy had produced cumulative data, illustrating common themes which were then summarised and made widely available in an unprecedented dissemination exercise. Research messages reinforced one another - 'like looking out of different windows and seeing the same view' (DHSS, 1985) - and seventies concerns about inadequate support for families, growing confrontation and controlling action on the part of statutory services plus a poor record of care for the children looked after by local authorities were all illustrated and emphasised.

In 1983/4 the House of Commons all-party Social Services Committee also chose to focus on childcare and drew both from the research evidence and the views of a wide range of providers and recipients of children's services. Champions of the child, like the National Children's Bureau, of families, like the Family Rights Group and the children themselves, through NAYPIC, were all heard - as well as the many statutory and voluntary providers of welfare services. Amongst the Committee's many observations, the low priority accorded to preventive work was deplored and the negative interpretations of prevention that were observed were sharply criticised. 'Care is not something like a disease or an accident: nor is it something to be regarded as a last-ditch solution such as imprisonment' (House of Commons, 1984, para.26).

The Committee also recommended an urgent review of the tangled web of childcare law. 'The time has arrived - indeed it arrived some time ago - for a thorough going review of the body of statute law, regulation and judicial decisions relating to children' (House of Commons, 1984, para.119) A thorough and massively detailed interdepartmental review followed hard on the Committee's heels.

In the meantime official enquiries into fresh scandals of child abuse were another source of potent but discordant criticism. Until the mid-eighties a series of reports attacked the childcare system on rather different grounds from those highlighted by research and the Commons Committee. Far from criticising the services for being over-controlling and unnecessarily confrontational, reports like those concerning the deaths of Jasmine Beckford (London Borough of Brent, 1985) and Kimberley Carlile (London Borough of Greenwich, 1987), castigated them for failing to act decisively. Their lack of knowledge of and commitment to the use of legal powers was deplored as was their perceived myopic focus upon parents and a misplaced trust in their goodwill and honesty. Prevention in the context of these enquiries was prevention of death or harm to children. The professionals' role was therefore to become experts in diagnosing and predicting such harm and protecting and rescuing children from situations of risk, using the full force of the law to do so. The messages concerning childcare services in general and child protection in particular appeared to have polarised, each demanding different approaches or even different service systems.

The Cleveland Report of 1987 (Department of Health, 1988) bridged the divide. Following one authority's removal within a few months of well over a hundred children suspected of having been sexually abused, professionals now stood accused of hasty and clumsy interventions, risking injustice and harm to parents and children alike. In the now hackneyed phrases 'too little, too late' had become 'too much, too soon'. Achieving a balance between these two positions had to become a central concern of the new legislation that was already being prepared.

The Children Act marks both an end and a beginning to any survey of childcare services over the last thirty years. Its hallmarks are comprehensiveness and a clear, unifying set of principles which bind it together. Its scope is signalled by the fifty five previous Acts (one dating from 1891) which are repealed in whole or in part. Private law, concerned with children caught up in the aftermath of parental separation or divorce and public law that governs the powers and responsibilities of welfare services for children and their families, are combined in the same statute. All children who are disabled - a group long-championed by the Bureau - are brought within its ambit and are defined as children 'in need'. Responsibilities towards older teenagers who are homeless or at risk and young people who have left local authority care are extended. Children in long-term hospitals and independent boarding schools also come under its protective umbrella. Only the young delinquents hover somewhat ambiguously on the fringe of the Act; no longer eligible for committal to care (though supervision with a condition of residence is a new option) - yet destined to be remanded to local authorities' facilities once their incarceration in adult remand centres is finally phased out. But the most recent alarms over grave and persistent juvenile offenders seem to threaten even these tenuous links with the care system.

The principles which pull together the many strands of this bulky Act are the paramountcy of the welfare of the child; the concept of enduring parental responsibility which may be shared but rarely extinguished; a preference for negotiated solutions rather than court orders; and the duty of public authorities to support families in their child-rearing tasks.

The child, rightly, is centre-stage and takes a more active role in defining his own welfare and asserting its paramount status. The child's wishes and feelings must be taken into account when any decisions are taken and, in certain circumstances he even has a right of veto over interventions that experts may construe as being in his interests. The Cleveland dictum 'the child is a person not an object of concern' has been heeded (Department of Health, 1988, p.245)

But the child's welfare is also seen as being firmly embedded in its family context and, furthermore, a family in its widest sense. Not only parents, but brothers, sisters, uncles, aunts, grandparents and even unrelated figures of significance to a child may therefore be involved in assessing or enhancing that child's welfare. But parents are likely to be the most crucial adults for most children and their role is recast in the legislation. The possessive term, parental rights is replaced by parental responsibilities, which remain even when parents separate, when their children live elsewhere, or are removed from them by the courts. Parents' responsibilities can be supplemented or shared but only through death or adoption can they be rubbed out.

Parental responsibility which may be shared and the Act's stated preference for negotiated solutions rather than court orders come together in Part III of the Act, where the responsibilities of family and state are conceived as complementary and non-confrontational. The presumption that children are usually best brought up in their own families, together with the recognition that some children and families have needs that they cannot meet unaided demands some kind of partnership between them. The legislative solution is the new local authority duty to support the families of children 'in need' with a range of services that includes accommodating the children.

Thus, through the Children Act we are brought full circle, to the place of prevention in the spectrum of childcare services. In its modern guise it is conceptualised more positively and generously than in the past. On paper at least the defensive stance at the gateway to care has shifted to the courtroom steps. A range of supports should be on offer to the children themselves as well as to other members of their families. Accommodating children ought not to threaten the exercise of parental choice or responsibility and should no longer be construed as a 'last resort'. In simple terms, the intention is to replace the double negative of 'prevention' as minimal intervention and 'care' as a necessary evil of last (and compulsory) resort, which was amply demonstrated in research - (see Fisher and others, 1986: Packman and others, 1986) with a new double positive. 'Support' is to encompass a wide range of services and 'accommodation' is reframed as a valued ingredient, to be shared in partnership with families.

It is under the Part III umbrella, also, that young offenders may gain some benefit. Local authorities are charged with reducing the need for criminal proceedings against children and must encourage them 'not to commit criminal offences'. Here there may be scope for further development of imaginative diversionary measures that some local authorities already support, in collaboration with police and probation colleagues, though these, in turn may now be threatened by current calls for a resurrection of the old approved school system.

Although partnership is not a term which is used in the Act itself, it is a concept which encapsulates the spirit of the legislation and is repeated time and again in the many volumes of guidance and regulation that accompany it. Separated parents are expected to remain jointly responsible for their children; parental partners, though no longer a marital pair. Local authorities must listen to the wishes of parents and children and must offer support services to families of children 'in need'. When they look after such children it is on behalf of the parents, whose roles and responsibilities must not be usurped. Even when children are harmed and are removed from their families they must still be informed and consulted and as involved as is consistent with their children's welfare. Services themselves must also work in partnership with other statutory, voluntary and private agencies, with individuals and with the community at large.

On the face of it, this seems to propel the professionals in local authorities and voluntary agencies into a largely untried area of practice - relying on the cooperation and trustworthiness of parents of children in need, including those who have harmed or neglected them. However, parents too face unknown challenges. Their official partners are themselves in some turmoil, with resource constraints and organisational upheaval disrupting established working patterns and machinery for coordination. In some authorities, long-established traditions of paternalism or coercion may make it difficult for parents and young people to have real influence. In others, however, the speed of change may be bewildering, with service-users thrust into roles not far removed from those of service providers, as resources for family support run short and managers seek to sustain their hard-pressed provision. Thus, partnership projects both sides into unknown territory and the early signs are that the transition will not be easy (Marsh and Fisher, 1992). The widespread fulfilment of its promises therefore awaits further experience, experiment and the evidence of fresh research and in each of these spheres the National Children's Bureau can be expected to play a valuable role.

References

Challis, L. (1990) *Organising Public Social Services*. Longman

DHSS (1985) *Social Work Decisions in Child Care*. HMSO

Department of Health (1988) *Report of the Inquiry into Child Abuse in Cleveland 1987*. HMSO

Department of Health (1992) *Capitalising on the Act. A Working Party Report on the Implementation of the Children Act 1989 in London*

Donnison, D.V. (1954) *The Neglected Child and the Social Services*. Manchester University Press

Fisher, M., Marsh, P. and Phillips, D. (1986) *In and Out of Care*. London: Batsford/BAAF

Fox Harding, L. (1991) *Perspectives in Child Care Policy*. Longman

George, V. (1970) *Foster Care: Theory and Practice*. Routledge and Kegan Paul

Griffiths, D.L. and Moynihan, F.J. (1963) 'Multiple epiphyseal injuries in babies' ('Battered Baby Syndrome'), *British Medical Journal*, 11, pp.1558-61

Harris, R. and Webb, D. (1987) *Welfare, Power and Juvenile Justice*. Tavistock Publications

Holman, B. (1981) *Kids at the Door*. Basil Blackwel

Holman, B. (1988) *Putting Families First*. Macmillan

Home Office (1960) *Report of the Committee on Children and Young Person (Ingleby)*. Cmnd 1191. HMSO

Labour Party (1964) *Crime - A Challenge to Us All*

London Borough of Brent (1985) *A Child in Trust*

London Borough of Greenwich (1987) *A Child in Mind*

Marsh, P. and Fisher, M. (1992) *Good Intentions: Developing Partnership in Social Services. Community Care into Practice Series*. Joseph Rowntree Foundation

Packman, J. (1981) *The Child's Generation*. Basil Blackwell and Martin Robertson

Packman, J., Randall, J. and Jacques, N. (1985) *Who Needs Care?* Basil Blackwell

Page, R. and Clark, G.A. (1977) *Who Cares?* National Children's Bureau

Parker, R.A. (1966) *Decision in Child Care*. George Allen and Unwin

Parton, N. (1985) *The Politics of Child Abuse*. Macmillan

Parton, N. (1991) *Governing the Family*. Macmillan

Pringle, M.K. (1974) *The Needs of Children*. Hutchinson

Seebohm, F. (1968) *Report of the Committee on Local Authority and Allied Personal Social Services*. HMSO

Trasler, G. (1960) *In Place of Parents*, Routledge and Kegan Paul

14. Children living away from home

Barbara Kahan
Chair, National Children's Bureau andChild Care Consultant

Children live away from home across the world

All children are of equal worth, whatever their race, ability, gender, sexual orientation, social class or religion.
Society has a responsibility to promote children's welfare and development, and to protect them from physical and emotional harm, deprivation or disadvantage (Values of the National Children's Bureau).

In a book to celebrate the National Children's Bureau's 30 years of work for children, it would be impossible to address the subject of children living away from home by concentrating only on children in Britain, ignoring others who, in varying circumstances, are living away from home worldwide. Shortly before its 30th year the Bureau established a European Children's Centre and immediately contacts began to be made with countries in which children away from home were in grave need and appalling conditions of life. Wars, despots, revolutions leave in their wake straggling armies of dispossessed people, among whom are many children who have lost not only their homes but in many instances their parents as well. Hunger, disease, violence and ignorance distort and cripple their lives and their future prospects, if they survive, can only be guessed at.

Outside of Europe's war areas even greater numbers of children struggle for existence away from home. Many die in famines, a slow and painful death with no resting place or medical care, while often corruption holds up relief. Others know only the shelter of the streets and have to prostitute themselves to survive. Yet others are picked off, like stray dogs, by police or soldiers with guns in an attempt to rid the streets of a political embarassment or to discourage others others who are homeless too. Across the world many millions of destitute children suffer and are exploited in child labour, child prostitution and beggary. Television in 1993 confronts us all with the realities of children's suffering in a manner not possible in 1963 when the National Children's Bureau was founded.

Has the Bureau any role to play in such massive need and problems? Can its work assist in upholding principles and values which are important to the welfare of children wherever they are?

We attempt to eradicate prejudice and discrimination against children as a group or because of race, disability, gender, sexual orientation, social class or religion.

Through research and in other ways, we identify and promote the best conditions for children whatever their circumstances, whether living with their families or apart.

We foster cooperation, collaboration and effective communication between all those who work with and for children (Principles of the National Children's Bureau).

Children living away from home in Britain

The history of childhood in Britain has included separation of children from home because of extremes of poverty, sold as labour; because of extremes of prejudice, abandoned or left as foundlings; because of ignorance and superstition, placed for life in institutions for the handicapped. It also records practices such as parents placing children in other households as part of their upbringing (as recorded in the Paston Letters), a practice reminiscent of modern placements of children in boarding schools from six years old and upwards. Many children in Britain currently spend significant periods of their lives away from home for reasons other than parental inability to care for them.

Who are the children living away from home in Britain? Information is incomplete because statistics are not collected or they are collected in different forms and at different times in England, Scotland, Wales and Northern Ireland. There are also differences between services concerned with education, health, childcare and delinquency. Such statistics as there are can be misleading because of differences between relatively static populations such as those in boarding schools compared with the throughput of children and young people in child care establishments, foster homes, hospital units and penal institutions.

In an attempt to illustrate the dimensions of residential alternatives to being at home the Bureau's own *ChildFacts No.2 - Children's Homes* gave statistics drawn from a variety of government publications or estimates. They show the approximate numbers on any day in 1990, and the period around it, in England:

Residential homes	13,200
Foster homes	34,400
Mainstream boarding schools	115,000
Special boarding schools for pupils with special educational needs	30,000*

*National Children's Bureau's estimate

Admissions to health facilities including NHS hospitals and psychiatric units cannot be stated but are additional to those already given.

These statistics relate only to a static situation on one day. Six times as many admissions to some childcare facilities may take place in a year as are present on any one day.

Child Care Now, a study based on six local authorities' placement patterns over two years, revealed 9723 placements in all forms of care and 9335 'endings' that is the child completing a placement. The researchers described these figures as 'quite staggering' and commented that 'one gets little or no idea of it from end of year statistics' (Rowe and others, 1989)

It must be a matter of concern that considerable numbers of children and young people in Britain spend significant periods away from home in the control of persons other than their parents yet the numbers are not able to be stated with any certainty. If the pattern of the six local authorities quoted above were typical of the whole of Britain it is clear that very large numbers of children move in and out of care during relatively short periods of time, while the numbers in various forms of boarding education are considerable.

When the Warner Committee began its inquiry into the 'selection and recruitment methods and criteria for staff working in children's homes' it found a dearth of information. In 1985 Berridge had pointed out that 'many of the decisions on residential care are taken on the basis of inadequate information' (Berridge, 1985). Six years later Utting (1991) said that 'information about the number of institutions accommodating children in care is poor'. The Warner Committee commissioned management consultants to provide an adequate information base for them to begin their work and in their report recommended that 'the Government should commission the compilation of a National Directory of children's homes ....and make arrangements to keep the Directory up to date'. In their opinion 'many placing decisions owe as much to grapevine, tradition and anecdote as to any strong base of factual information about homes' and 'allowing the market in residential child care to change in a totally unplanned way is unacceptable. It produces the maximum uncertainty' and 'changes too often appear as sudden and catastrophic and produce angry reactions from staff and children. A sense of powerlessness is engendered....and morale can be seriously affected by uncertainty' (Warner, 1992)

This is a situation familiar in war zones, but why should it obtain in Britain's state supported and controlled and legally required childcare services?

A similar lack of information characterises boarding education facilities, provision for children in the NHS and private health services. Why should this be so? Who does it benefit? What problems arise from the lack of knowledge thus created?

Internationally there is also little knowledge of how different nations and cultures address the needs of children living away from home. One of the first books to attempt to draw together certain basic material *Residential Child Care: An International Handbook* was edited in 1991 by Meir Gottesman, an Israeli. It was published jointly by FICE (International Federation of Educative Communities) and SCA (Social Care Association) in Britain. In broad outline 'it encompasses and analyses the history, present state and future prospects of 22 residential child and youth care and education systems ...including 19 from Europe, two from North America and one from the Middle East'. In most of the countries represented a boarding school network exists alongside the residential care system described. The editor claims that in relation to residential childcare the 22 national chapters:

...testify to two almost parallel processes: on the one hand, during the last quarter of a century residential child care has changed worldwide in almost all respects, mostly for the better; on the other, seemingly independent of this progress and quite paradoxically, the reservations, antagonisms and even hostility to residential care have grown markedly during the past few years, causing it to pass through its deepest crisis since the end of World War II.

FICE, an organisation with which the National Children's Bureau has established links, had its origins in the UNESCO's 1947 General Conference in Mexico City when the following resolution was adopted:

1.7.   War Handicapped Children. The Director General is instructed:
1.7.1. to draw up a plan of study and action on the educational problems of war-handicapped children, in collaboration with the national and international organisations concerned;
1.7.2. to obtain from experts in different countries information and factual reports, and to institute a field survey of the most significant experiments made in that field;
1.7.3. to analyse the documents and draft a report.

This resolution was the basis for a UNESCO report *Childhood as a War Victim - A Study of the Situation in Europe* by Dr Therese Brosse. An international conference which followed was the starting point for a multidisciplinary team model of psychology, pedagogy and psychiatry responsible for children's and adolescents' establishments as commended by UNESCO. The Director General in 1948 recalled that 'our duty is not merely to reconstruct and restore that which has been destroyed, but to rebuild the very foundations of our civilisation'.

In England in the same year the foundation stone of the modern childcare service, the Children Act 1948, was laid. The multidisciplinary focus required to meet children's needs was a major reason for the foundation of the National Children's Bureau in 1963, after the specialised service in children's departments revealed gaps in overall provision and the links which had to be made.

In Britain, unlike in a number of European countries, there has traditionally been a sharp and wide division between education and welfare in relation to children. Boarding schools have had an educational and character building focus which was the distinguishing mark of nineteenth century public schools and still remains part of the accepted objectives of many similar schools in the twentieth. Living away from parents, in groups of peers, in a controlled environment and carefully programmed lifestyle, has been regarded by parents and teachers alike as a benefit which offers not only an undistracted educational opportunity but also considerable social advantages in life after school. Meir Gottesman (1991) speaks of 'the United Kingdom (as) the cradle of residential education'.

Although boarding education has traditionally been part of the British class system (it would be an interesting study to examine how membership of a few boarding public schools by a significant proportion of Britain's leading politicians and senior civil servants has affected our national political scene), in recent years it has become a desired resource for aspirant families, particularly some whose lives are affected by mobility or marriage breakdown. A curious example of official ambivalence is the support given for many years by the central government defence department to boarding education for over 20,000 children of armed services personnel, while the central government department responsible for social services has, until recently, reinforced professional rejection of residential childcare, as a potentially damaging experience, for children from similar population groups to many of those supported in the boarding schools.

Boarding schools, even those of mediocre or poor standard, have never faced the emotive rejection meted out to even high standard residential childcare establishments. Yet for many years there has been implicit acknowledgement that whether a child is received into care or becomes a resident in a special needs boarding school may be a matter of organisational accident. The special boarding schools have made less staffing or other care provision for the needs of children outside classroom hours than is customary in children's homes. Yet in the dramatic decline of residential childcare during the 1980s, the population in special boarding schools did not decline. Instead by 1990, as has already been shown, nearly three times as many children were in the schools as the numbers living in children's homes. It has often been questioned whether there may be a link between social services policies which discourage admissions to care and the use of special boarding schools by professionals in other services, for example educational psychologists, who believe certain children need to be removed from home. The authors of the National Children's Bureau's study of the now well known Warwickshire childcare policy described in *Closing Children's Homes - An End to Residential Care?* (Cliffe with Berridge, 1991) commented:

We expressed concern.... about the national situation of children defined as having emotional and behavioural difficulties (EBD). Overall, although reliable statistics are difficult to come by, it seems that the numbers of these pupils living and being educated in *residential* schools continues to grow. There are significant - and quite worrying - disparities between local education authorities on this subject, yet this overall increase seems to be completely at odds with trends affecting residential care for children more generally ...so far there has been no overall view as to whether or not it is a desirable development.

Residential childcare, unlike boarding education, has been dogged by ghosts of long past Poor Law policies and theories concerning total institutions drawn from models which bear little resemblance to modern children's homes. The Warner Committee, in demonstrating that the average size of children's homes in 1992 was 11-14 beds, and that the numbers of children in them averaged nine, most of whom except those excluded by education services, go out daily to school, has merely described what those responsible for the homes and those who use them knew already. They could scarcely be described as 'total institutions'.

Berridge's study of children's homes (1985) seven years earlier had demonstrated from personal experience and careful research in a sample of twenty establishments in the local authority, voluntary and private sectors, that:

...the quality of *individual* care offered in the homes visited was, generally, of acceptable standard and in several establishments extremely impressive ...Most staff were deeply committed to their task and children were usually appreciative of their residential experience.

A similar conclusion was reached in the Social Work Service (now Department of Health Social Services Inspectorate) study of children's homes:

The great majority of (children's) homes ...in most cases covering wide age ranges, were judged to be meeting the needs of children well and there were many examples of sensitive handling by staff in a homely and acceptable environment. The problems of control noted in some homes for adolescents were not generally found in these homes, with the exception of those few where the mix of children, in terms of both age and problems, had not been carefully considered (Social Work Service, 1985).

Traditionally final decisions about admissions to individual homes have lain within the power of agency staff outside of the homes themselves.

In the Inquiry reports of 1991 and 1992 (Pindown (Levy and Kahan); Utting, Howe and Warner) senior social services management has been unanimously seen to have failed dismally to support, understand, develop and value residential childcare services. Public allusions to Goffman and total institutionalism to justify the relegation of children's homes to the status of a last resort are now seen to be inaccurate, misleading and unfair. The neglect of responsibility for a service attempting to care for very needy children and young people, damaged in many cases by unrealistic and rigid expectations of fostering as a cure-all method of care, can no longer be concealed.

The National Children's Bureau, from its earliest years, demonstrated concern about children living away from home. Only four years after its inception in 1967 two important books were published, *Residential Child Care - Facts and Fallacies* and *Foster Home Care - Facts and Fallacies* both by Dinnage and Kellmer Pringle, then Director of the Bureau. In each case they provided a review of research in the United States, Western Europe, Israel and Great Britain between 1948 and 1966. (A similar volume was published on *Adoption - Facts and Fallacies* (Pringle, 1967)). Looking back at these impressive volumes is both a salutary and a depressing experience. Twenty-five years ago the volume on residential care contained the following:

All those giving substitute care have the task of giving the best care they can while knowing that it is a substitute; and perhaps the more the problem is acknowledged the less of an obstacle it may become. Residential care in particular has been depreciated in two ways: it has been considered the poorer alternative to foster care (partly as a result of research on old fashioned orphanages and on very young children in nurseries) and it has consequently become the accepted placement for difficult children who cannot be fostered - a kind of double substitute care, neither own home or foster home. Whether or not the *good* foster home is always better than group care, such homes will probably always be in short supply, and the research reviewed in *Foster Home Care -Facts and Fallacies* indicates the hazards of foster home breakdowns for a large number of the children cared for in families (Dinnage and Kellmer Pringle, 1967b).

The writers' commentary on research on residential care concludes as follows:

It has been said that the most difficult of all human activities is to change human attitudes. It is this and not lack of knowledge which is holding back advance. If even half of what is now clearly known were accepted with feeling and carried out with understanding by all, the picture of residential child care could be transformed.

The impetus for the foundation of the National Children's Bureau sprang from the experience of children's departments set up following the Curtis Committee report, and the Children Act 1948 which implemented it. The Committee had seen the remaining effects of the Poor Law in childcare and condemned it. They had also seen examples of the alternative service of foster homes, many of which seemed to them to present a better alternative. They were not forgetful, however, of the foster home scandals which lent support to the initiative they represented. Their view of the use of fostering and residential care was balanced and remarkably realistic considering the paucity of professional experience and research knowledge available to them.

The primary requirements of the children for whom the substitute home must be provided are affection and stability. There is no doubt that these essentials have been secured in many foster homes, but we wish to say emphatically that no risk should be taken in this very serious matter ....It must be remembered that supervision and the possibility of removing the child from a bad or indifferent home are not a satisfactory safeguard because the removal itself is bad for the child who has already had at least one complete change of environment. *Children undergoing several changes of foster parents are often worse off than if they had never been boarded out at all* (Curtis, 1946, para.461).

They went on to conclude that:

...it would be wrong, in view of the limitations placed on boarding out ...not to develop side by side with boarding out, an alternative form of compensation for the loss of normal home life (para.462).

Their concept of one desirable alternative was 'family groups' (homes) not exceeding twelve children in number with ages and sexes mixed, similar to the homes in Berridge's research.

Nevertheless the Children Act 1948 embodied a priority for fostering to be considered for each child in care before other forms of care. The Select Committee on Estimates in 1952 was the first in a series of postwar public statements that fostering was not only best for children in care but was also cheapest! This statement was repeated in the late 1980s by the Audit Commission which could have been expected to be better informed. The research of Dr Martin Knapp has challenged it and drawn attention to the dangers of founding policies for children on inadequate data. He has pointed out that the more specialised fostering becomes the more closely its costs as a whole (instead of merely the cost of allowances) approximate to residential costs, although fostering remains cheaper in varying degrees according to supply and demand (Knapp and Robertson, 1989).

In the 1950s the Home Office Children's Department Inspectorate (the body responsible until 1970 for monitoring the childcare services) put heavy pressure on children's departments to increase their boarding out of children as well as to improve their residential facilities. Such was the pressure, combined in those early years with the difficulties of establishing a new service, that foster placement breakdowns became unacceptably high and the Association of Children's Officers themselves set up a research study to examine the problems and make recommendations.

By the mid 1960s the childcare service was fully aware of the need for a balance in provision and for a spectrum of services which would include residential care, fostering, adoption and intensive preventive work with families to help them care for their own children. This preventive work was not aimed primarily at reducing numbers of children in care but at supporting, rehabilitating and assisting families with overwhelming difficulties to maintain an acceptable level of care for their children to remain at home.

In 1963, the year the National Children's Bureau was established, the Children and Young Persons Act 1963 became law. Children's departments had made a major contribution to its development and it embodied two particularly important policy changes they had desired. The first was the location within the departments of legal responsiblity for prevention of neglect and ill-treatment of children, for prevention of reception into care wherever possible and for prevention of children and young people appearing before juvenile courts. The second was the removal of the requirement that fostering must be the first consideration in any placement of a child in care. From 1963 the method of substitute care most suited to an individual child was to be the required choice.

In 1970-71 children's departments were absorbed into the new social services departments and most social workers quickly became generic, that is non-specialist. This meant that many staff responsible for children away from home had had no experience or training to prepare them for this part of their overall task. The new departments had a much higher profile than the small departments they had absorbed and for a time resources were more readily available. It could be argued that a combination of freer resources and less skill in the social workers handling young people led to greater use of residential accommodation than pre-1970 and many new homes were opened. Competitiveness in building programmes took the place for a time of competitiveness in boarding out percentages when directors of social services met together.

The reorganisation of local government in 1974, only three years after the new social services departments had been set up, brought greater upheavals even than the Seebohm reorganisation. Continuity between professional workers and consumers was almost totally extinguished. Many staff, including many directors, either had to find or accept different jobs. It was a time of great stress and disruption. Childcare had indisputably been the best qualified and most professional service brought within the parameters of the reorganised departments in 1970. This sometimes militated against, rather than ensured, the preservation of what had been learned in 22 years of caring for children away from home. Some who experienced the change saw what they believed to be irrational rejection of the past which prevented the new organisations from benefiting from former specialist experience and knowledge. In addition, by the mid 1970s, the economic climate was becoming much bleaker and economies had to be faced by social services as well as by other local authority services.

In the United States of America a new policy of 'permanency' in relation to children away from home was being promoted. Its professional credo was that individual children needed stability and permanence and if that could not be readily achieved in their own family, alternatives should be energetically sought, particularly adoption or long term fostering. Every child needs a home and a family was the underlying principle. The economic virtue of the policy was that return home, or adoption (in particular) by alternative parents was far less costly than remaining in public care. In Britain *Children Who Wait* (Rowe and Lambert, 1973) postulated that there were significant numbers of children under 11-years-old in residential accommodation who could be adopted or placed in foster care. These two professional threads, the American model and the British research, helped to fuel a strong drive to reduce residential care again and to place as many children as possible in families. The fact that the children who were the subject of *Children Who Wait* were under eleven years of age was readily overlooked and the drive towards foster placements rapidly encompassed all ages and conditions of children and young people. The much publicised Kent experiment in professional fostering of adolescents became a major focus and once more residential care began to be relegated to the status of a last resort, while as many units of accommodation as possible were considered for closure.

Professional concerns about the quality of public care of children separated from their families was being clearly expressed to the National Children's Bureau by 1973 when ABAA (Association of British Adoption Agencies) proposed a wide ranging investigation. In the event a narrower brief was established, complementing the DHSS working party on foster practice and the Court Committee on child health services. The brief was:

...to consider the care, welfare and education of children separated from their families for recurrent or long periods. In particular, to examine the means of planning for these children so as to promote continuity and quality in their care, education and welfare.

The National Children's Bureau working party set up to explore this brief, was chaired by Professor Roy Parker. Membership came from a multidisciplinary field and their report was published in 1980 entitled *Caring for Separated Children*.

The report drew together much of the current good practice wisdom, asked penetrating questions and illuminated areas where thinking was confused and practice not geared to children's needs. The overall message of the report was by then disturbingly familiar. It reminded readers that the Personal Social Services Council (later abolished by government action) had pointed out, in the context of promoting intermediate treatment, that 'for too long the emphasis has been fitting the child or young person into existing forms of provision'.

The working party supported the idea of intermediate provision because it was 'at the heart of our desire to see less rigid lines drawn between residential and community care and to have resources used flexibly'.

They argued that:

...the penetration of practice by well-grounded theory still seems to be a painfully slow process ....We actually know a good deal about the characteristics of good care ....it is unnecessary to feel our way forward in ignorance on all fronts ....Yet even when the knowledge base is more generally appreciated its successful application demands sensitivity and commitment ....Knowing, feeling and doing cannot be separated out in good practice (Parker, 1980).

A major function of the National Children's Bureau over 30 years has been to bring together research as a basis for 'well grounded theory' and to relate this to practice. Developmental work, seminars, publications and training materials have all been used in both specialist and interdisciplinary settings and groups. This function has continued to be needed as later events and practice have demonstrated.

The hard truth of Roy Parker's message in 1980 was painfully illuminated again in 1987 when the Director of the Bridge Child Care Consultancy Service described its work at a BAAF (British Association of Adoption and Fostering) Conference. Set up to help local authorities and others to assess the needs of 'hard to place' children, the Bridge 'encourage(d) social work staff to identify accurately:

- the number of changes a young person experiences year by year;
- the number of separations a young person experiences from parents or parent figures;
- the number of changes of sets of carers a young person experiences;
- the number of new sets of carers a young person experiences.

John Fitzgerald, the Director, reported that:

...taken overall the young people with whom we have had an involvement, will experience changes as follows by the age of 13:

average number of changes	136.6
average number of changes of sets of carers	33.5
average number of new sets of carers	22.5

...Many of the changes occurred before admission to care and life in care seemed to mirror the earlier experiences

...In every case the staff involved with the young people were surprised at the extent of change and ....horrified at the number of sets of new carers they had experienced (Fitzgerald, 1987).

Fitzgerald blamed rigid professional attitudes which failed to address the needs of individual young people:

We must get back to focusing upon the individual young person and pose the question 'What does this young person need?' not 'What do I want to happen?'

A year earlier, in 1986, Warwickshire County Council had taken the unprecedented and radical step of closing the last of its children's homes and other local authorities were moving in a similar direction. The policy in Warwickshire effectively removed choice of placement from social workers and children. The research study found that suitable or not, there was often only one foster home available for a child in need and that the incidence of changes in placements was higher than the national average (Cliffe with Berridge, 1991).

During the same period a childcare law review was taking place which resulted in the Children Bill and subsequently the Children Act 1989. The National Children's Bureau was fully involved in the debates and consultations which took place as the Bill was prepared and became law, and contributed, with others, to the influence on the Act of current research which significantly helped to shape its provisions.

The year before the Children Act was implemented (October, 1991), the 'Pindown Inquiry' had investigated a method of care in Staffordshire children's homes intended, it was claimed, to convince 'difficult' children that it would be preferable to behave well enough to remain at home. A service intended to provide for children in need of care away from home was distorted into a punitive and humiliating system which reinforced the deprivation the children had already suffered. Contributory factors in its creation and continuation were successive years of reduction in residential accommodation; unrealistic objectives for remaining homes; disregard for national standards and legal requirements; careless and flawed staff recruitment methods; and uncaring attitudes on the part of some elected politicians and some senior managers.

The Experience of Pindown and the Protection of Children (Levy and Kahan, 1991) focused attention on a group of children away from home and sharply reinforced the much wider focus of the Children Act 1989. During the rest of 1991 and 1992 a series of other reports was published (Utting, 1991; Howe, 1991; Welsh Office, 1991; Warner, 1992; Skinner, 1992). They produced a national consensus of demand for higher standards of residential childcare in all respects, more attention to children's and parents' choice, and recognition that children away from home require a spectrum of services to meet their individual needs rather than professional beliefs and bureaucratic convenience.

Meanwhile the Children Act 1989 was implemented from October 1991. Its emphasis on the welfare of the child, on seeing 'accommodation' away from home, whether in residential or foster care as a support to a child's own family life, on listening to children and their families and giving them choice in placement decisions has incorporated many of the lessons to be learned from past mistakes. The changes of attitudes required to implement the spirit of the Act into detailed good practice were recognised in the guidance and training materials provided to assist managers, practitioners and professionals in other services. In developing these the National Children's Bureau has played a major part.

The next 30 years

1993 marks a greater opportunity than ever before for children away from home in Britain to receive the sensitive and positive care they require. Greater awareness of the diversity of need has been embodied in legislation - brothers and sisters together, those leaving care, children with disabilities, children in boarding schools, children from minority ethnic groups and others are all identified as having need for special attention and consideration. This greater awareness must include determination to use knowledge, skill and opportunity wherever they exist to develop ways of helping children away from home.

The *Sunday Times* , 3 January 1993 estimated that 1.4 million children were victims of the Balkan war alone: 'Studies carried out since the second world war suggest war-related trauma is unlikely to heal for two generations'.

In striving to improve our services for children away from home in Britain the even greater needs of other children elsewhere must never be forgotten. During the 1990s National Children's Bureau staff and Board members have developed many links, not only with European countries, but with countries as far apart as China, Australia, America, Africa and India. Their activities have included encouraging the development of organisations on a similar model to the Bureau, adapted to different cultures; sharing experiences and achievements on a range of services for special needs; and offering advice to planners of new services.

All children are of equal worth ...(we have) a responsibility to promote (their) welfare and development, and to protect them from physical and emotional harm, deprivation or disadvantage (Values of the National Children's Bureau).

References

Berridge, D. (1985) *Children's Homes.* Oxford: B.H. Blackwell

Cliffe, D. with Berridge, D. (1991) *Closing Children's Homes - An End to Residential Care?* London: National Children's Bureau

Curtis, M. (1946) *Report of the Care of Children Committee.* London: HMSO

Dinnage, R. and Kellmer Pringle, M.L. (1967a) *Foster Home Care - Facts and Fallacies.* London: Longman

Dinnage, R. and Kellmer Pringle, M.L. (1967b) *Residential Child Care - Facts and Fallacies.* London: Longman

Estimates, Report of the Select Committee (1952) London: HMSO

Fitzgerald, J. (1987) Young People in the Care System, *Adoption & Fostering*, 11(4)

Goffman, E. (1968) *Asylums: Essays on the Social Situation of Mental Patients & Other Inmates.* Penguin Books

Gottesman, M. (ed.) (1991) *Residential Child Care - An International Reader.* London: Whiting & Birch/SCA

Howe, E. (1991) *The Quality of Care.* Local Government Management Board

Knapp, M. and Robertson, E. (1989) 'The cost of services' in Kahan, B. (ed.) *Research, Policy and Practice.* Hodder and Stoughton for the Open University

Levy, A. and Kahan, B. (1991) *The Pindown Experience and the Protection of Children.* Staffordshire County Council

National Children's Bureau *Values and Principles*

National Children's Bureau (1992) *Child Facts No.2 - Children's Homes.* London: National Children's Bureau

Parker, R.A. (ed.) (1980) *Caring for Separated Children - Plans, Procedures and Priorities* Macmillan

Pringle, M.K. (1967) *Adoption - Facts & Fallacies.* London: Longman

Rowe, J. and Lambert, L. (1973) *Children Who Wait.* Association of British Adoption Agencies

Rowe, J. et al. (1989) *Child Care Now.* Research, Series 6. British Agencies for Adoption and Fostering

Skinner, A. (1992) *Another Kind of Home.* London: HMSO

Social Work Service (1985) *Study of Children's Homes.* Department of Health

Utting, W. (1991) *Children in the Public Care.* London: HMSO

Warner, N. (1992) *Choosing with Care.* Report of the Committee of Inquiry into the Selection, Development and Management of Staff in Children's Homes. London: HMSO

Welsh Office (1992) *Accommodating Children.* Cardiff: HMSO

Appendix:
Some highlights from the history of the National Children's Bureau 1963-1993

Oct 1963 The National Bureau for Cooperation in Child Care established with Mia Kellmer Pringle as director.

1964 Bureau commences the National Child Development Study (NCDS), research into 17,000 children born in one week of March 1958. This presents an unparalleled opportunity to increase knowledge of children's development nationally and to assess how far social, medical and educational factors affect this development over time.

1967 Publication of *11,00 Seven Year Olds*, the first follow-up report of the NCDS. Reveals the major importance of a child's home background on his/her early educational achievement.

1968 First issue of Bureau's house journal *Concern*.

1969 Initial findings of second NCDS follow-up report looking at the children at age 11, reveals the first clear evidence of the detrimental effects of maternal smoking during pregnancy on a child's later development.

1970   Publication of *Living With Handicap,* which was to greatly influence future action for children with disabilities. Calls for the urgent need for special social security allowances to meet the high costs of care; emphasises that the personal, family and social needs of disabled children are being overlooked.

1971   Name changed to National Children's Bureau.

Born Illegitimate highlights some of the problems that can emerge for children, particularly where mothers are young, where ante-natal care has been unsatisfactory and for families with poor housing and insufficient amenities.

1972   *From Birth to Seven,* the second NCDS report, arouses great national interest by bringing to light the extensive social, educational and health differences between children from different social classes.

1973   The Bureau's *National Study of Further Education, Training and Employment of Handicapped School Leavers,* the first national enquiry of its kind, finds that, for every type of handicap, facilities available for progress after schooling are seriously lacking.

Born to Fail? clearly outlines for the first time the problem of transmitted deprivation. By revealing that six per cent of Britain's children are disadvantaged (two in every classroom), the problem is seen to be greater and more extensive than had previously been envisaged.

The first *Highlight* is published - on the Halsey Report on Educational Priority and the pre-school child.

1974   The establishment of a new department to promote development and dissemination work signals a shift in the Bureau's priorities.

1975 Start of the *Who Cares?* project, which, for the first time, asks children in care to give *their* views on the care they receive. This project was to lay the foundations for much future work with children in care and led to much greater emphasis being placed on children being allowed to participate in decisions about their own futures.

Publication of *The Needs of Children*, an account of what was known about the needs of children and the effects of not meeting these needs. New editions have subsequently been published and it has been translated into several languages.

1975 Launch of the *Voluntary Council for Handicapped Children,* in response to one of the recommendations of the Living with Handicap publication for an independent resource and information centre for professionals and parents concerned with all aspects of disability.

The Council's first initiative was to publish *Help Starts Here,* a free booklet giving advice on sources of information and help. Hundreds of thousands have been distributed and it was revised and republished in 1993.

1976 Release of the initial findings of the third sweep of the NCDS, *Britain's Sixteen Year Olds,* reveals that effects of maternal smoking during pregnancy on child development can still be identified at age 16.

A further NCDS report, *Growing Up in a One Parent Family,* confirms the multiple disadvantages suffered by one parent families. Whilst the children did less well educationally, the report shows that the effect of the parental situation in itself on the children was relatively slight.

1977 *Who Cares? Young People in Care Speak Out,* published, leading many local authorities and voluntary organisations to review their policy and practice on this issue.

1980   *Caring for Separated Children,* the report of a national working party is published.

1980   The NCDS report, *Progress in Secondary Schools,* compares the progress of 16-year-olds in comprehensive, secondary modern and grammar schools. The study finds that children in comprehensive schools are doing as well as those in grammar schools and better than those in secondary moderns.

1981   *Combined Nursery Centres* is published, the first detailed research study of nurseries providing both care and education.

       Bureau asked by government to take over some of the work of the axed 'Children's Committee' which had been set up 'to advise on the coordination and development of all health and care services as they affect children'.

1982   Publication of *Unqualified and Underemployed,* on the employment experiences of handicapped school leavers, reveals the great lack of supportive services and further education provided appropriate to the needs of disabled young people at this difficult stage in their lives.

1983   The *Policy and Practice Review Group* is established.

1984   Bureau begins servicing the *All Party Parliamentary Group for Children* - a forum for discussion by MPs and Peers of policy matters relating to children.

       The first nationwide information source on Solvent Misuse is established at the Bureau.

       The Needs of Parents, examines what it is like to be a parent in the 1980s at a time when family structures and roles are changing rapidly and looks at the skills involved in parenting. This publication is still regarded as a seminal work on preparation, education and support for parents, and is currently being updated.

The first major study of children growing up in step families is published, using NCDS data.

1986 Launch of the *Under Fives Unit,* as a national centre for advice, guidance and information on current practice, thinking and research on under fives. Responding to extensive work the Bureau had already done into this area and the need to improve service provision for this age group.

1987 Launch of Bureau's *Sex Education Forum* to provide a unified voice to help develop sex education for all children at school.

The Bureau expands its work in the area of child sexual abuse by working with *TAGOSAC (Training Advisory Group on Sexual Abuse of Children)* to promote greater action on child abuse and to produce new training materials for professionals. This was to lead to the establishment of the Bureau's *Child Abuse Training Unit.*

Policy and Practice Review Group publishes *Investing in the Future,* a study of children's health services ten years after the Court Report, and stressing the importance of 'preventive health care'.

The first issues of *Children & Society*, the Bureau's academic multi-disciplinary journal and *Who Cares?*, a magazine by and for young people in care, are published.

1988 The first report of the Under Fives Unit, *Services for Under Fives: Developing a Coordinated Approach*, paints a national picture of early years provision in the UK which provides the basis for work with central and local government in implementing the coordinated review required by the Children Act.

1988-89 The Children Act 1989 is generally regarded as the most wide ranging reform of childcare law this century. The National Children's Bureau acts at the major focal point for inter-agency consultations on the Children Bill as it goes through Parliament. The All Party Parliamentary Group for Children is used as a highly effective means of discussing suggested amendments (nearly 500 in all) in a non-political, non-party forum.

1989 Publication of *Achieving Adoption with Love and Money,* the report into the temporary adoption allowances scheme for people on low incomes. A unanimous vote in Parliament introduces these allowances as a permanent measure in line with the Bureau's recommendations.

Working Towards Partnership in the Early Years, provides a theoretical framework, case studies and training materials for developing partnership between parents and professionals.

Escape from Disadvantage, reports on those children in NCDS who were 'born to fail' but who, against the odds, succeed in the education and job market.

1990 The publication of *Child Poverty and Deprivation in the UK,* shows that child poverty has increased by more than 50 per cent in the last 15 years. Following on from this book and subsequent work by other organisations on this issue, previously frozen child benefit allowances are increased.

HIV, AIDS and Children: A Cause for Concern, pinpoints the lack of information available to children and parents infected and affected by AIDS. This was to lead to the establishment of the *National Forum on AIDS and Children.*

Establishment of the Bureau's *Under Fives Unit in Wales.*

Working for Children? Children's Services and the NHS Review, takes a critical look at changes proposed in the government's White Paper 'Working for Patients' and makes recommendations to ensure children's health needs are fully met.

In the light of the UN Convention on the Rights of the Child the Bureau joins forces with UNICEF-UK to organise a National Summit for Children. Young people present a communiqué to 10 Downing Street outlining their demands for the 90s.

1991   The Bureau publishes *The UN Convention and Children's Rights in the UK* urging health and local authorities to adopt the UN Convention. Britain's existing childcare laws do not wholly fulfil the UN's minimum standards.

Young Children in Group Day Care, is published in both English and Welsh, providing innovative national guidelines for good practice in day nurseries.

The *European Children's Centre* is launched, aiming to play a major part in the development of children's policies within the EC.

Two training packs commissioned by the Department of Health as part of the Children Act implementation are published, and sell in their thousands: *Ensuring Standards in the Care of Young Children* and *Child Protection*.

The Under Fives Unit name changes to the *Early Childhood Unit.*

1992   Publication of *Closing Children's Homes: An End to Residential Care?,* highlights the urgent need to review the whole issue of residential care.

The Voluntary Council for Handicapped Children changes name to *Council for Disabled Children.*

The *National Voluntary Council for Children's Play,* representing thirty organisations, publishes *The Charter for Children's Play.*

Children in Wales is formed, bringing together organisations concerned with children and young people in Wales, and affiliated to the Bureau. In Scotland, a similar partnership is created with SCAFA (Scottish Child & Family Alliance), to be renamed *Children in Scotland* in 1993.

Racism in Children's Lives reports on research into racism in mainly white primary schools, part of a wider Bureau commitment to challenge discrimination.

*Investing in Young Children: Costing an Education and Day Care Service i*s published, providing a carefully costed framework for the expansion of early childhood services.

The Silent Minority recommends improvements in service provision for children with disabilities in Asian families.

Two groupings of organisations are formed to work collaboratively on the 1992 Education Bill - the Special Educational Consortium, convened by the Council for Disabled Children; and the Early Childhood Education Forum convened by the Early Childhood Unit.

The research report *Leaving Care and After* and the first of the new ChildFacts series, *Young People Leaving Care* are published.

The training pack *Making Assessment Work: Values and Principles in Assessing Young Children's Learning,* is published to join earlier training materials on working with parents and curriculum development.

The National Forum on AIDS and Children is launched, with over fifty member organisations.

1993 *Children and the Environment* is published, calling for urgent action to protect children from polluted air and drinking water.

A conference on *Children with Emotional and Behavioural Difficulties* highlights the situation of the 8,000 such children living in residential special schools.

The new *Practice Development Department* is launched with the establishment of the *Residential Childcare Development Unit.*

The Bureau collaborates with the East London and City Health Authority on a major project to develop a child health strategy.

The Editor would like to thank Lorraine Hunter, Ron Davie and Nicola Hilliard for their help in compiling this Appendix.

Index

The index covers Chapters 1 to 14 (excluding end-of-chapter lists of bibliographical references) and the Appendix. Entries are arranged in letter-by-letter alphabetical order (in which spaces and hyphens between words are ignored for filing purposes). Where an entry contains several page references, any principal reference is printed in bold type.

D

E